T0373214

Z A P R U D E R E D

ZAPRU

UNIVERSITY OF TEXAS PRESS ⌵ AUSTIN

DERED

THE KENNEDY ASSASSINATION FILM
IN VISUAL CULTURE

ØYVIND VÅGNES

First edition, 2011

Portions of Chapter One were first published as "Quoting Zapruder," in *U.S. Icons and Iconicity*, edited by Walter W. Hölbling, Klaus Rieser, and Susanne Rieser (Vienna: LIT Verlag, 2006). Chapter Three appeared in a different form as "Inside the Zapruder Museum," *Working Papers on Design* 2 (2007). An excerpt from Chapter Six was published in the 51st Belgrade October Salon Catalog (Belgrade: Cultural Centre of Belgrade, 2010). Chapter Eight was originally published as two essays: "Remembering Civic Trauma: Narratives of Cultural Authority," *Journal of American and Comparative Cultures* 25, nos. 3–4 (2002): 347–356; and "'Chosen to Be Witness': The Exceptionalism of 9/11," in *The Selling of 9/11: How a National Tragedy Became a Commodity*, edited by Dana Heller, 54–74 (New York: Palgrave Macmillan, 2005).

Requests for permission to reproduce material
from this work should be sent to:
Permissions
University of Texas Press
P.O. Box 7819
Austin, TX 78713-7819
utpress.utexas.edu/about/book-permissions

LIBRARY OF CONGRESS CATALOGING-IN-PUBLICATION DATA

Vågnes, Øyvind, 1972–
    Zaprudered: the Kennedy assassination film in visual culture / Øyvind Vågnes.
        p.   cm.
    Includes bibliographical references and index.
    ISBN 978-0-292-724525-4
    1. Kennedy, John F. (John Fitzgerald), 1917–1963—Assassination.   2. Kennedy, John F. (John Fitzgerald), 1917–1963—In motion pictures.   3. Zapruder, Abraham.   4. Amateur films—Texas—Dallas—History—20th century.   5. Memory—Political aspects—United States.   6. Motion pictures and history.   I. Title.
    E842.9V35 2011
    973.922092—dc22   2011014036

First paperback edition, 2012

Zaprudered into surreal dimensions of purest speculation, ghost-narratives have emerged and taken on shadowy but determined lives of their own.

WILLIAM GIBSON, *PATTERN RECOGNITION*

CONTENTS

ACKNOWLEDGMENTS

THIS BOOK WOULD NOT HAVE BEEN WRITTEN if it were not for a generous invitation from Edward Ingebrigtsen, of Georgetown University, to come to the Library of Congress as a Fulbright fellow in 2001–2002. I owe many thanks to both him and the Fulbright Foundation for early support and encouragement and for an immensely inspiring research stay. Thanks also to the Faculty of Arts at the University of Bergen for financial support. I have had the pleasure of working as a visiting scholar in two of the greatest libraries in the world, the Library of Congress and the New York Public Library (in the summer of 2003), and want to extend my thanks to several staff members in both places who were always helpful. I also want to thank the University of Washington in Seattle for welcoming me as a visiting scholar in 2004 and for providing me with perfect facilities in which to get much writing done.

Several segments in *Zaprudered* have been previously published in slightly different versions, and I want to thank the publishers of those books and journals for granting permission to reprint passages and segments. Some of the chapters have benefited greatly from insightful commentary from readers as well as from audiences at conferences where I have presented my work, and I appreciate all their input. My reading of Don DeLillo's *Underworld* in the fourth chapter was improved by lively discussions at a conference in Hatfield, England, in 2005, "Show and Tell: Relationships between Text, Narrative and

Image," arranged by the tVAD research group at the University of Hertford-
shire; many thanks to Grace Lees-Maffei and an anonymous reviewer for
their comments when I was preparing the paper for publication. Panel discussions at two conferences where I presented parts of the sixth chapter (the
American Studies Association in Washington, D.C., in 2005 and the Society
of Cinema and Media Studies in Chicago in 2007) were immensely helpful
and inspiring to me (special thanks to Ann Fabian and Deirdre Boyle). The
discussions at the PCA/ACA (Popular Culture Association/American Culture
Association) conference in New Orleans in 2003 and at the brilliant photograph conference that the editors of *Mosaic* put together in Winnipeg in 2004
were in different ways important to me in writing the last chapter of this
book (thanks to Arthur Neal in New Orleans).

I wish to thank helpful members of the staff at the various museum in-
stitutions I visited while working on *Zaprudered*, including the Yale School of
Architecture Gallery in New Haven, the Spencer Collection at the New York
Public Library, the Whitney Museum in New York City, and the Sixth Floor
Museum in Dallas. Chip Lord mailed me a VHS copy of *The Eternal Frame*
in 2001. The video came to transform my work, and it is difficult for me to
imagine what this book would look like if I had not received that package.
Thanks also to Zoran Naskovski for providing me with material and images.
Marquard Smith and John Beck made incisive comments to an early version
of the manuscript. I am grateful to Jim Burr at the University of Texas Press
for recognizing my work. I was also fortunate to benefit from valuable input
from Kip Keller, two anonymous readers, and others at the Press.

It has been my privilege to work in two departments at the University of
Bergen over these last few years, the English Department and the Department of Information Science and Media Studies. Two colleagues and friends
have been instrumental in helping me shape and refine my thoughts over the
years. I want to thank Orm Øverland for diligent readings and inestimable
guidance and for helping me find my own voice. I have been extremely fortunate to be able to work closely with Asbjørn Grønstad on project after project
during the first decade of the new millennium, and it has never been anything but a joy. Finally, I want to use this opportunity to extend my thanks to
my nearest family for their constant support: to my mother, who made me a
passionate reader; to my wife, Birgit, for her unending patience and kindness;
and to my two boys, Eskil and Amund, for all the joy. My father never failed to
show great interest in my work, but passed away before he could see this book
come out. I dedicate it to his memory.

ZAPRUDERED

FIG. I.1   Frame 262 from the Zapruder film. © 1967 (renewed 1995) The Sixth Floor Museum at Dealey Plaza. Used with permission of the Sixth Floor Museum.

FIG. I.2   Frame 375 from the Zapruder film. © 1967 (renewed 1995) The Sixth Floor Museum at Dealey Plaza. Used with permission of the Sixth Floor Museum.

Introduction

During our negotiations, Zapruder said again and again how worried he
was about possible exploitation of his 26 seconds of film. He told me about
a dream he'd had the night before: He was walking through Times Square
and came upon a barker urging tourists to step inside a sleazy theater to
watch the President die on the big screen. The scene was so vivid it made
Zapruder heartsick. Later, while testifying before the Warren Commission,
which was investigating the assassination, he wept as the film was shown.
"The thing would come every night," he said of the dream. "I wake up and
see this." // Richard B. Stolley, "Zapruder Rewound"

THE MOTORCADE TURNS ONTO HOUSTON STREET, and in the backseat
of one of the cars sits President John F. Kennedy, smiling and waving to the
crowds that have gathered along the road, his wife next to him. The car disap-
pears behind a road sign, then appears again, and the president seems to be
fumbling with his collar, clutching his throat, while Jackie Kennedy is watching with increasing attention (Fig. I.1). He glides slowly to the left, and then
his upper body is jolted violently, his head exploding in a spurt of blood, and
his wife crawls across the back of the car as a Secret Service man climbs up on
it (Fig. I.2). She turns back and looks for a moment in the direction of the now
slumped, partly invisible body, then the view is obstructed again by bushes
and another road sign before we see the car speeding up, disappearing under
the overpass.

When I awoke in my West End hotel room in Dallas, Texas, on the morning of November 22, 2003, and turned on the television set before getting
out of bed, only a minute or two passed before I saw these images on the
screen. I cannot recall precisely which channel I happened to be watching,
but I remember switching for a few minutes and observing without surprise
that the anniversary of the Kennedy assassination had made the headlines
on a number of Saturday-morning shows, all running similar footage from

the Kennedy years and the day of the assassination. It felt strange to see the motorcade turn again and again on Houston Street, knowing it had all happened only blocks from where I was staying.

On that day, forty years had passed since Kennedy was murdered in the city I had been visiting for half a week. In the course of those few days in Dallas, I found that what had at first been a strange and unfamiliar sensation—that of being in a city where all the major networks were present to cover an event—gradually came to feel routine. When I eventually saw a friend and myself on the screen, I observed it without any of the enthusiasm or excitement one usually feels at suddenly being caught on tape at the periphery of some television report. By that time, it had come to seem inevitable that our faces would end up being broadcast during that weekend. With cameras everywhere around us, I would have been surprised if we had not ended up being photographed or filmed at some point.

The first morning I arrived in Dealey Plaza, where Kennedy was shot, the area was almost empty. A few people were walking around and pointing up at the sixth-floor window of the former schoolbook depository building from which Lee Harvey Oswald had allegedly fired the rifle shots that killed the president. They took photographs of the building, of the giant X painted in the street at what is believed to be the exact spot where Kennedy was shot in the head, and of the picket fence from behind which one or more shots had been fired, according to numerous so-called conspiracy theorists. Two or three of the more dedicated of these had silently placed themselves in the area, offering videotapes and homemade publications for sale. To them, it was just another working day. One told me that three or four of them came to Dealey Plaza fairly regularly to spread their information. The traffic roared matter-of-factly down Elm Street and through the plaza, with the occasional driver smiling at what for her must have been a familiar sight: people on the curb mimicking the tilting movements of Kennedy's upper body as he was shot, eagerly pointing at and photographing the window, the mark in the street, the fence.

That same afternoon, when I returned to the site a few hours later, a woman had positioned a hotdog stand at the corner of Elm and Houston. A few more people had gathered. I had read in the newspapers that there would be several television specials on the assassination, but I was nevertheless surprised when I came back to the plaza the next day, Thursday, to see the impact of the arrival of the networks. The site had changed profoundly. With the coming of the television crews, larger numbers of people had arrived and were arriving. A section of the plaza and the parking lot of what is now the Sixth Floor Museum, located in the former Texas School Book Depository building, were closed off to accommodate television news trucks, all flashing the familiar logos of the major networks. That evening, I watched news reporters get their makeup on, prepare before cameras in the white light with notes scribbled on cards, and then report live. On the cover of the Metropolitan section of the *Dallas Morning News* the following day there was a color photograph of the ABC News anchor Peter Jennings, who had used the plaza as a backdrop for a report, with the schoolbook depository building behind him. In addition to Jennings, Dan Rather flew into town and found his way to the plaza. I had counted more than a dozen television specials dedicated to Kennedy and the assassination during the last few days. However, it was with the arrival of the crews and the well-known reporters that one got the feeling that an entire nation would be watching *us*, the crowds who, for various and widely different reasons, had gathered in Dealey Plaza forty years after a president was slain there.

When I left my hotel and walked down to the plaza on the morning of November 22, hundreds of people had gathered already. The entire area was closed to traffic. For a couple of hours, people poured into the plaza from all directions. The *Dallas Morning News* had reported the previous day that the entire nation was now focused on Dallas; several events were expected to "occur spontaneously"; others were planned and "sponsored by private groups."[1] Local visitors seemed pleased to run into friends, people they had not seen for a while. Otherwise, people were standing around, not doing much except for one thing. All seemed to have cameras and were either photographing or filming. I have never seen such extensive recording. Families gathered on the curb in front of the mark in the road for a pose. The window, the fence, the pergola: people were positioning themselves, taking pictures, and filming, and as they did so, they were looking, gesturing, pointing. Television crews were reporting live. The whole site was steeped in nervous energy. Pictures were being discussed; pictures were being made.

There was one point in the plaza that seemed to attract particular attention that day. Hundreds of people climbed a small concrete abutment on the north hill of the plaza, halfway between the Sixth Floor Museum and the underpass. They climbed up and photographed or filmed Elm Street, many with a gliding movement, as if following the motorcade down the stretch of road that morning forty years ago. Some photographed the abutment itself, an unremarkable piece of concrete. At one point, a cameraman from CNN climbed up on it, carrying all his gear, and positioned himself there in order to shoot some images of Elm Street and the gathering crowds.

Of course, it was not only the excellent view of the plaza that made this climb look so inviting to camera-carrying amateurs and professionals alike. They were doing this because a fifty-eight-year-old manufacturer of ladies' dresses, Abraham Zapruder, had made that same climb forty years earlier and accidentally filmed the assassination. The story of how that happened has become a contemporary legend. On the rainy morning of November 22, 1963, Zapruder went to work at his office on Elm Street. Although excited about the president's visit, he had left his 8 mm camera at home, since the weather conditions did not seem to invite filming. However, at ten o'clock the skies cleared. When the sun broke through, several people in his office who knew him to be an eager amateur filmmaker suggested that Zapruder go home and get the camera. In the future, a film of the presidential visit would undoubtedly find a special place in his collection of home movies. Zapruder went home and got the camera and returned to his office. After deciding not to film the motorcade from his office window, as he had originally planned to do after reading about its route in the morning newspapers, he went down to Dealey Plaza to find a better angle and, after looking around a bit, settled on the concrete abutment in the pergola. He suffered from vertigo and was afraid to climb up on it. The receptionist from his office, Marilyn Sitzman, who had found her way down to the plaza too, offered to hold onto his coat to steady him. They both climbed the pillar. At twelve thirty, the president's motorcade came down Houston Street and turned onto Elm Street. Zapruder kept filming the car the president was sitting in until it disappeared from view to the right, under the overpass. He never took his eye away from the telescopic lens that magnified everything he saw.[2]

One can only imagine what Zapruder would have thought if he had been able to see the abutment forty years later, knowing that his film and its story were engaging people in collective reenactment in Dealey Plaza. I felt dizzy when I eventually made the climb myself: from that vantage point, the world indeed did seem to me "increasingly filmic," to borrow the words of Joel Black, a literature and film scholar; the plaza itself was "recorded, registered, and increasingly recognizable only as a series of mediated events."[3] Watching the hordes of people made me feel as if I had climbed into the television set in my hotel room and become part of what I had watched earlier that morning, zapping from one channel to the next, encountering the same images again and again. A few people were lining up, waiting to get a chance to do exactly what I now found myself doing. All around me, people were filming—or they were being filmed as they *pretended* to film, in order to get their own simulations documented.

This book begins here, in Dallas on the day of the fortieth anniversary of Kennedy's death. *Zaprudered* explores how the cultural status of Zapruder's accidental footage has been transformed in the decades following the event and how it has contributed in producing a collective and compulsive impulse to visualize that today defines Dealey Plaza and the commemoration that goes on there. For more than a decade after the assassination, Zapruder's images were visible to the public only as a series of stills published in a magazine and were broadcast on national television first in 1975. Scrutinized for years as photographic evidence and an indexical record of one of the most controversial murders of the twentieth century, the Zapruder film has never yielded a conclusive version of what happened in Dealey Plaza, and its meaning remains contested for that reason. Over the years, however, the images have increasingly come to figure heavily in a range of diverse cultural expressions, including movies, television series, documentaries, video artworks, performances, plays, gallery installations and exhibitions, prints, paintings, video games, novels, and comic books. The fact that the original film that was inside Zapruder's camera has been converted into public property—becoming the highest-priced photographic artifact in the world in the process—both reflects and contributes to this transition from an evidentiary to an aesthetic image, which calls for a shift in critical focus to the performativity of the images.

Before addressing the nature of this transformation, however, it is pertinent to raise the fundamental question of what "the Zapruder film" *is*. Indeed, the compound noun and proper noun are only deceptively simple: even if the definite article suggests reference to a particular object, a film, and identifies it by transforming the name of its maker into a proper adjective, no one would protest or find it peculiar if I were to say that I woke up in my Dallas hotel and "saw the Zapruder film on television." In the vernacular, then, "the Zapruder film" simultaneously refers both to a photographic artifact—the original film that was inside Zapruder's camera when he recorded the assassination—and to one of the most recycled film clips of contemporary visual culture. Even if the distinctions between these two different meanings of the phrase are so familiar that we only seldom pause to reflect upon them, it is nevertheless significant to address them before contemplating the cultural status of what has simply come to be called "the Zapruder film."

A master and three copies of the film were distributed to four different cities on the afternoon of the day that followed Kennedy's death. "From then on," David Wrone points out, "the original and each copy would have separate and distinct histories."[4] Even the briefest account of the Zapruder film's early history thus raises questions of object, naming, and cultural status that echo those Walter Benjamin reflected upon in his essay on the status of the artwork in the age of "technological reproducibility."[5] Indeed, the original film has been seen as imbued with a complex sense of aura, even if it is not an artwork in any traditional sense of the word and remains vaulted and will never be exhibited. It is significant, however, that the cultural status of the Zapruder film depends not merely on the journeys of objects, whether originals or copies, but also on something less quantifiable, namely, how its images have appeared in a variety of media and spread virally through culture. That is the subject of this book, which, as the title suggests, explores the journey of Zapruder's images rather than his film.

ZAPRUDER'S IMAGES AS A RORSCHACH OF CULTURAL MEMORY

Every time we watch the footage today, the images have been transformed into something new. They keep floating hither and thither in what is popularly referred to as a torrent of images and sounds, and are endlessly recycled in what Jay David Bolter and Richard Grusin call "remediation," the mediation of mediation.[6] If we see them in a clip in one of the televised specials that map the major events of a century, they are placed within a larger narrative structure that is specific to the medium of television. If we see them in a theater, they have been edited into a movie and figure there in a way that is integral to a corresponding logic of storytelling. If we see the images on the Internet, on a website like YouTube, amateurs have played around with them on their desktops before posting something that yet resists generic description. If we watch a DVD at home, digitization has transformed the images, and we are invited to watch repeatedly. Unlike the film, which seems to have reached its final destination in a vault at the National Archives, the journey of Zapruder's images has no end.

Although he could never have anticipated such a comprehensive projection, Zapruder instantly understood that his images were bound to cross technological boundaries and appear in a number of media, that they inevitably had to be projected on a grand scale rather than in the private sphere of his living room. Richard B. Stolley, who bought the film for *Life* magazine from Zapruder the morning after Kennedy died, describes how, during their negotiations, Zapruder worried about the exploitation of his film. Zapruder told him about a dream from the previous night in which "he was walking through Times Square and came upon a barker urging tourists to step inside a sleazy theater to watch the President die on the big screen."[7] What Zapruder realized was that he had created images that neither he nor anyone else would ever be able to control entirely. Even if he could only sense it, there is something almost uncanny about how his nightmare of a Times Square spectacle predicted the manifold ways that his images would spread. In a way, this book may thus be said to explore the depths of Zapruder's early intuitions.

The cultural status of the Zapruder film derives in part from the fact that its projection is shaped by the realities of contemporary visual technology, but it is more complex than technological facts alone can explain. In a sense, Zapruder's images were seen first by their maker, who looked at them through his viewfinder as they were caught on Kodachrome II Safety Film, an outdoor color film. His footage came into being as what is known in photographic processing as a "latent image," but at the same time, a mental image was shaped, a memory that would keep Zapruder awake many a night in years to come. Wrone describes how Zapruder found himself in a state of shock after he saw the car disappear under the overpass and climbed down, only to wander around the chaotic plaza for a while before making it back to his office. After placing his camera on a filing cabinet, he sat down at his desk and began to weep. Traumatized by what he had seen, he nevertheless knew that he had to begin to deal with what to do with his recording.

His film was the subject of deep speculation before anyone saw it; several reporters had spoken with Zapruder before and immediately after he left the plaza. The images were thus imagined before the film had been projected or even developed; a description that immediately began to travel by word of mouth, spreading like wildfire, brought the strip of celluloid mythic status even in its early, embryonic state. Zapruder's traumatic experience was thus characterized by the paradoxical fact that the very images he wanted to forget were the same that he had to share with a mass audience, a fact that placed a heavy responsibility on his shoulders. A struggle for ownership preceded the first projection of the film, and its status as a unique record was recognized before it had been seen by anyone.[8]

As these initial observations indicate, the question of the identity of the Zapruder film is related to the question that W. J. T. Mitchell raises in the introduction to his *Iconology*, namely, "What is an image?" In listing the various meanings we attach to the word, Mitchell suggests that we think of images as a family: a rough distinction is normally made between material images and what he calls mental and verbal images.[9] Likewise, in more recently proposing a new approach to iconology, Hans Belting insists that images "are neither on the wall (or on the screen) nor in the head alone" and observes that the discourse of images is characterized by "contradictory conceptions of what images are and how they operate." Both Mitchell and Belting problematize how material and mental images have come to belong exclusively to specific institutional discourses (semiology, art history, psychology, neurobiology); as a result, the interactions between these two kinds of images, Belting argues, remain "largely unexplored."[10] A central reason that we tend to have a problem with the very notion of mental images, Mitchell argues, is that although we share the capability to project mental images (when we remember or dream, for example), we cannot point to the physical presence of a mental image.[11]

Indeed, questions concerning how our minds work visually are significant for how we remember in a culture of images. In recent years, several articles and books that address the complex relations between the past, memory, and history have sought to theorize the boundaries between material and mental images, and a new concept, "cultural memory," has come to present an alternative to that of "collective memory." "All memory is individual, unreproducible—it dies with each person," writes Susan Sontag in *Regarding the Pain of Others*. "What is called collective memory is not a remembering but a stipulating: that *this* is important, and this is the story about how it happened, with the pictures that lock the story in our minds."[12] Work on the idea of cultural memory has renewed recognition of the French sociologist Maurice Halbwachs, a student of Emile Durkheim and the author of *La Mémoire Collective* (published posthumously in 1950), a study that for years made him a primary theoretical reference point for any study that addressed how memories are shared collectively. However, several critics have come to suggest that emphasis on the social construction of memory brings with it a neglect of the significance of individual memory, and the need to address the way memories are "tangled," as Marita Sturken puts it, has led to a critical reformulation of Halbwachs's influential concept.[13] Theorists have increasingly recognized how the past, in one way or another, must always be culturally mediated.[14] Even though human memory may be an anthropological given, Andreas Huyssen argues, memory is nevertheless necessarily based on representation. The past does not simply reside in memory; it must be articulated before it can become memory.[15] Sturken sees cultural memory as different from, yet entangled with, individual memory and historical discourse; likewise, Mieke Bal describes the past as something always articulated in the present and thus as fundamentally an expression of the moment of articulation.[16] To these theorists, memory is a phenomenon that is not merely individual or social but also, significantly, cultural.

To a tremendous degree, cultural memory of the Kennedy assassination is shaped by the photographic record of the event, both directly and indirectly, in the centers as well as at the margins of culture. In *The World's Tribute to John F. Kennedy in Medallic Art*, published three years after the assassination, Aubrey Mayhew describes the timeworn tradition of medallic art as a privileged form of memorialization because it is tangible and material—it represents a "permanent record."[17] One of the medals in Mayhew's book is a double representation of the deaths of Kennedy and Oswald. One side copies the famous press photograph, taken by Jack Beers, of Jack Ruby shooting Oswald in the stomach, a picture that was circulated by the Associated Press and featured in *Life* magazine a week after the assassination. The other side depicts Kennedy's death. Positioned in the back seat, he clutches his neck in pain after the impact of the first bullet. At his side, Jacqueline Kennedy, wearing her pillbox hat, a familiar detail of assassination iconography, turns toward him. John Connally and his wife, Nellie, are placed in the seat in front of them, the governor also about to turn around; behind them, the Texas School Book Depository towers against a gloomy, dark sky. Engraved in metal, the image nevertheless has a photographic quality, and it clearly draws from the visual information of several photographic sources.

However permanent a record, and however much it may inspire collectors' nostalgia, the medal does not in any sense represent a defining or authoritative cultural memory of the assassination, as Mayhew suggested, or perhaps rather wished. Instead, the collectible seems to invite comparisons between different media of exchange and the shifting symbolic value we attach to them. Even if a medal differs from a coin, both are pictures that rest in the palm of a hand, and thus both raise questions concerning the transforming concept of "currency." In what Mitchell (echoing Benjamin) calls "the age of biocybernetic reproduction," images as well as money have come to circulate in global economies.[18] As this book amply demonstrates, this transition implies neither the gradual disappearance of Zapruder's images nor a cultural "devaluation," but rather a widespread and complex proliferation.

Whatever its form, it is difficult to imagine the cultural memory of the assassination without the Zapruder film; according to Sturken, it is impossible.[19]

Increasingly, future encounters with Zapruder's images will thus produce what Marianne Hirsch calls "postmemory," which is characterized not by recollection but rather by an interaction with cultural memory that depends on "imaginative investment and creation."[20] Significantly, cultural memory has the power to become infused with or replace real memories.[21] Sturken thus predicts plausibly that it is through Oliver Stone's *JFK* (1991) that a majority of people will come to see the Zapruder film in the future.[22] Whereas Zapruder's images evoke the memories of one generation, they are bound to shape the postmemories of the next.

A scene from Wolfgang Petersen's *In the Line of Fire* (1993) illustrates well the significance of these observations for the analysis of how Zapruder's images appear in culture. The movie tells the story of how Frank Horrigan (Clint Eastwood), one of the Secret Service agents who rode with the motorcade and failed to protect Kennedy in Dallas, gets another chance to take a bullet and save a president three decades later. (Describing himself wryly as a "living legend," "the only active agent who ever lost a president," Eastwood's character was inspired by real-life Secret Service agent Clinton J. Hill, the agent who ran after Kennedy's car and climbed up on it.) During a routine investigation, Horrigan searches an apartment and finds a wall covered with photographs and magazine articles of the assassination. The resident is clearly obsessed with the event, but is he dangerous? Horrigan returns a day later to find that there is just one photograph still pinned to the wall, one of him riding with the presidential motorcade in Dallas (a manipulation of James Altgen's well-known photograph for the Associated Press). Eerily, there is a red circle drawn around his head. From then on, he becomes personally involved, and the film describes the cat-and-mouse game that ensues between the aging agent and the would-be assassin, Mitch Leary (John Malkovich), a former CIA contractor grown bitter.

One night Leary (who calls himself Booth, after Lincoln's assassin) calls Horrigan at home and says, "I'm watching your movie." Isolated in one of the bare rooms where he spends much of the movie plotting a presidential assassination, Leary is watching footage from Kennedy's Dallas trip on his television set. As he talks to the agent, the camera zooms in on Horrigan's face; images from Dallas are superimposed over Eastwood's stony expression. Simultaneously, we see a young Eastwood manipulated into the footage; he has been given a digital haircut and can be spotted behind the Kennedys in the terminal at Love Field. "Only one agent reacted," Leary says, knowing which buttons to push, "and you were closer to Kennedy." Silently, Horrigan

FIG. I.3 A Secret Service agent, played by Clint Eastwood, visited by the ghosts of November 22, 1963. From *In the Line of Fire* (Wolfgang Petersen, 1993).

listens to Leary's droning voice asking him: "Late at night, when the demons come, do you see the rifle coming out of that window, or do you see Kennedy's head being blown apart?" Superimposed over Horrigan's face, Zapruder's images flash across the screen (fig. I.3).

Horrigan stares intently into what we gather is his memory of the assassination. The images he sees are identical with those Leary is watching as he slyly remarks, "That could have been your head blown apart." The scene shows one man remembering, then, and the other watching; it shows us that Zapruder's images are both mental and graphic images, that they are projected as both human and cultural memories. They have a diegetic function in the narrative of *In the Line of Fire*, since they come to represent the memory that Horrigan is haunted by and that he seeks to confront actively by asking to be reassigned to the presidential security team: the images are traumatic for him not only because they reflect how he shares in a collective sense of loss of a national leader, but also because they have come to symbolize his professional failure. The movie's use of the images thus reflects its makers' recognition of the prominent status of Zapruder's images in the formation of memory in the broadest sense of the word. Petersen was undoubtedly aware that they would be familiar to the audience, since they figure prominently in Stone's box-office success, which would still have been fresh in the minds of many moviegoers when *In the Line of Fire* premiered in the summer of 1993.

In the Line of Fire is thus a story of redemption, and Zapruder's images have a function in its narration. This reflects another fundamental aspect of the images: whenever they are projected, they are framed by a narrative. Indeed, in less than half a minute, the Zapruder film tells a story of its own, of how a man seated in a car with his wife is shot to death. Its 486 frames move with inevitability toward a double closure of film and life. In *Shooting Kennedy: JFK and the Culture of Images*, David Lubin suggests that the film's structure thus inevitably conforms to the three-act structure of mainstream cinema.[23] The film has proved immensely attractive to filmmakers, who frequently quote and reinscribe it; film scholars have been fond of proclaiming it a "cinematic ur-text."[24] Zapruder's images have thus lent themselves to a particular kind of meditation on the filmic image and, in recent years, more specifically on the documentary image. In addressing the relationship between the Zapruder film as record and as representation, Stella Bruzzi argues that the footage is "mutable" in the sense that it is always reinterpreted and recontextualized, and thus always incomplete, a fact that profoundly informs its status as archival evidence.[25] The footage can be considered a "fragment seized from reality," in the words of Michael Chanan; it is always already both index and icon, both objective and subjective, in the way that it necessarily shows a truth, but not the whole truth.[26]

Zaprudered represents a shift in focus and scope from the above-mentioned chapter-length discussions of Zapruder's footage in several ways. It explores the images in depth rather than merely describing how they are quoted in a variety of media. It addresses the ways in which the footage reappears in a range of narrative situations that are distinctly characterized by verbal-visual tensions, but it does not limit its discussions to questions concerning the properties of the image in fiction and nonfiction film. Whereas the 8 mm film that Zapruder recorded had no sound, we always encounter the images in a word-image interplay—words, whether spoken or written, shape our understanding of them—and this fundamental fact has implications far beyond the ontological debates that tend to inform medium-specific writings on the importance of the footage. To achieve a greater understanding of how Zapruder's images have increasingly taken on an allegorical character over the last decades, it is therefore vital to address how their incessant movement across media informs and even defines their shifting performativity in visual culture.

The most basic definition of allegory reflects how it says one thing and means another, as Angus Fletcher observes in his classic study, how it undermines our expectation that our words "mean what they say."[27] A couple of years before Fletcher's comprehensive book came out in 1964, J. L. Austin's *How To Do Things with Words* was published, a book that addresses the performativity of words—how they in fact not only *mean* more than or something different from what they say, but also *do* more than just say things.[28] In much of his work, Mitchell insists on a sustained critical reflection on the ability of images to take on a similar agency. This book represents an attempt to address Zapruder's images from such a perspective, namely, that what they do is every bit as important as what they are or mean. This shift in focus is significant for our understanding of the extensive allegorical reach of the images because the many attempts to impart knowledge about the assassination from the footage ultimately have contributed profoundly to their transformation into allegory.

How the assassination has been represented visually, Art Simon argues, reflects more than anything a fundamental instability, and the Zapruder film plays a particularly significant role in this, since ever-new attempts to discover some hidden truth in the images through rotoscoping, rephotography, and frame enlargement ultimately have achieved abstraction in the place of precision.[29] The definitive moving image of the assassination, the Zapruder film provides a time frame of the event and has inspired endless and contradictory theories about what happened when Kennedy was shot; bodily movements have been scrutinized in search of evidence of a second shooter. The film has been used to argue both for and against a wealth of conspiracy theories.[30] Indeed, as the forensic gaze has continued to reveal the immense number of dots of which a photographic image ultimately consists, and as the epistemological status of the film consequently has been threatened by this removal from figurality to abstraction, artists have increasingly turned to its expressive aspects, to its allegorical potential.[31] The epistemological crisis described by several cultural theorists thus simultaneously produces and reflects a transformation of the performative function of Zapruder's images from the evidentiary to the aesthetic. The images hide as much as they reveal, making the spectator look hard for what they seem to conceal, for what is there but seems to be invisible. The effect of the many investigations into the film's frames—whether they have been viewed in slow motion or had their colors enhanced or been projected forward or in reverse or, more recently, been digitally manipulated—is that the footage has become "a work of artistic abstraction," Lubin argues.[32] As John Beck observes, a history of the uses and abuses of the footage thus offers critical insight into a culture that has increasingly lost faith in the indexicality of photographic representations. In a sense, Zapruder's images have simultaneously caused this distrust in the veracity of images and called for innovative interpretive methods with which to approach visual information now and in the future.[33]

The scene from Petersen's movie suggests that a perspective on Zapruder's images as a reemerging, traumatic representation and an involuntary memory is significant, but as this book demonstrates amply, their allegorical quality involves much more, finally, than a "return of the dead," in Roland Barthes's well-known formulation.[34] Christopher Brown's painting *Elm Street* (1995) illustrates this point well (fig. I.4).

Significantly, remembering is a process not merely of recall but inevitably also of distortion; there is a difference between the mental images we produce in moments of seeing and those involved in remembering, and the scene in Petersen's movie does not address this distinction—which is precisely what interests Brown. Obviously, *Elm Street* differs from the film scene in that it is a painting exhibited in a gallery; however, it also distinguishes itself by transforming Zapruder's images more radically, to the extent that this transformation constitutes the painting and makes it predominantly allegorical. It does not merely depict a scene; it insistently invites us to reflect upon its depiction and to question more deeply the processes of imaging, imagining, and picturing. If the advent of photography has taught us much about how imprecise memory is, as Alison M. Gingeras suggests, about how it is "nebulous, malleable, ever changing," then the painted image, materially sensual and tactile, can be seen as corresponding "more closely to the imprecision of the human brain's mnemonic functions."[35] However, Brown's painted image of a human memory shaped by the photographic record of an event insists that these processes are entangled, that the technology of photography deeply informs mnemonic functions.

Brown paints his own individual memory of the film, not the event of Kennedy's death. *Elm Street* is part of a series of paintings which all allude to Zapruder's images in similar ways, echoing the filmic properties of the original (blurs, visible frame edges, sprocket holes). *Elm Street* can thus be placed in a tradition that addresses not only the increasingly contested mnemonic function of photography but also, by extension, various contemporary art debates. The painting illustrates Beck's observation that what makes the

FIG. I.4   Christopher Brown, *Elm Street* (1995). Oil on linen. 88 × 95 in. (223.52 × 241.3 cm.). Collection of the Kemper Museum of Contemporary Art, Kansas City, Missouri. Gift of the E. Kemper Carter and Anna Curry Carter Community Memorial Trust, 1996.3. Used with permission of the Kemper Museum of Contemporary Art.

Zapruder film such an important text in the history of American visual culture is that the film and the history of its reception have contributed significantly to the very criteria of what has constituted art since the 1960s.[36] *Elm Street* thus invites reflection not only on the formation of human and cultural memory but also on abstraction and figurality, on the properties of painted and photographic images, and ultimately on what we conceive of as art.

Certainly, Brown's painting suggests that the Zapruder film, widely regarded as symbolic of a crisis of representation, must also be considered as representative of a specific period in cultural history. In his "report on knowledge," Jean-François Lyotard defines the postmodern as "incredulity towards metanarratives," that is, toward the grand narratives of history and science.[37] Fredric Jameson refers to the Kennedy assassination as no less than the defining moment of this paradigm shift, the "inaugural event."[38] Such a sentiment has been echoed by critics who have conceived of it paradoxically as "the first postmodern historical event."[39] Indeed, Kennedy's death seems to resist narrativization, and yet only inspires more of it; it threatens to atomize any model theory of narrative. This has led Hayden White to refer to it as an example of how historical notions of "the event" have been dissolved, a condition in turn giving rise to "new genres of postmodernist parahistorical representation."[40] The assassination, White argues, can be considered a "modernist event," one that resists traditional methods of categorization as well as ways of assigning meanings to events.[41] The Warren Commission's multivolume report on the assassination becomes a postmodern symbol of such a dissolution of the event, a "novelization of the Zapruder film," in the words of J. G. Ballard, or, as one of the characters in Don DeLillo's *Libra* describes it, "the megaton novel James Joyce would have written if he'd moved to Iowa City and lived to be a hundred."[42]

ZAPRUDER'S IMAGES AND THE PICTORIAL TURN

It is not my intention here to invoke the postmodernism debate or to dwell further on the question of whether the Zapruder film is a genuinely postmodern phenomenon. The point, rather, is that the technological realities of the period in question are bound not only to shape any cultural study of the Zapruder film, but also to transform how we think and write about images and about the material conditions in which they are made to appear. In what follows, Zapruder's images will therefore be analyzed against the background of what Mitchell calls the "pictorial turn."[43] The pictorial turn, Mitchell posits in *Picture Theory*, is complexly related to the postmodern; it is less a beginning of something new at the end of postmodernism than it is a continuation or constituent of the postmodern. What are the consequences of this observation of a pictorial turn for how one should address Zapruder's images critically? Most significantly, the images should not be analyzed exclusively from the perspective of one of the "models of textuality," Mitchell insists. The pictorial turn entails "a postlinguistic, postsemiotic rediscovery of the picture as a complex interplay between visuality, apparatus, institutions, discourse, bodies, and figurality" that engages us in a critical rethinking of the theoretical models we have constructed to make sense of how we look at images. Of course, this does not mean that these theories cannot provide insights that are important (as indeed they do throughout this book). Rather, it suggests that we need to recognize that spectatorship is as deep a problem as reading and that "visual experience and 'visual literacy' might not be fully explicable on the model of textuality."[44] The pictorial turn thus stimulates interest in the very question of what vision is, a "fascination with the senses, perception, and imagination"—in short, an interest in an aesthetic complexity that cannot be addressed with a "reliance on linguistic and discursive models" alone.[45]

The medal, the movie, and the painting: all these illustrate how Zapruder's images are in a sense graphic, mental, and verbal images that shape and distort human as well as culturally produced memories with imagery that is, ultimately, also expressive, a quality that makes the film latently allegorical. All three expressions suggest that Lubin is right when he insists that the Zapruder film today must be analyzed as "more than a forensic or historical document, more than a home movie."[46] This book consists of analyses of how a variety of cultural expressions have projected Zapruder's images in ways not unlike these initial examples, which I have merely touched upon briefly. *Zaprudered* is thus a study of how images appear in a variety of media and have distinct performative functions that shape and are shaped by a variety of material practices in producing pictorial representations. Both image-in-motion (abstract) and object-in-motion (concrete), the Zapruder film evidently calls for a kind of analysis that addresses the aesthetic, social, political, and ethical aspects of the film's migratory identity. Zapruder's images appear in an expansive object domain and can never be fixed by any one object. They seem to exist epidemically rather than endemically, leaving the analyst forever a step behind, troubling the very sense of "object" in a way that threatens to critically undermine systematic book-length study. Indeed, *Zaprudered* represents less an attempt to overcome these problems than to work with them—in the belief that valuable insights are produced in the process.

Not only to acknowledge, but also to take critically into consideration this fleeting movement between the concrete and the abstract that characterizes the unruly identity of Zapruder's images, this book proposes to think of them as "traveling images." It follows from this conception, which seeks to reflect how the images move across and between the media in which they appear, that the present work can be considered an extended argument for the view that an image-picture duality is fundamental to the Janus-like identity of the Zapruder film as well as to its cultural status. Whereas the word "picture" in these pages refers to the material image, the word "image" will be used to describe the immaterial image.[47] The metaphoricity of the phrase "traveling image" is intended to suggest that Zapruder's images consequently invite a movement between disciplines, that they call for the Latin prefix "inter-": neither the traveling image nor the study of it can ever reach a final destination. Embedded in the phrase is an acknowledgment that images cannot belong to any one discipline and, furthermore, that an analysis of this kind is profoundly dialectic, since it can begin and end only with temporary conclusions that must be amended in an ongoing process.

Close readings of how Zapruder's images "travel" allow me to address the transition of the cultural status both of the images and the film; the one informs the other. Images have always traveled, and I should state that I do not think of "traveling images" as exclusively photographic; neither their appeal nor their reach are confined by the visual technology of any given period. Traveling images are notable for their iconogenerative power, for how they persist to be projected, imagined, and described through an extended period of time and in very different ways.[48] For widely different reasons, images have traveled because they had to be seen and to be seen again.

With such a scope, there is no one "field" of scholarship, no single discipline of the humanities, from which one can approach and address Zapruder's images. The success of the present endeavor depends on the validity of an interdisciplinary approach—a meeting of perspectives and discourses—for the critical analysis of a phenomenon of contemporary culture. As Mieke Bal points out, there are two basic reasons for invoking interdisciplinarity, "either because the object requires it, or because the approach is more productive when not confined to disciplinary traditions."[49] Critics of interdisciplinarity sometimes see it as a hollow gesture, as an irresponsible declaration of a Feyerabendian "anything goes" attitude, or simply as an autostatement of unclear implications. In a symposium on interdisciplinarity in the *Art Bulletin*, Carlo Ginzburg reminds us that "there is nothing intrinsically innovative or subversive in an interdisciplinary approach to knowledge," and in the same forum, Mitchell observes that interdisciplinarity "may be nothing more than a euphemism for something else, a term that permits us to feel good about what we do and to avoid thinking about it too precisely."[50]

However different in their thoughts on "being interdisciplinary," Ginzburg, Mitchell, and Bal agree that the point must be that interdisciplinarity is performed not routinely or ritualistically—that, in the words of Ginzburg, the critic is not "unchallenged by the objects"—but rather that it provokes new methods, new ways of looking and thinking.[51] *Zaprudered* draws on insights from articles and books that can be placed in disciplines and fields such as visual culture studies, cultural analysis, American studies, history, iconology, and narratology. Furthermore, several of my readings are informed by preceding genre- and medium-specific studies with which they enter into a dialogue, and a number of works I consult in the pages that follow address the Kennedy images or the Zapruder film more specifically. Indeed, a number of these texts, hard to categorize in any rigid way, could thus be said to belong in more than one discipline. To engage with this multitude of texts meaningfully, I have been inspired by what Bal calls a "concept-based methodology."[52]

Bal's idea is that the analyst not only addresses the etymological and intellectual history of a critical concept, but also engages with it in analysis as a "traveling concept." With reference to an article in which Jonathan Culler traces the concept of "the performative" across disciplinary borders, Bal proposes that the concept itself is not only performative, but also potentially productively so in analysis.[53] Echoing Austin, she suggests that a concept used as an analytical tool benefits from always being in a process of becoming: "While groping to define, provisionally and partly, what a particular concept may *mean*, we gain insight into what it can *do*."[54] This heuristic strategy informs the analysis of *Zaprudered*. It was Edward Said who observed that ideas and theories travel, just like people and schools of criticism: they travel "from person to person, from situation to situation, from one period to the other."[55] A failure to critically address how this profoundly conditions analysis, Said insists, can result in theoretical stagnation and irresponsible appropriation. In the introduction to her *Reader*, Bal insists that concepts can offer "miniature theories" only if scholars use them to confront, rather than apply, the cultural objects under examination.[56] This point is instrumental in a book about Zapruder's footage, since the history of its appropriations reflects strongly how cultural objects are "amenable to change and apt to illuminate historical and cultural differences."[57] The aim of *Zaprudered* is to enact and engage with these ongoing transformations of images as well as concepts. An ongoing reflection on traveling images thus provides this book with the miniature theory around which it revolves.

Even if Zapruder's images travel, they cannot, as Art Simon argues in *Dangerous Knowledge*, be regarded merely as "free-floating signifiers." Rather, they need to be addressed with attention to how they inform and are informed by the debates around Kennedy's assassination, the discursivity of which is defined by very specific media forms.[58] As Simon observes, the journalistic texts and their deployment serve as a fitting starting point because it was in those pages that the cultural memory of the assassination was publicly initiated and most thoroughly developed in the early years.[59] Every time Zapruder's images appear, they do so in what Bal calls an "expository discourse." Gestures of showing, she suggests, can be analyzed as discursive acts that are analogous to speech acts.[60] "Exposition" is a word we traditionally connect with "exhibition"; normally, since the aftermath of the Industrial Revolution, both terms have referred to public fairs or displays of material objects, whether industrial products or artworks. In my first chapter, however, I borrow Bal's notion of "exposition," which extends to a much broader, partly metaphorical use. By analyzing three narratives that in different ways "project" Zapruder's images, the chapter discusses how the immediate transformation of the Zapruder film into private property was the effect of a distinct pressure to visualize the event of the assassination in the news media. Ownership was motivated solely by this pressure; the cultural status of the Zapruder film was thus entirely conditioned by the ability of its images to produce the account of the assassination that the privileged photographic record offered. The achieving of "expository agency" thus implied the cultural authority that is ascribed to the main narrator and interpreter of the past.[61] In effect, the modes of display of these journalistic discourses were defined by a show-and-tell strategy that is troubled by any large-scale projection of traumatic footage.

In Chapters Two through Four, *Zaprudered* considers how Zapruder's images have been treated artistically and how this changes the way we look at them. Artistic expressions have had a tendency to be neglected in studies of how collective memories are shaped. In *Covering the Body*, her comprehensive study of how journalists have shaped the cultural memory of the assassination, Barbie Zelizer describes in a brief epilogue how the premiere of Stone's *JFK* put the assassination debates back on the national agenda at the very moment that her book was going to publication.[62] As Zelizer argues in her brief coda, Stone's film supports and extends the central arguments of her book, namely, that journalists have used the assassination story in order to attain cultural authority. The impact of Stone's film was unprecedented, and the need to address it in a book about how journalists have shaped the collective memory of the assassination is obvious—not least since the success of the film contributed to a significant transfer of authority from the historian (as well as the journalist) to the filmmaker. Yet Zelizer's epilogue leaves the reader wondering whether popular culture—or the art world, for that matter—had not also shaped human and cultural memory of the assassination before the release of Stone's film—and if so, why this is practically absent from her study.

"Culture, popular or otherwise," David Lubin writes, "is not a mere side effect of history or a glittering distraction from it but is instead integral to it, playing an active role in the making of that history."[63] Chapters Two through Four not only reflect this sentiment, but also take it seriously by performing in-depth analyses of how Zapruder's images appear in Ant Farm's video *The Eternal Frame* (1975), in Don DeLillo's novel *Underworld* (1997), and in an episode of the sitcom *Seinfeld* (1992). The second chapter, "Eternally Framed," introduces "quotation" as a key concept for exploring how Zapruder's images travel through these widely different cultural expressions. The paradox *The Eternal Frame* theorizes, I suggest in Chapter Two, is that whereas bodies and pictorial representations are subject to destruction, images are only empowered by acts of iconoclasm. By presenting Zapruder's images theatrically, the performance troupe Ant Farm insists that the images cannot be made to disappear, that they have taken on a powerful life of their own. *The Eternal Frame* theorizes about how Zapruder's frames of film are constantly reframed in mediation, both metaphorically and quite literally, by enacting it.

Description can indeed be called an expository mode of writing. In Chapter Three, the concept of exposition can thus be said to "travel" into the realm of novelistic discourse. In a close reading of Don DeLillo's description of an artistic multiple-screen projection of Zapruder's images in *Underworld*, I argue that the images are projected as both verbal image and memento mori. The fact that the art installation DeLillo describes is his own invention is less significant than the capacity of his fiction to performatively analyze the transition of Zapruder's images from evidentiary to aesthetic image: whereas in *Libra* they are analyzed by assassination researchers who are unable to read any epistemological truth in them, they are projected as aesthetic image in *Underworld*. In Ant Farm's video as well as in DeLillo's novel, Zapruder's images thus appear in what Mitchell calls "metapictures," pictures that theorize about pictorial representation.[64] In Chapter Four, in an analysis of how "The Boyfriend" (1992), an episode of the sitcom *Seinfeld*, quotes the projection of Zapruder's images in Stone's movie in order to perform a genre parody, I observe how the images have traveled even further away from their status as historical images. Quotation here transports me into theories of postmodern intertextuality and Linda Hutcheon's notion of parody as "stylistic confrontation."[65]

In the fifth chapter, I consider how two events in the nineties both reflected and contributed to what I describe as a transformation of cultural status. In the summer of 1998, the Zapruder film was released commercially on a DVD, *Image of an Assassination*, and later that same year, the U.S.

government used eminent domain to take Zapruder's camera-original footage from the Zapruder family and into its own possession. These events reflect how Zapruder's images are now widely recognized in U.S. culture as predominantly aesthetic rather than evidentiary images, I argue in the chapter. The sixth chapter then traces the images into the museum. In a close reading of Zoran Naskovski's *Death in Dallas* (2000), I consider how the installation is not only informed by how it is situated—in the exhibition narrative of which it is a part, or as a particular form of institutional poetics—but also marked as an event by factors that have to be identified outside the museum building. Zapruder's frames are now being projected in the same sphere as the finer arts; how does this change how we look at the images?

The seventh chapter returns me to Dealey Plaza, where I pay a visit to the Sixth Floor Museum, arguing that a pressure to visualize troubled their poetics of preservation in the years leading up to the fortieth anniversary of the assassination. The public outcry against a video game that invites the player to imagine herself as the assassin—as the corner-window exhibit does, however differently, in the museum in Dealey Plaza—can in part be said to reflect how the museum's institutional authority to narrate and stage events of history remains so strong that it often goes unquestioned.

All these chapters reflect how "no set of imagery has toured the cultural landscape as much as that referring in some way to the death of JFK," as Art Simon observes in *Dangerous Knowledge*, a book dedicated to analyzing how this imagery (and not exclusively the Zapruder film) informs Pop art, avant-garde art, and several movies.[66] For very good reasons, Zapruder's footage has tended to be regarded as metonymical in its relations to the event of the assassination and various broader cultural and historical phenomena that are integral to and surround it. Like several of the articles and books mentioned in the previous pages—whether by Marita Sturken, David Lubin, Stella Bruzzi, or Michael Chanan—Simon's book features a chapter-long discussion of Zapruder's footage and uses it as a lens through which to address a very specific problematic. However, the time seems overripe for a study that concentrates consistently on the impact of Zapruder's images on culture, as well as on the film's transformed cultural status, over the length of a whole book. *Zaprudered* is the first publication to do so, a strategy the range of these phenomena presently seems to insist upon.

Even if the history of the Zapruder film is unique, it is evoked regularly with reference to contemporary events in visual culture. However different from their representational predecessors, the frames resemble such earlier images as Emanuel Leutze's history painting *Washington Crossing the Delaware*

(1851) and Timothy O'Sullivan's *A Harvest of Death, Gettysburg* (1863) in that they reflect how historical events have always been pictured.[67] But the immense proliferation of pictures and the steadfast progression of contemporary visual technology in our present age, I would hold, urge us forcefully to consider with particular attention the specific subcategory of traveling images to which Zapruder's belong: those that originate in a photographic record of traumatic events captured by amateurs. It is pertinent not only to remember that the Zapruder film is indeed such a record, but also to reflect upon the implications of its transition into aesthetic image that *Zaprudered* analyzes. My book thus concludes by addressing a selection of more recent images shot by amateurs—images that have only just begun their journey through culture—and by reflecting upon the fact that such images at present seem to increasingly define cultural memory. These concluding observations are meant to invite further theoretical thinking on images that travel—for if there is no ending for this kind of analysis, there are certainly many beginnings.

Owning, Showing, Telling

These memories, like those of every previous national tragedy, would
eventually fade into the dry pages of history, were it not for the camera's
eye that recorded with immediacy and color the event of those 72 hours.
And with this record, future generations shall also become privileged witnesses to the actual event, to be present and shaken and reawakened as we
were. // John F. Kennedy Memorial Edition of *Life* magazine, December
6, 1963

IN THE AFTERNOON OF NOVEMBER 25, 1963, the day of Kennedy's funeral,
Hughes Rudd and Richard C. Hotelett were speaking on CBS Radio when Rudd
suddenly exclaimed, "Dick, ah, Dan Rather just came into the studio." Rudd
went on to ask Rather, "What do you have that's new—anything?" Struggling
to find the proper words, Rather began to explain that he had just attended
a projection of the Zapruder film. "I . . . have just returned from seeing a . . .
a movie . . . which clearly shows in some great detail the exact moments preceding, the exact moments of, the president's assassination," he hesitantly
said, uncertain of what Rudd and Hotelett had been talking about before he
entered the studio. "I think it fits right into the context of what we've been
saying," Hotelett suggested, and invited Rather to share his experience, upon
which the young reporter said: "Well, let me tell you, then, give you a word
picture of the motion picture that we have just seen."[1]

In a sense, the "word picture" that followed represents the first public
projection of the Zapruder film. When Rather went on the air with his description, the film had not been broadcast and individual frames were yet to
be printed. His narrative reached thousands of Americans listening in their
homes; several of these and many more would turn on the television later
that same day to see Rather appear there too, giving a similar depiction after

a lead-in from news anchor Walter Cronkite. By that Monday, Rather had already become a familiar sight to the national television audience, since he had been reporting from Dallas throughout the weekend following the assassination. This chapter addresses how Zapruder's images were described in Rather's on-air narratives and how they were then displayed in a series of magazine photo-essays and on a late-night talk show. All these modes of display are treated as forms of what Mieke Bal calls "expository acts" or "gestures of showing."[2]

The mass media began to shape the cultural memory of the assassination almost as soon as it happened; the news of Kennedy's death spread to most Americans within half an hour.[3] Stores were closed, classes were interrupted and cancelled, and workers left their jobs and went home, where they would listen to and watch Cronkite, Rather, and a small group of other anchors and reporters excessively. Many viewers devoted a full four days to following the coverage of the assassination and the surrounding events.[4] The media thus inevitably came to shape how an event felt collectively to be traumatic was experienced and continues to be remembered as such.[5] The particular circumstances that surrounded the early projections of the images are addressed in this chapter. Zapruder's original film as well as the print and motion-picture copyrights became owned by a leading magazine publisher, and this is of great significance for how they were to be projected in the years that followed. The narratives I analyze established the composite cultural status of Zapruder's images in the first years as they appeared as verbal images, in image-texts, and eventually as moving images. The fact that the images were projected, then taken out of public view, then projected again in a new and different way is important, since this oscillating movement between acts of concealing and revealing produces a way of looking that ultimately helped transform the images from forensic data to aesthetic representations. Furthermore, I argue, the earliest Zapruder narratives sought to render their own acts of projection "invisible" and, in effect, to produce what I propose to call a transfer of witnessing, whereas later projections increasingly directed attention toward the Zapruder film, contributing to a mythologization of it.

Exposition is "always also an argument," Bal insists, since it entails an act of showing, which implies seeing, an authority conditioned by "the visual availability of the exposed object."[6] The Zapruder film, the ultimate visual record, presented itself as a key expository object even before it was developed: it immediately laid claim to this position because it enabled privileged display or, rather, the possibility of several privileged modes of display. Owning the film and, more significantly, the copyrights to it meant controlling the distribution of its images and the traveling they would undertake. It involved expository agency on a large scale and over an extended period of time. To obtain the object, one had to have the power to do so, and control of the object in turn increased one's power, symbolic as well as real. Thus, expository agency is embedded in power structures. "Only those who are invested with cultural authority can be expository agents," Bal holds, since they "are able to address an audience, routinely, that is numerous and anonymous to the agent."[7]

Addressing such a vast audience, however, involves a host of problems when the expository object is a film that depicts the brutal assassination of a national leader, and from the very first, the agency that a projection of Zapruder's images involves was troubled. "What can be shown, what should not be shown—few issues arouse more public clamor," Susan Sontag observes in *Regarding the Pain of Others*.[8] Zapruder's images confront the viewer with what W. J. T. Mitchell calls "the frontiers of the unimaginable and the unspeakable, the place where words and images fail, where they are refused, prohibited as obscenities that violate a law of silence and invisibility, muteness and blindness."[9] With reference to Ludwig Wittgenstein's axiom "Concerning that about which one cannot speak, one must remain silent," Mitchell reflects upon the meanings of the word "cannot"—is it a "grammatical" or a "moral prohibition"? He arrives at an important distinction between the inability to speak and the refusal to do so.[10] The first reflects how a traumatic scene is, in the words of Ruth Leys, "unavailable for a certain kind of recollection."[11] Bal treats such a recollection narratively, thinking of memory as an act of visualizing the past—an act that it becomes impossible to share when the traumatized subject cannot make a story, when it lacks words.[12] Certainly, when the assassination was widely felt to be such an "unspeakable" event by many, it was in part because of the sheer brutality of Kennedy's death, the suddenness of it—exactly the aspects the Zapruder film uniquely captures.[13]

In the professional news media, questions did not so much concern whether the images were to be projected, but rather how and, even more importantly, by whom. Indeed, the unlikely fact that none of the television networks had recorded what happened created a formidable panic in their newsrooms. Thinking back, Rather remembers in his memoir (aptly titled *The Camera Never Blinks*) how he responded to this information: "If you are a TV newsman, almost your first thought, your first instinct is: *film*. Was there film?"[14] This immediate interest in the existence of a visual record, a unique expository object, produces a pressure to visualize that is so tremendous that,

to Rather and other members of the media, it becomes the governing principle of reporting.[15] Although trauma "is supposed to be the unrepresentable in
word and image," Mitchell observes, "we incorrigibly insist on talking about
it, depicting it, and trying to render it in increasingly vivid and literal ways."[16]
Indeed, the exposition of Zapruder's images is contested by this double and
contradictory, but deeply human, sense of prohibition: the conflicted urge to
describe or project the unspeakable, to share it, to structure it into narrative.
When analyzing the earliest instances of a pressure to visualize the assassination by projecting images of it, we should keep this in mind. The point
here is not, with the considerable benefit of hindsight, to moralize. The news,
Michael Schudson reminds us, "is produced by people who operate, often unwittingly, within a cultural system, a reservoir of stored cultural meanings
and patterns of discourse." This does not imply that one neglects questions of
individual responsibility, but it seems to require an analysis of how the power
of the media "lies not only (and not even primarily) in its power to declare
things to be true, but in its power to provide the forms in which the declara-
tions appear."[17] Zapruder's images, as we are about to see, have shaped as well
as been shaped by these forms of appearance.

THE CAMERA AND THE EYE

Indeed, the profession of reporting is often described as one of overcoming
the double prohibition Mitchell describes. "In the midst of mourners," Rather
writes in a chapter about his reporting of the Kennedy assassination, "a reporter can feel his pulse race." In language colored by visual metaphors, he
goes on to describe a person who is risk taking in the name of truth telling, a
figure who is so driven to see and to show that he "will sometimes walk closer
to the flames, so he may use the light." Looking back, Rather writes, this reporter may come to think that he "was lucky to have been in that place at
that time."[18] Rather's figure of the reporter, it would seem, places himself as
a witness in order to translate individual experience into one that is shared,
and considers this no less than a call and a privilege. Indeed, such a profession
places a heavy responsibility on its practitioners.

In *The Power of News*, Schudson asks the question, what is a reporter?
Reading the autobiographies of two members of the profession, Lincoln Steffens (1866–1936) and Harrison Salisbury (1908–1993), he observes a shift
between two eras in journalism as the reporter is transformed from a person
"with a mission" to one "with a role." Whereas the former is "confronting

politics," Schudson argues, the latter is "detached," since he is "confronting a career in journalism and a name for himself."[19] Rather's career reflects this shift, as does his autobiographical account of it, which, however unlike those of Steffens and Salisbury, similarly provides insights into not only his self-understanding but also his self-representation.

Indeed, Rather's account of how he came to cover the Kennedy assassination is particularly illuminating in this respect. It is described as a transitional event in his life and in his career, and yet the narrative is defined by a peculiar mixture of pride and guilt. This is because Rather's reporting in Dallas remains controversial; it continues to be narrated both as success and as failure. The controversy revolves around two incidents. First, Rather has consistently been credited with providing the unconfirmed report that eventually led to one of the most famous moments in the history of live broadcasting, namely, Cronkite's composed yet tearful declaration on CBS television that Kennedy was dead. However, Rather did not deliver the report.[20] Second, and more significant here, his on-air description of Zapruder's images misdescribed the shot to Kennedy's head: "Given the circumstances I would like to think my description was good," he writes, but adds, "regrettably, it was not without error, in terms of what was unsaid about the movement of the President's head. . . . I failed to mention the violent, backward reaction."[21]

In her book about how the media covered the assassination, Barbie Zelizer describes how CBS has systematically misrepresented these events over the years in order to add to rather than complicate the legend of "being first"—a legend that has been constitutive not only of Rather's fame, but ultimately also of the reputation of CBS News.[22] In his frequent appearances in television retrospectives, Rather has "reinforced" his "role as an authoritative interpreter of the assassination story," an authority that, in turn, made him a "journalistic celebrity," Zelizer claims. When I was visiting Dallas for the fortieth anniversary of the assassination, I was thus not surprised when I read in a paper one morning that Rather had arrived to sit down, with a lighted plaza as a backdrop, and reminisce about the assassination and how he came to cover it. He seemed to be the perfect guest for any of the several television shows being broadcast from the city.

With the news of Rather's presence, Dealey Plaza yet again visibly became a site of struggle for cultural authority. Zelizer gives a detailed account of how the assassination was "mainly witnessed by amateurs, not professionals," and how this "challenged journalists' professionalism."[23] Reporters and media institutions sought to recover that sense of professionalism not only in Dallas during those November days in 1963, but also, in the following decades, by producing and participating in anniversary television retrospectives.[24] Analyzed as a collective effort, as by Zelizer, these strategic attempts to claim ownership of an event and its representation should give us pause. In Dealey Plaza in 2003, eleven years after Zelizer wrote her book, Rather once again demonstrated his persistent power as a key narrator of the assassination, in spite of evidence showing that he forty years earlier had failed to report the event according to his own ideals of reporting.[25]

In my reading of Rather's reports, however, I would like to shift the focus from Rather the reporter (or his career or his legacy) to his expository account of Zapruder's images: to what the images did for Rather and what he did for the images. Only thus can one begin to address the power of the account and the position Rather has had as interpreter-narrator. The forms of discourse that inform the work of reporters, Schudson observes, have an "extraordinary power" to control both narrator and audience.[26] As Zelizer points out, "retellings of the assassination were shaped by how journalists decided to narratively reconstruct its event," one implication being that the narratives "accommodated the narrator's inclusion within the assassination story."[27] Rather's word pictures entail a particular form of such inclusion; they were so powerful precisely because they invited a form of visualization that depended equally on the imaginative powers of both narrator and listener. "Description," Schudson points out, "is always an act of imagination."[28] In Rather's case, such an act reflected an attempt to overcome Mitchell's double prohibition, to speak where both words and images fail.

When Rather joined Rudd and Hotelett in a radio studio on the afternoon of November 25, 1963, he had just returned from Zapruder's offices, where he had attended the screening that preceded negotiations for the motion-picture copyrights to the film. He describes in his memoir how he did not sit down while watching the film and rushed off immediately afterward to consult CBS News executives in New York, who had the authority to make an offer.[29] In effect, Rather ended up describing the film while losing the rights to broadcast it, since Time Inc. purchased them just after he left. However, whereas Rather neither witnessed the assassination himself (he was located outside Dealey Plaza, waiting for the motorcade to pass through, when Kennedy was shot) nor was able finally to purchase the film from Zapruder, his description still enabled him to construct a first-person narrative of indirect witnessing. This resulted in a particular form of expository discourse—in what can be called a contemporary form of ekphrasis.

An ancient Greek term that means to speak (*phrazo*) out (*ek*), the concept of ekphrasis has its roots in the field of rhetoric, but has been appropriated by literary critics and art historians—it is a typical example of what Bal would call a traveling concept.[30] Consequently, it has inspired both the crossing over and the reinforcement of disciplinary boundaries.[31] In art-historical discourses, an ekphrastic description vividly evokes absent sculptures and paintings in words, but seldom objects outside the realm of whatever passes as art.[32] In visual culture studies, however, several attempts have been made to broaden the perspective considerably, and to think of ekphrasis as a concept that enables the critic to frame and situate the analysis of a wide variety of word-image relations.

Indeed, Rather's narratives on radio and television can fruitfully be considered verbal representations of a visual representation, what Bal calls an "evocation of absent images."[33] Like Bal, Mitchell points out that in an ekphrastic description, what is described "cannot literally come into view."[34] An ekphrastic gesture thus evokes an absent picture by replacing it with a verbal image. The absence of the expository object calls for a compensatory projection. Indeed, this expository tension lends to Rather's depiction a troubled descriptive mode: it implies not only that significant details were lost in translation, but also that an alteration of the concept of witnessing threatened to corrode the reportorial ethos he describes in his memoir. But, simultaneously, such expository tension lends that same description a different kind of power, since it calls for a collective attempt to imagine what the Zapruder film shows. It evokes Zapruder's images, but creates a thirst in the listener to see the film.

Because Rather's description on radio was coherent and remarkably detailed, it differed significantly from a traumatic eyewitness account; it suggests that Rather saw the film more than once before he described it.[35] In passing, the narrative addresses the act of projection, the fact that Rather looked at a filmed record of an event, rather than the actual event: "At almost the instant the President put his hand up to his eyebrow . . . on the right side of his face, with Mrs. Kennedy looking away . . . the President lurched forward just a bit, uh, it was obvious he had been hit in the movie, but you had to be looking very closely in order to see it."[36]

Throughout most of the narrative, however, Rather manages to describe the images so vividly that he makes the listener momentarily forget that he is describing a film. This is not because his narrative resembles that of "a camera if it could talk," but rather because the descriptive mode, which does more than register, is informed not merely by the Zapruder film but also by other information that was publicly known. Rather describes his memory of watching the film, but details from elsewhere seep into and infuse the narrative. Thus, when he says that Kennedy's head went forward even though the film clearly shows the opposite, it is likely that he assumed this was the movement he had observed, since he had learned that Oswald had fired from behind. But one can, of course, also attribute this mistake to carelessness, fatigue, or the considerable pressure involved in describing these images live on the air.[37]

Rather's narrative veers between the informative and the expressive. Its detail contributes to its dramatic effect; several images are striking and memorable. The narrative includes descriptions of facial expressions as well as gestures ("Mrs. Kennedy stood up immediately, her mouth wide open").[38] It combines this precision with a sense of the chaos of the moment, since it bears the mark of an oral account; it is sometimes grammatically incorrect and contains a certain amount of confused stammering. As a source of significant forensic information that can be gathered from Zapruder's frames, then, Rather's radio narrative ultimately fails—but as an act of the imagination, it is tremendously successful.

Reading the transcripts of his depiction on both radio and television, one is struck by how similar the television report is to the radio report. The phrases are similar, the detail is the same, but there is one notable difference that cannot be detected in the transcript: on the screen, we see Rather's upper body, we meet his eyes. The cultural authority of the talking head is defined not only by his trustworthiness in interpreting an event, but also by his performance, by what Schudson calls "form." Today, of course, it is difficult to imagine reportage of this kind, which consists exclusively of a reporter's verbal description. We have become accustomed to a form of television news that is different from the style prominent in 1963. "Slow-paced, talking-head imagery" has been replaced by a "rapid-fire succession of shots," and thus what Geoffrey Baym calls the "packaging" of television news has been transformed.[39] Of course, CBS would have broadcast Zapruder's images in 1963 if it had been able to, but since the film was not in the network's possession, the audience instead got Rather describing them. When the reporter appeared on television, the compensatory nature of verbal description was transformed by the visible presence of the narrator in a powerful example of what Zelizer describes as the accommodation of the narrator's inclusion within the story of the event.[40] The reporter persona became significant as a witness and an interpreter. It was through his eyes that the viewer "saw" the Zapruder film ("The films show

. . .”; “President Kennedy could be seen to . . . ”; “you could see him lurch forward,” Rather says).[41] He conditions our own images of the event, showing us what he sees as well as what we should think about it. The reporter persona is now not merely a voice, but also a face that asks us to take his words for truth, to imagine the images he describes and make them our own.

It is, of course, significant for this compensatory projection that Rather is reporting live to Cronkite. As Jane Feuer points out, television can be “live in a way film can never be,” since “events can be transmitted as they occur”; this enables television to play “upon the connotative richness of the term 'live,' confounding its simple or technological denotations with a wealth of allusiveness.”[42] In observing how Rather reported on a plane crash on CBS in 1987, Mary Ann Doane suggests that in the reporting of unfilmed traumatic events, television seeks to compensate by activating a “discourse of eyewitness accounts and animated reenactments of the disaster—a simulated version.”[43] Rather's ekphrasis was such a simulation and, in effect, an example of what Roland Barthes calls the “reality effect.”[44] The reporter persona was elevated to the status of key narrator—ironically, in an oral narrative describing a visual narrative, broadcast in what has increasingly become a footage-fuelled genre of narrative, television news.

Indeed, a transfer of witnessing is embedded in the narrative form of Rather's “word pictures.” In describing Zapruder's images so vividly, he rendered his own act of exposition invisible, unfiltered. This is of some consequence for Rather's central presence as a narrator of the assassination through the years. The reporter was not close enough to the flames to use the light, to stay with Rather's own metaphor, but he managed to weave together a compensatory narrative nevertheless. In thus reducing Zapruder to an unblinking eye from which one can adopt the gaze, the expository tension that characterizes Rather's performance serves as a proleptic warning of the far more important narrative that would be published when Zapruder's images were seen for the first time by millions of Americans—in the pages of *Life* magazine.

LIFE'S GALLERY OF PICTURES

Rather describes in his memoir how his “heart sank” when he ran into Richard Stolley, the Pacific Coast regional editor of *Life* magazine, on the morning that he lost the motion-picture copyright to the Zapruder film.[45] Stolley had gotten on a plane to Dallas upon hearing of the shooting, and while en route he learned that Kennedy had been declared dead.[46] The editor immediately understood the status of the film; as he explained later, he knew that he simply "had to have" it the moment he found out about its existence.[47] In Stolley's and Rather's accounts of what happened in Dallas, both describe hearing about the Zapruder film in much the same way (although Stolley offers a more detailed memory of the events). However, the urge to possess the expository object defines the narratives of both.[48]

Shortly after he arrived in Dallas, Stolley learned that a "garment manufacturer" whose last name began with a z had filmed the assassination.[49] He looked Zapruder up in the phone book and called his number every fifteen minutes until he finally reached him at home late in the evening. Zapruder told him that he could watch his film the next morning at nine, when there would be a gathering of prospective buyers. Stolley, however, showed up an hour earlier and thereby managed to see the film before the rest of the press. When the time came to negotiate the sale, Zapruder told the group assembled there that he would talk to Stolley first, since he had arrived first.[50] Shortly after, *Life* bought the print rights for $50,000. When Rather ran into Stolley two days later, on Monday, the latter had already secured print rights. Stolley drew up an additional contract that secured for Time Inc. the original film as well as all rights—including television and movie rights, which were sold for $150,000 plus royalties.[51] As Wrone argues convincingly in his book on the Zapruder film, *Life*'s ownership of what should have been recognized as significant evidence of a crime (and hence public property) raises questions concerning the status of legal principles in the handling of a particular kind of recorded footage.[52] The fact that the Zapruder film and the copyrights to it went into private ownership from the very beginning determined the journey of its images in distinct ways. "Because of the circumstances of its production," David Lubin suggests, the film "immediately acquired a commodity status and has maintained it ever since."[53]

Life's handling of the film and its presentation of it through the years remain every bit as controversial as Rather's reporting from Dallas.[54] Owning the Zapruder film and the rights to print the images put *Life* in a unique position to define the cultural memory of the assassination; this privileged status as interpreter and narrator, however, also confronted the makers of the magazine with a human and cultural prohibition against projecting images of trauma and would continue to do so in the years that followed. *Life*'s unique expository object became something of a double-edged sword. "Television news producers and newspaper and magazine photo editors make decisions every day which firm up the wavering consensus about the boundaries of public knowledge," Sontag observes; "often their decisions are cast as judgments about 'good taste'—always a repressive standard when invoked by institutions."[55] Indeed, a paragraph in Stolley's contract stated that Time Inc. would present the film "to the public in a manner consonant with good taste and dignity," a contractual obligation Zapruder insisted on, but one ultimately so open to interpretation that it is, at least in juridical terms, meaningless.[56]

Life printed selected frames from the film in four issues in the early years after the assassination, the first time in black and white a week after the event, on November 29, 1963, in a news report. A week later, on December 6, frames appeared again, now in color, in a memorial edition. A year later, the magazine made use of a selection of frames a third time when it presented the findings of the Warren Commission on October 2, 1964; on November 25, 1966, enlarged frames were then used to question those very findings. Read chronologically, these *Life* narratives tell the story of how Zapruder's images came to perform different and indeed contradictory functions in the magazine's pages during this three-year period. Initially, presented as news items and memorial images, they were projected in the 1964 and 1966 issues to express faith and then doubt in their own status as evidentiary images. Indeed, it was in this period that Zapruder's strip of celluloid became "the Zapruder film"—whereas the early narratives did not address the act of exposition, thereby contributing to yet another transfer of witnessing, the later narratives shifted the focus to the expository object *Life* owned and in the process came to render it mythic, describing it as a "famous movie."

Each issue of *Life* was a gallery of pictures available at any newsstand for twenty-five cents. Certainly, it is hard to overestimate the significance of the fact that the images for years kept appearing exclusively in a magazine, a form of expository discourse that engages spectators in a very particular kind of looking. We do not only move around with magazines, we also in a sense move around inside them—we flip through, read a bit here and there, show pages to one another, borrow a friend's copy—in short, we inhabit a magazine's world every now and then, and often over an extended period of time. A magazine lies around on a table for a while, and is then either thrown away or placed in a drawer or on a shelf; the issues that contain stills of the Zapruder film fall into the latter category. Repeated display in *Life* also made the images a recurring topic of conversation, for as Siegfried Kracauer suggested, the reconstruction of memory depends on recollection through "the oral tradition," not merely the image alone.[57] Indeed, the images in *Life* were in this respect described ekphrastically en masse; like Rather's verbal descriptions, they led to a persistent thirst for seeing "what others were talking about." This is of some consequence for the immense reach of the images. It has been estimated that each issue of *Life* was read by up to forty million people, and in 1963, as in earlier years, the magazine had a "unique position to transform modes of vision within the more privileged sectors of the United States."[58] These circumstances determined not only how Zapruder's images appeared in the early years after the assassination, but also how they came to be remembered by many as still rather than moving images—for Time Inc. held on to the film and denied any public projection or broadcasting of it for twelve years after the event.[59]

A "mixed medium" dedicated to showing and telling, the photographic essay is an excellent example of what Mitchell calls an "imagetext," since it is normally structured to involve a dynamic verbal-visual relation: "texts explain, describe, label, speak for (or to) the photographs; photographs illustrate, exemplify, clarify, ground, and document the text."[60] Instead of separating image and word and analyzing one or the other, or stating the difference between them, an analysis should, Mitchell suggests, ask, "Why does it matter how words and images are juxtaposed, blended, or separated?"[61] In the four issues of *Life* in which Zapruder's images appear, this matters because it is through their contested image-text relations that the narratives derive what I observe to be an "expository tension."

In addressing agency in *Life*'s imagetexts, one must consider the implications of the fact that these were products of collective effort and struggle. This adds to the distinctly componential shape of expository agency, since the narratives were constructed by several internal (and often conflicting) forces. There is no reporter persona showing us the images; rather, we are instructed to look in a particular way by the faceless but nevertheless subtly authoritative voice that is *Life*'s. Photographers for the magazine were to see and record a particular vision ("objectively"), then the writers and, ultimately, the editors were to show that vision to the magazine's readers ("subjectively") by adding words; it was the picture editor who had the last word and decided which pictures would be used.[62] Wendy Kozol points out that the editors had the power not only of selection, but also of shaping the layout.[63] The outcome of these processes was a tremendously consistent aesthetic, a fact that often is attributed to the lasting impact of the magazine's founding editor, Henry Robinson Luce, and his "pictorial vision."[64] As Art Simon observes, this vision "implied that images nearly spoke for themselves, that knowledge, perhaps truth, was ensured by the camera's expanded vision."[65] Ironically, however, it was *Life*'s own narratives that finally represented a change from initial belief to increasing doubt that the Zapruder film could produce such a vision.

The imagetext of the November 29, 1963, issue of *Life* describes what happened when Kennedy was shot (figs. 1.1 and 1.2).

The verbal narratives of these pages enter into a contested relationship with the images they accompany. Indeed, by creating a sense of "being there," the words seem to compensate for a lack of the sense of "liveness" that defined Rather's broadcast and, perhaps more strikingly, for a lack of the movement and sound that define the moving image. On page 26, the accompanying text, "Jackie Crawled For Help," tries to add sound as well as movement to the silent pictures on the page: "'Oh, no!, Oh, no!,' Mrs. Kennedy cries (*top row of pictures*) as she sees the blood flowing from the President's head." The verbal narrative shifts from the past to the present tense on this page, with an insistent reference to blood-soaked verbal imagery: "As the President lies dying, Jackie scrambles out of her seat and crawls onto the trunk of the car in a pathetic search for help. As she crouches on hands and knees, the President's head presses against her, staining her skirt and stockings with blood." This powerful verbal image seems almost to compensate for the absence of the graphic frame of Kennedy's head being shot, which is not depicted in the imagetext, not only because such a thing would have represented a breach of the contract with Zapruder, but undoubtedly because it would also have been widely considered a tasteless attempt to overcome the moral prohibition against projecting trauma at a moment when the incident was yet fresh in people's minds. It is likely that this troubled narrative also reflects the emotional distress felt by its writers, who, like everyone else, were marked by what had happened. Indeed, the verbal narrative of the imagetext in the November 29 issue strives to argue for its own necessity, for why else does it tell us in this way what we see in the pictures? Why does it describe the images as if they were absent, unseen by the reader? The result is that the imagetext is marked by what Mitchell calls a "paragonal struggle," a struggle between word and image for domination in a confrontation with the unspeakable.[66]

Zapruder's accidental photographic record was perfect as a resource for *Life*, for as Erica Doss points out, most of the magazine's photographers "tended to 'hide' their cameras, mediating the experience of looking at pictures as a naturalized occurrence and consequently helping to define photovision as visual truth."[67] Zapruder's photographic record was not that of a

SPLIT-SECOND SEQUENCE AS THE BULLETS STRUCK

On these and the following two pages is a remarkable and exclusive series of pictures which show, for the first time and in tragic detail, the fate which befell our President. The caravan had just passed through the downtown area of Dallas and made a sharp left turn at the corner of Elm and Houston Streets, where it headed down an incline into an underpass. First came the police motorcycle escort (*above*) and then the big Lincoln bearing the Kennedys and Texas Governor John Connally and his wife. The crowds were thin at this point, but the President and Mrs. Kennedy were smiling and waving as their car passed the brick building where the assassin lurked, and disappeared momentarily behind a highway sign.

Then came the awful moment. In these pictures, which run consecutively from left to right, it begins as the car comes out from behind the sign (*fifth picture*). The President's wave turns into a clutching movement toward his throat (*seventh picture*). Governor Connally, who glances around to see what has happened, is himself struck by a bullet (*ninth picture*) and slumps over (*tenth picture*). As the President's car approaches a lamppost (*13th picture*) Mrs. Kennedy suddenly becomes aware of what has happened and reaches over to help (*large pictures below*) while Governor Connally slumps to the floor. The President collapses on his wife's shoulder and in the last two small pictures the First Lady cradles him in her arms.

FIG. 1.1 Selected frames from the Zapruder film appeared for the first time in *Life* a week after the assassination. *Life*, November 29, 1963, 24–25 and 26–27.

JACKIE CRAWLED FOR HELP

"Oh, no!, Oh, no!", Mrs. Kennedy cries (*top row of pictures*) as she sees the blood flowing from the President's head. But the convoy keeps going, past the onlookers and photographers who stand frozen or fall to the ground as they hear the shots.

As the President lies dying, Jackie scrambles out of her seat and crawls onto the trunk of the car in a pathetic search for help. As she crouches on hands and knees, the President's head presses against her, staining her skirt and stockings with blood. A Secret Service man leaps on the bumper to protect the First Lady and get her back into the car.

FIG. 1.2   Selected frames from the Zapruder film appeared for the first time in *Life* a week after the assassination. *Life*, November 29, 1963, 24 and 26.

professional posing as an accidental witness, but the real thing. It was not difficult for *Life* to present the images as if they had in fact produced and not bought them, since the magazine did not typically give credit to photographers; a writer or a photographer would get a byline only on occasion, Kozol observes, and photographers "rarely participated in writing the text."[68] Zapruder's name is not mentioned in what in effect becomes another transfer of witnessing; it is *Life* that has captured the moment. Whereas photographers had consistently been rendered mute, Zapruder was already silent, as was his film. The amateur filmmaker merely provided the frames of film that could be appropriated into the larger verbal-visual framework that was a *Life* gallery of pictures. This transfer of witnessing also informs the December 6 issue of *Life*. The magazine came with a separate "John F. Kennedy Memorial Edition" in which a list of photographers and agencies are credited on the first page. Zapruder's name does not appear; we learn that the pictures were taken by an unnamed "Dallas clothing manufacturer."[69] Zelizer points out that it was *Life* that was "hailed" for these narratives, not any individual person within the magazine.[70]

The memorial edition arguably represents the first major example of what would become an extensive production of cultural artifacts in the name of assassination commemoration. Zapruder's images appeared in close-up and color in a four-page spread. The verbal narrative that accompanies the images differs markedly from the one published a week earlier. It lacks dramatic momentum, undoubtedly because of the expressive charge of the images themselves. The imagetext presents itself as the primary shaper of memory as well as postmemory, as the provider of the definitive account of the moment of trauma implicitly (through the aesthetic properties of the carefully designed "memorial edition") as well as explicitly (through the editorial introduction, which asserts that the edition will enable "future generations" to "become privileged witnesses to the actual event, to be present and shaken and reawakened as we were"). It depends on Zapruder's images in doing both.

Suggesting that Larry Burrows's Vietnam photography in *Life* fortified war protest, Susan Sontag points out that he was the first photographer to "do a whole war in color—another gain in verisimilitude, that is, shock."[71] In *Life*'s aesthetic, Chris Vials suggests, color photographs were meant to "increase pleasure."[72] It is difficult to look at the imagetext of the memorial edition today and not conclude that at this early stage, it had already produced a way of looking at Zapruder's images that had less to do with their evidentiary than their aesthetic properties. The mode of display in the memorial edition implies that they were meant to be looked at again and again; they were transformed accordingly by the *Life* aesthetic. In effect, the issue became a commodity-relic (in fact, it remains so, since I bought my own copy on eBay, where a few are available in "mint condition").

In the two issues of *Life* from 1964 and 1966, the Zapruder film is used not merely to describe the event of the assassination as a news item or a historical event; instead, Time Inc.'s expository object is now prominently displayed as the top story. Whereas a portrait of Kennedy and a funeral picture of the mourning Jackie Kennedy adorn the front pages of the 1963 issues, frames from the film are displayed on the front pages in 1964 and in 1966. On the cover of the 1964 issue, a selection of frames rolls across the page, as if in projection. The page alludes to a narrative inside the magazine, "Piecing Together the Evidence," by Gerald R. Ford, at the time a member both of Congress and of the Warren Commission. As Ford describes his work with the commission, eight enlarged frames illustrate his argument and, in effect, support the commission's conclusions; the film is referred to by the editorial staff of *Life* as "one of the most important pieces of evidence." Zapruder is named by *Life*, but not mentioned by Ford, who describes witness accounts and testimonies, concluding that the report is "the truth as we see it."[73] Whereas the imagetext of the 1963 memorial issue left frame 313 out of its imagetext, the editorial staff chose to include it in its issue on the commission's report (fig. 1.3).

The page reprinted here is from one of the three versions of the magazine to go to press.[74] The magazine first decided to print the violent image of Kennedy's exploding head, but then stopped the press run to replace it—and then, after having resumed printing, stopped it yet another time to change the caption. A year after the assassination, the magazine's makers were uncertain whether the printing of frame 313 would break with "good taste," whether the blood spray would offend or even hurt readers.

In the November 25, 1966, issue of *Life*, a comprehensive spread of frames supports Governor Connally's argument that he and Kennedy were hit by two different bullets. The Zapruder film, now referred to as famous, is the center of attention. The magazine shows a single frame, 230, on its cover, against a black background. A photograph of Connally poring over single frames of the Zapruder film with a magnifying glass takes up the whole of the issue's page 39. This suggests that Zapruder's images can render vital information when magnified or enlarged dramatically (fig. 1.4).

As Simon observes, the film at this point had come to appear both "unimpeachable"—a word that is used to describe it in the 1966 issue—and "highly suspect" as evidence, "at times unreadable, and constantly open to

FIG. 1.3 A year after the assassination, *Life* printed the graphic frame that depicts the president's head exploding. *Life*, October 2, 1964, 45.

FIG. 1.4 Enlarged details of frames appeared in *Life* in 1966 in an article questioning the findings of the Warren Commission. *Life*, November 25, 1966, 46.

multiple interpretations."[75] "The evidence," the November 25 issue concludes, "particularly that given by Governor Connally and his interpretation of the Zapruder film, does not prove that Oswald had a co-conspirator. Nor does it disprove it. It does show that reasonable—and disturbing—doubt remains."[76]

This epistemological crisis produced a new way of looking at the images, which nevertheless make a strong impression in the 1966 issue. Thirty-one frames are displayed across nine pages. The reader is likely to do as Connally did and lean over them with a magnifying glass. Whereas the magazine had invited readers to look at the images in earlier issues, it now insisted that they be studied. Yet there was no guarantee of what would come out of such a study. Looking at these pages today, it is hard not to agree with David Lubin that the film "unlocks no mysteries but only creates more of them." "Under 'scientific' analysis and technological reconstruction," he argues, "it ends up as blobs of color, not revelation."[77]

By regulating the frequency with which Zapruder's images appeared, in ever-new arrangements of frames, and by supporting contradicting theories of what had happened in Dealey Plaza, *Life* not only reported on the ongoing assassination debates but also staged and produced them. Ownership of the Zapruder film enabled it to do so. The ensuing rhetoric, which shifts between strategies of exposure and concealment, lends not only a contested but also a mythic and aesthetic quality to the images. Readers' thirst for further disclosure, further projection, was multiply and complexly motivated. Gradually, the burden of shaping this expository discourse outweighed the privilege of doing so. However inevitable, the first projection before a mass audience nevertheless did not take place until almost a decade after the 1966 issue; Zapruder's images were broadcast on national television for the first time in 1975.

"DON'T WATCH THIS FILM"

"At the time of its birth, *Life*'s only real rival in the visual representation of news were the newsreels," Chris Vials writes.[78] By the time Kennedy was assassinated, however, television—the president's modus operandi, a fact I will return to in the next chapter—lighted up the living rooms of America, and *Life* had to compete with the new medium and its ability to show and tell. Furthermore, the period immediately following Kennedy's assassination is widely considered one of the most tumultuous in postwar American history, a period of cultural and political conflict, and the ongoing assassination debates were marked by being situated in such a period. The assassinations of Martin Luther King, Jr., and Robert Kennedy, the Vietnam War, the Kent State shootings, and the Watergate scandal: all evoke a sense of political and cultural malaise. The war in Vietnam was the first to be televised, and this, Sontag argues, "introduced the home front to new tele-intimacy with death and destruction."[79] The war, as Sturken observes, was collectively witnessed in every living room in the United States.[80] It was against such a background that Geraldo Rivera screened a Zapruder copy on the late-night talk show *Good Night America* on March 6, 1975, and broadcast Zapruder's images on national television for the first time.

Rivera's show was yet another example of composite expository agency, one in which host and guest address their viewers. Rivera's guests that night were Dick Gregory, the comedian and human rights activist, and Robert J. Groden, who brought a copy he had made from one of *Life*'s prints in early 1968, when he worked at a film lab in New Jersey that had been hired by the magazine. He had spent six years working with this copy, seeking to enhance its quality so that he could analyze its frames better; in early 1975, he began screening his treated version publicly.

Rivera addressed a double audience, the one present in the studio and the one at home. The event had a character of liveness, but it differed from reporting; it was organized around an interaction staged within the television studio. The setting was one of conflict and confrontation. *Life* had not sanctioned the screening, and Groden was present as a critic of the Warren Commission's conclusions. Thus, Zapruder's images were now exposed as conspicuously withheld evidence. They had been concealed because of what they, upon scrutiny, reveal, Groden argued.

Rivera's function was to be both moderator and provocateur.[81] He stages the act of exposition and shapes it; the scene was defined by the assumption that these were images the audience would want to turn away from but simultaneously could not resist. Knowing this, Rivera built momentum by warning his audience about what was about to be broadcast:

> It's become very chic among television producers to put a disclaimer at the head of any film that the film you're about to see might be shocking, might be horrifying, you might not want your kids to watch it. And I think the unfortunate net effect of that is to make more people watch it. Well, I'm telling you right straight out that if you are at all sensitive, if you're at all queasy, then don't watch this film. Just put on the late-night movie, because this

is very heavy. It's the film shot by the Dallas dress manufacturer Abraham Zapruder, and it's the execution of President Kennedy, and Bob and Dick, would you please narrate what we're seeing as we show this film.[82]

Rivera first plausibly described the paradoxical logic of a "disclaimer," only then to illustrate it himself as he told the viewer that what would be exposed was sensational, unique, and then advised the meek-hearted to look the other way. These are images of the unspeakable, the warning says—and here they are.

As the grainy images of the copy were projected into American homes, Groden explained to the audience what Zapruder's images show and what he found to be the indisputable implications: Kennedy's head is thrown backward when his head explodes, proving that there must have been a second shooter, since that bullet could not have been fired from behind. For years, the public at large had seen only frames; when projected, however, the film leaves no doubt. Indeed, this is the same argument that was delivered during the only public projection of the film in the years when it was in *Life*'s possession, a courtroom screening in 1969.[83]

Kennedy's head explodes, there is an audible gasp from the studio audience, and Rivera comments, "That's the shot that blew up his head. It's the most horrifying thing I've ever seen in the movies." Then we see the film one more time, now as an "extreme blowup," so that Kennedy's head and torso fill the screen. After this second screening, Rivera says, "That's the most upsetting thing I've ever seen, and we'll talk about it in a minute," before the screen fades to black for a commercial break.

Whereas *Life*'s hesitation to show a national audience the president's exploding head marked its conflicted displays in the sixties, an entire program now revolved around the projection of the same image. Images that previously had been felt to be unspeakable were followed matter-of-factly by conversation. Exposition here was exposé, spectacle: by declaring the image forbidden, it appealed to the guilty voyeur, the viewer who watches in spite of being warned. In the weeks that followed this broadcast, Rivera presented new programs devoted to an ongoing critique of the findings of the Warren Commission. To Groden, the show was a "media coup," Richard Trask suggests, since the broadcast was followed by "a flurry of bookings and interest." Many came to credit Groden for the congressional resolution that in September 1976 called for the creation of a select committee of the House of Representatives to reopen the investigation of the assassination.[84]

In a commentary on Rivera's various programs that spring, John O'Connor wrote sourly in the *New York Times*:

> No real new evidence is exposed. . . . In the aftermath of Watergate and its stunning revelations, the whole of recent American history has been opened to re-examination. The darkly improbable can no longer be casually considered impossible. At the same time, easy sensationalism becomes more seductive. Mr. Rivera's ends are his own concern, and he hardly tries to conceal them. . . . His means, however, can be questioned closely. He is not content to discuss the Kennedy assassination. He feels forced to dramatize, evidently for the sake of production values. . . . No one doubts Mr. Rivera's sincerity. But his judgment in the never-ending quest to "grab" an audience demands challenge.[85]

Again, the projection raised questions about "good taste" that have continually been raised ever since Zapruder was concerned with it in signing his contract with Time Inc. The images revealed on Rivera's show, however, were not the same ones displayed on the pages of *Life* days after Kennedy died; by this point, they had already "come to signify a whole range of disparate meanings," as Lubin points out, and the film "was at once a holy relic of presidential martyrdom, a document of the last moments of American idealism and innocence, and a testament to governmental ineptness at best, nefarious conspiracy at worst."[86] The film's cultural status, constantly in transformation, involved a radically extended performativity of the images, which were increasingly beginning to mean different things, depending on how they were projected.

"As its mode of existence changed[,] so, too, did the boundaries of its meaning," Simon writes about the Zapruder film.[87] Although Zapruder recorded the assassination on 8 mm film, the medium merely represented a starting point for the images. A distinct parallel rhetoric of concealment and exposure finally gave the film a cult identity and created a persistent thirst for further disclosure. As the images found their way into the living rooms of America in descriptions on radio and television, in state-of-the-art magazines, and finally in television broadcasts, they gradually took on a life of their own and began their journey.

TWO

Eternally Framed

Because I must function only as an image, I have chosen in my career to begin with the end, and to be born, in a sense, again, even as I was dying. // The Artist-President, *The Eternal Frame*

THE CAMERA ZOOMS IN QUICKLY on a bronze bust of Kennedy, and we hear a man declaring solemnly with a distinct British accent: "Ladies and gentlemen, the president of the United States has been the victim of an assassination." Then there is a deep, collective sigh of disbelief as a rather poor black-and-white copy of the Zapruder film dated "November 22, 1963" fills the screen. Even if what we are seeing is clearly video, the sound of a projector can be heard vaguely in the background, and the dating lends a strange archival or even archeological feel to the scene, a sense that what we are watching could have been taken off a dusty shelf or dug out of the ground sometime in the future, very much like the bronze piece. Associations with an earlier era in the history of recorded film, a time when gesture was everything and no sound was to be heard, seem inevitable as the shadowy black-and-white images flash by. Or perhaps this is what a newsreel will look like to a viewer in the distant future? Finally and somewhat more prosaically, the sequence exposes the act of transmission and thus illustrates that the Zapruder film is much more than a reel of 8 mm film. The images have been transferred onto a spool of magnetic tape. What we see both is and is not the Zapruder film.

This is a short description of the opening moments of *The Eternal Frame*, a video by Ant Farm, a collective of architects who also worked as video, performance, and installation artists in the Bay Area in the late sixties and early seventies. Doug Michels and Chip Lord founded the group in 1968, and were joined by Curtis Schreier, Hudson Marquez, Douglas Hurr, and other short-time members who came and went (the group split up in 1978). The video was recorded in 1975 in cooperation with T. R. Uthco, another performance group in the area, which consisted of Doug Hall, Diane Andrews Hall, and Jody Procter.[1]

Performed, recorded, and produced not long after Geraldo Rivera's late-night broadcast of Robert Groden's copy of the Zapruder film, and undoubtedly in part as a response to that screening, *The Eternal Frame* is nevertheless much more than a commentary on Rivera's sudden exposure of Zapruder's images to a nationwide audience. A Chinese box of sorts, the video revels in its own conundrums and never quite allows the spectator to figure out whether it is a performance about a film, a film about a performance, a film about a film about a performance, and so on. "What it is," Doug Michels says in a scene, "is figuring out what it is." In its climactic moment, a reenactment of the assassination in Dealey Plaza toward the end of the video, Ant Farm performs not so much Kennedy's death as Zapruder's recording of it, as Marita Sturken observes.[2] Leading up to this, staged appearances resemble televised presidential press conferences, and several scenes describe Ant Farm's studio preparations for its upcoming on-location reenactment. Finally, toward the end, the video includes audience commentary after a San Francisco screening of the reenactment.

What happens when Zapruder's images travel into art, when they appear in a video such as *The Eternal Frame*? Indeed, if all our encounters with Zapruder's images take place through remediations, we can in a sense only see them quoted—Jay David Bolter and Richard Grusin remind us that no medium "can now function independently and establish its own separate and purified space of cultural meaning."[3] "The meanings of the Zapruder film continue to shift each time it is reenacted," Sturken points out.[4] But in stressing this point, *The Eternal Frame* confronts us with a reuse of the images that differs markedly from that of *Life*'s imagetext or Rivera's late-night show. Here, Zapruder's images are profoundly transformed, and in a way that suggests that the artist wants to reveal and focus on the very act of quoting. As expository discourse, then, the kind of artistic quotation Ant Farm staged is metareflexive. To be recognized as a quotation, it had to expose itself as such.

A traveling concept, quotation stands at the intersection of iconography and intertextuality, and hence of the disciplines of art history and literary analysis, both of which uncover the "re-use of earlier forms, patterns, and figures."[5] Indeed, video art has always been addressed from such intersections between disciplines, since its lineage, Doug Hall and Sally Jo Fifer suggest, "can be traced to the discourses of art, science, linguistics, technology, mass media, and politics."[6] In the words of Doug Michels, everything that Ant Farm did was informed by "mixing disciplines and not having a leader."[7] Its playful video work reflects this hybridity. It is not entirely performance or film or documentary, and at the same time, it is all of these; clear-cut distinctions collapse or, perhaps more precisely, are exposed as unstable. In *Media Burn*, recorded on Independence Day 1975 in an asphalt field outside San Francisco, members of the group drive a customized Cadillac, the "Phantom Dream Car," through a wall of burning television sets. As much about the desire of the attending news media to cover the event as it is about the image of the car crashing through the wall, the video shows how news crews captured this iconoclastic performance. However, the hybrid quality of Ant Farm's production extends far beyond its work in one medium. Its early architecture engaged "the possibility of splicing things that in conventional atmospheres would be impossible to join," as Michael Sorkin puts it; the group designed inflatable structures—buildings, objects—for a "mobile lifestyle."[8] Likewise, the reassemblage of what is probably their most famous work, *Cadillac Ranch* (1974), joins images of the prehistoric and the modern in a way that changes how we look at the iconography of both Stonehenge and the Cadillac. On a ranch alongside Route 66 (today Interstate 40) in Amarillo, Texas, a row of ten Cadillacs are partially buried, nose down, at an angle corresponding to that of the pyramids in Giza, Egypt. The piece is seen by an estimated 280,000 who pass by each year.[9]

To quote is always to manipulate, to actively reshape something from the past in the present. From such a perspective, quoting is both a creative and a destructive act; something is added, so "the work performed by later images obliterates the older images as they were before that intervention and creates new versions of old images instead."[10] Thus, even if they are very different artistic expressions, Christopher Brown's *Elm Street* and Ant Farm's video are both artworks that quote Zapruder's images in a way that is constitutive for how they are experienced. Regarded as "pictures about pictures," they can be considered what W. J. T. Mitchell refers to as "metapictures," "pictures that are used to show what a picture is." Both the video and the painting can be said to "theorize" pictures or, as Mitchell would have it, to "picture theory."[11] In *The Eternal Frame*, Zapruder's images are "performed" in order to address their latent performativity, their quotability. But the video is also about the

Kennedy image, about the politics of performance as well as the performance of politics. It pictures theory by mock-ritually staging an iconoclastic event and, in the process, raises the ambiguous question, what happens to images when we make and break pictures?

Whereas the video is a meditation on how not only Zapruder's images but also our vision of the assassination are conditioned by framing, *The Eternal Frame* is itself framed in a particular way when exhibited. This chapter engages with these multiple acts of framing. Two different ways of looking at *The Eternal Frame* define how I frame my own analysis in what follows: whereas most of this chapter consists of a close reading of the video based on repeated watching over an extended period of time, the experience of a gallery screening—specifically, at the Yale University School of Architecture Gallery in New Haven on the last day of October, 2005, to which I will turn toward the end of the chapter—was shaped by the overall narrative of that exhibition. Like the images they quote, then, the quotations of *The Eternal Frame* are also finally defined by acts of framing.

IMAGES AND MASKS

The zoom-in on the bronze bust serves as the keynote of *The Eternal Frame*. Its abruptness suggests an analogy between our gaze and the assassin's bullet, both aimed at Kennedy's head, implying that the two are related. Kennedy's head, cast in (probably fake) bronze, is simultaneously lifelike and lifeless, characterized by its stillness—the kind of stillness Kenneth Gross observes in statues, that of "a once-living thing whose life has been interrupted."[12] The bust can thus be considered a plastic image of death that is juxtaposed with the moving image of death that is the Zapruder film. Observing the cult of the dead in archaic societies, Hans Belting suggests that the function of pictorial representation mainly was to replace the bodies of the dead and produce a compensatory visibility; the dead "were kept as present and visible in the ranks of the living via their images."[13] This reference to ancient times is far from irrelevant in addressing *The Eternal Frame*'s initial juxtaposition. Indeed, Belting's words echo André Bazin's suggestion that film is able to capture not merely stillness, but indeed duration—and thus the final transformation, the event of death. Film, Bazin thus deduces, is "change mummified."[14] Unlike the photograph, in which Roland Barthes sees an instant "return of the dead"—photography's "noeme," its essence, according to Barthes, is "that-has-been"—film captures dying.[15]

However, the opening serves as much more than a metapictorial reflection on death and image in the age of technological reproducibility; just as significantly, it reminds the viewer that what Zapruder intended to capture on film was the "Kennedy image." The zoom-in suggests that what draws the gaze to the bust is what draws it to the body in the car: a particular kind of desire. Zapruder, *The Eternal Frame* suggests, wanted for once to cast a star in his home movie, the contemporary version of the bust on the mantelpiece. The abrupt zoom-in also suggests that within this ongoing creation of an icon, its destruction is implied. "The process through which the camera and 'Jack' found each other and stayed with each other is charged with meaning, as is our relentless attention to his image," writes Thomas McEvilley in an essay about Kennedy:

> Picture the view-finder, twenty-five years ago [in 1963], dissolving into a rifle sight and zeroing in on Camelot. What did it see? It saw something that we loved in the first act, when the play was romance, but that made us insatiable in the second. . . . There was a deeper meaning in our attraction to Kennedy's poise than we acknowledged. . . . We couldn't see it until it had forced itself upon us and them: like movie stars, through whose heads the winds of disaster play at an early age, these people were being set up for sacrifice. . . . Hidden like voyeurs, we gazed at them safe in our invisibility.[16]

In its opening, *The Eternal Frame* confronts the viewer with the implications of this gaze by inviting the viewer to share it, and thereby raises the question whether it not merely captured but also produced Kennedy's death.

Indeed, the video is as much about the picture Zapruder wanted to capture on film as the one he ended up capturing. After this initial juxtaposition of bust and moving image, military music introduces a segment dated "Independence Day, 1975." Made up to look like Kennedy, actor Doug Hall arrives in a black Lincoln, climbs the stairs to a podium, and gives a speech to an awaiting audience: "What has gone wrong with America," he says, "is not a random visitation of fate. It is the result of forces which have assumed control of the American system. . . . These forces are militarism, monopoly, and the mass media." Uncannily similar to the diction of the late president, Hall's speech, delivered in a mock-Bostonian accent, complete with pauses and stresses, is also highly stylized. Close up, we can see that Kennedy's trademark tan—one of the effects of Addison's disease—is overdone with makeup.[17] Hall's role is not so much a portrayal of Kennedy, we gather, as of the Kennedy image, a personification aptly named the "Artist-President" in *The Eternal Frame*.

The parade music suggests that we are witnessing a reenactment of the kind of "production" that was typical of the Kennedy presidency, which was known for its "regal and spectacular" events.[18] The Kennedy team had a keen understanding of how public image could be reconceptualized in the twentieth century.[19] The "Kennedy image," John F. Hellmann observes in *The Kennedy Obsession*, was "designed both to express and elicit desire," it was a "doubling" of Kennedy "into something like a fictional character."[20] A commentator who early recognized the creativity involved in the making of such a mythic persona was Norman Mailer, who ambivalently contributed to both mystifying and demystifying the Kennedy image.[21] Kennedy, Mailer insisted, had to be understood as a "metaphor," an "empty vessel."[22] The Kennedy persona was thus what S. Paige Baty, in a book on Marilyn Monroe, calls a "representative character," a mass-mediated figure that "operates on a site on which American political culture is written and exchanged" and that ultimately is "remembered as product or story or some hybrid of the two."[23] Such a persona, of course, is not a novelty of the television age. Its massive reach, however, is. The Kennedy image was projected beyond the specific borders of media such as books, articles, and television into what Hellmann calls an "unbounded cultural space, a kind of national screen encompassing the mass-communications network of the twentieth-century United States."[24] The Kennedy image, in other words, was designed to travel.

The Eternal Frame animates this traveling image by allowing it to speak to us through the medium of television, albeit in a way that both mimics and defamiliarizes that medium's conventions. In the guise of the Artist-President, the Kennedy image comes across as a profoundly uncontrollable phantasm that operates on the basis of collective desire. An image can "set loose a flood of attention and desire and take on a life of its own," McEvilley writes about the Kennedy charisma, and after this, it is no longer an image "that can be maintained or dissolved"; it becomes "part of an onrushing dynamic."[25] The Artist-President addresses us from within this state, inviting us to ponder what kind of image we are looking at: A picture on the television screen? A mental image appearing in memories and dreams? A public image performing official functions? The Artist-President is all this and more.

Kennedy's rise to political power and stardom was inextricably linked with the rapidly increasing cultural domination of television in the sixties.[26] Throughout *The Eternal Frame*, the Artist-President continues to address his audience as the "television president" did in speeches and press conferences.[27]

In a "broadcast" dated September 9, 1975, which follows the excerpt from his Independence Day appearance, we find him seated behind a desk, from where he delivers a short speech:

> As your honest president, I have addressed you on several other occasions through the media, and I have always valued this opportunity. It is truly fitting that I am only able to communicate to you tonight via television, for like all presidents in recent years, I am in reality nothing more than another image on your television sets. I am in reality only another face on your screens. I am in reality only another link in that chain of pictures which makes up the sum total of information that is accessible to us all as Americans. Like my elected predecessors, the content of the image that I present is no different than the image itself. Because I must function only as an image, I have chosen in my career to begin with the end and to be born, in a sense, again, even as I was dying. I suffered my image death on the streets of Dallas, Texas, August 10, 1975, in order to render my ultimate service to the media, which created me and without which I would be nothing. I did this to emphasize the fact that no president can ever again be anything more than an image and that no image could ever be in the past, nor can ever be in the future, anything but dead.[28]

This "image death"—which we are yet to see, in the form of a series of reenactments in Dallas—implies, the Artist-President claims, a form of rebirth, and will be performed in service to the media, without which he cannot exist. It is a ritual. A sacrifice will be performed to emphasize that although he may appear human, the Artist-President is, in fact, "dead." He has always and only appeared in the realm of the lifelike: what the audience relates to is an image, a likeness, not a person but a persona, a construct designed to express and elicit desire. The Artist-President can die again and again, his sacrifice being that he must continue to render his service to the media through which he must appear. He is caught forever in the eternal frame.

Ironically, this declaration of death depends on a simulation of the "liveness" of television. What is toyed with here, of course, is the theatrics of the live televised presidential press conference, introduced by the Kennedy administration after press secretary Pierre Salinger came up with the idea.[29] According to David Halberstam, the televised performances demonstrated how Kennedy was "way ahead of most working politicians" in understanding that television was "not just substance, but it was style, it was as much theater as it was reality."[30] The Artist-President is all style and no substance; he is able to communicate only through the media. His very existence depends on projection, on play.

The Artist-President invites us to take part in a charade, then, in which the medium is hostage of the image. *The Eternal Frame* adds to the sense of theater that it so firmly establishes from its beginning by making explicit reference to its own play with masks and personas, to its own rituals. The effect is that the spell is doubly broken: as the Artist-President utters the words "the content of the image," there is a cut to actor Doug Hall, reflected in a mirror as he is putting on his makeup to perform as the Artist-President. "Every image, in a way, could be classified as a mask," Hans Belting writes, "whether transforming a body into an image or existing as a separate entity beside the body."[31] Mid-speech, we are taken back in time to Ant Farm's rehearsals and preparations before its journey to Dallas and the image death to be staged there, by an interruptive cut that explores the mask as metapicture. The actor is working on his lips, and his upper body is naked; he is concentrating on putting the final touches on his mask before donning the wig. The specific effect of this juxtaposition of theatrical elements relies much on a contrasting of sound with image. Whereas what we hear is still the Artist-President, what we see is the actor's sealed lips being lipsticked. The speech continues as the mask of the Artist-President is replaced by the bare face of the actor. To add to the effect, we do not so much see Hall as we see the reflected image of him in the mirror, which he stares at blankly and purposefully.

A cut then leads us to the first studio reenactments of the Zapruder film, in black and white. Seated in a Lincoln, Hall is joined by Michels, who is dressed up as Jackie Kennedy. The gestures and movements are familiar: Hall clasps his throat, then Michels crawls back over the back of the car; the light sound of handclaps replaces that of gunshots. What we see are actors at work, studiously timing their performance according to the assassination time line established by the Zapruder film. Immediately recognizable yet different, Zapruder's images are now being performed.

Another cut interrupts these preparations as *The Eternal Frame* returns to self-reflexivity and we move to another address being given by the Artist-President, again seated behind a stately desk. He makes the following brief statement: "I am happy to be here in Texas today and to have this opportunity to speak to you via television. Texas is a great state, and it is appropriate that we have come here to make these statements about the American condition." *The Eternal Frame* purports to be about much more than the Zapruder film or the assassination that it is a record of. But in what sense is it about "the American condition"?

Another cut leads us to a backstage interview in black and white; a smiling reporter interviewing the Artist-President tries to get to the meaning of it all:

Reporter: Do you consider yourself a martyr for art?

Artist-President: No, I don't.

Reporter: How would you characterize this act of yours?

Artist-President: It's difficult to characterize. It's crazy, yes. It is crazy. I understand that part of it.

Reporter: Is this a "freedom of speech" statement?

Artist-President: No, it isn't. Ask me what it is, and perhaps together we will be able to figure it out.

Reporter: Is this a confrontation with death?

Artist-President: No, it isn't. It's close though. It's . . . But it's not really a confrontation with death, no. Ask me another question.

Reporter: Is this . . . would you call this art?

Artist-President: It's not *not* art.

Reporter: Where do you think you're gonna go from here?

Artist-President: To heaven. To celebrity heaven.

Reporter: Is this opposed to rock 'n' roll heaven, or . . .?

Artist-President: No, they may be the same, but I think they're different.

Reporter: So you'll be up there with Jimi Hendrix and Janis Joplin?

Artist-President: No, I'll be there with Charles de Gaulle, King Henry VIII . . .

Hinting at his own genealogy, the Artist-President suggests that he is but one in a line of images, that royalty and national leadership have always been visible only as image. By turning the questions back on the interviewer, the Artist-President invites him to join him in figuring out what *The Eternal Frame* is about; by extension, that invitation reaches us as we watch the film. Adding to *The Eternal Frame*'s increasingly self-reflexive mode, the conversation addresses the video's doubly negative status as "not *not* art" and exposes its own metapictoriality.

By first staging a mock televised press conference, then taking a backstage approach, and combining black-and-white with color images, *The Eternal Frame* becomes an interplay of sixties documentary conventions, Patricia Mellencamp points out.[32] In many respects, it is typical of the video art of its period, and particularly so in its play with the narrative conventions of television.[33] Ant Farm grew out of radical sixties culture, and this informed its artistic practice.[34] The group bought its first black-and-white Sony Portapak in 1970, equipment that enabled Ant Farm to record its performances on location without incurring high production costs.[35] Its members were influenced by and worked with contemporary peers; Michael Shamberg and his influential book *Guerilla Television*, published in 1971, is of particular significance here.[36] Shamberg, a member of the New York group Raindance and one of the editors of a magazine by that name, envisioned "guerilla television" as an intervention, as a way of critiquing from within, rather than at a distance from, the medium of television, and this spirit evidently infuses *The Eternal Frame*.[37]

The style of these camera-carrying video artists also inevitably echoes that of cinema verité directors such as Dziga Vertov, Jean Rouch, and Edgar Morin—and Robert Drew, who had made his Kennedy documentaries, *Primary* (1960) and *Crisis* (1963), a few years earlier. If these directors were after the truth, Bill Nichols writes, "it is the truth of a form of interaction that would not exist were it not for the camera."[38] The Artist-President recalls the man-in-the-box who pops up frequently in Drew's *Primary*, the televised Kennedy image. Increasingly, *The Eternal Frame* thus turns into a guerilla take on Drew's Kennedy films as press conferences and speeches abruptly shift to backstage sequences.

During the reenactment rehearsals, *The Eternal Frame* continues to intercut them with rehearsals staged and recorded in various formats, shifting between black-and-white and color. The first of these is taped in front of a rear-screen projection, bringing to it a weird Hitchcock-like feel (fig. 2.1).

In contrasting the iconographic site, in which the sky is cartoonishly blue and the grass just as green, with the equally iconic and eye-scarringly pink costume of Jackie Kennedy, this scene highlights its own projection of Dealey Plaza as a theatrical mise-en-scène. This intensity of color, which suggests a mock-baroque style, is then juxtaposed with another cut of the ensemble filmed in black and white, in which the actors are watching their own rehearsals on a television monitor; eased in a chair, Hall allows himself to fall back in laughter, exclaiming, "This is really bad taste."

The Eternal Frame goes on to introduce camp elements into this heady mixture of stylistic elements.[39] In one of the defining moments of the video, in which the rehearsals are filmed from behind a parked car in the studio in which they take place, what we can call "the Jackie Kennedy image," played

FIG. 2.1 Doug Michels as Jacqueline Kennedy and Doug Hall as John F. Kennedy in *The Eternal Frame* (Ant Farm and T. R. Uthco, 1975).

by Michels, crawls across the hood and winks flirtingly at the camera in a moment that is less shocking than it is peculiarly charming in its irreverence. Again, there is a sense of defamiliarization, of recognition of the difference between historical and reenacted images, the first tragic, the second now comic. Michels is then interviewed outside an elevator in Dallas, where he shares some of his thoughts about his role in the reenactment. The playfulness is modified by Michels's own worries about what they are about to do. "I've been waking up every night," he claims, and admits to being "puzzled," "uncomfortable" in the clothes and the makeup. "But I only relate to it as an image, you know. I don't relate to it as acting as Jackie," he adds as we see him dressing up.

The "essence of camp," Susan Sontag claims in her famous essay on the subject, "is its love of the unnatural: of artifice and exaggeration." Essential to perceiving camp, she insists, is to understand "Being-as-Playing-a-Role." "Camp is the triumph of the epicene style," of "the convertibility of 'man' and 'woman.'"[40] The Jackie Kennedy image—that of a first lady widely recognized for her taste—is exposed as a performance in its own right in these scenes. By casting a drag Jackie, *The Eternal Frame* further explores the implications of Belting's contention that masks transform bodies into images, and addresses the question of gender.[41] Not only is the body "the rhetorical instrument of expression," Judith Butler writes, but performative acts are also "influential rituals by which subjects are formed and reformulated."[42] Demasked, Hall and Michels present a marked contrast with what otherwise is a narrative of excess, and this verité element also arguably hints at the cliché of the sadness and seriousness behind the mask of every clown. For all its irreverence, however, *The Eternal Frame* has implications that are serious: the desire for the image, for that which keeps us looking, these scenes suggest, depends as much on what the image conceals as on what it shows. What drew the gaze to the Kennedys was this duality, McEvilley argues, "their masklike quality."[43]

"In acting terms," Arthur Miller said, the presidency is "a heroic role" and transforms the actor into something that resembles "a real star."[44] The Kennedy family came to be considered an American equivalent of European royalty. Gil Troy argues that the main challenge for any modern presidential historian is to transcend "the false polarities between policy and personality, between the roles of commander-in-chief and celebrity-in-chief."[45] The Artist-President embodies the breakdown of these polarities. He takes on mythic proportions and echoes superhuman creations from legends old as well as more recent ones, including those of Faust and Frankenstein; he is a ghost in a machine, a human-made image spun out of control. Ant Farm suggests that the cumulative effect of the chains of image making it describes in its first part, with its mix of bust, masks, and televised images, is to elevate the Artist-President into an icon, into a ritual image. In its second part, its reenactment of Zapruder's images, it goes on to raise the question, what are the implications of biological death for this ritual image?

STAGING IMAGE DEATH

As the performance group arrives in Dealey Plaza, *The Eternal Frame* finds a more charged pace. Verité-style street interviews are mixed with site-specific performances as the mise-en-scène changes; the group moves from rehearsing against background projection to filming on location. The video's identity as a document of a performance is also more central here than in the earlier sequences. Richard Schechner's axiom that performance can take place either in "a totally transformed space" or in a "found space" informs Ant Farm's take on what he calls the "theatrical event," or, as it has come to be called, "site-specific performance."[46] To be true, such performance has to stage an interaction that allows the unexpected to redefine it. Without authorization, Ant Farm staged its performance on the site where the assassination happened, but the effect feels less like a remove into the realm of the real than a reflection of the fact that the plaza itself has been transformed by its own image, steeped in its own iconography.

Before the reenactments in Dealey Plaza begin, however, we see, once again, the grainy images of the Zapruder film that silently introduced *The Eternal Frame*. It is these images, we understand, that are going to be quoted; then, with "The Battle Hymn of the Republic" as sound track, the video reaches its prolonged climax as the limousine circles through Dealey Plaza and the actors stage Kennedy's death again and again. We see this in a variety of formats and from different angles, first in black and white, then in color. Through the rehearsals as well as the reenactments in Dealey Plaza, the same gestures are repeated: the clutching of the neck, the bodily contortions, the crawling across the back of the car. Hall and Michels perform their roles as if they were images caught in a loop; each time it looks similar yet different. The effect of this gestic theater is that the performance becomes what Walter Benjamin, in a short piece about epic theater, describes as interruptive. The actors continue to quote their own gestures and thus expose the very theatricality of the performance.[47] For what we see is the staging of a performance, *The Eternal Frame* insists, not of the historical event of the assassination.

As in *Media Burn*, cameras turn on cameras, and we see several bystanders filming the event. There is a segment shot from the "grassy knoll," another from the opposite side of the plaza. Soon, half the people standing on the curb and watching the Lincoln circling the plaza are holding cameras, photographing or filming what they see. Watching seems to breed visual recording, and vice versa: already at this early point, before the plaza has come to serve as a scene for numerous anniversary specials for the networks, it seems to be transformed into what has been called televisual space.[48] Amateurs and artists meet, carrying their Portapaks, filming each other, creating images of the creation of images.

It is with some trepidation that the performance group meets its accidental audience, the visitors who happen to be there in the plaza, as they arrive to stage an event that is "not *not* art." This confrontation is a central element of this second part of *The Eternal Frame*, since it stresses the ambiguity and spirit of inquiry that informs the video as an artistic undertaking.

The bystanders do not turn away from a reenactment that the actors find to be in poor taste, but instead engage themselves with what is happening, and several document it by recording it. Not knowing what to make of what they see, a number of people who happen to be in the plaza think it is an official reconstruction. "Reporters" talk to the people who begin to gather. A woman is moved to tears: "It looks like the real thing," she says. "I'm glad we were here—that was a beautiful reenactment. I wish we had a still camera so we could have caught it, to show it." The impulse to preserve the moment of reenactment has come to characterize the site, but at the same time, several bystanders begin to think back to where they were on November 22, 1963, and are moved by being transported back in time to that morning; an elderly man points at the motorcade and describes to his grandchildren what happened all those years ago. "How can they enjoy it so much?" a baffled Hall asks after the ensemble has left the plaza, realizing that the images his group has performed are out of their control as well.

The shock of recognition that the interviewed woman gives expression to presents a marked contrast to Hall's professional irony. It would be too easy, however, to conclude that this upsurge of feeling and collective reminiscence is a naive confusion of realism and parody. In fact, the bystanders seem to be strongly aware of the theatrics of reenactment and of their own involvement in it. The woman describes the performance as "beautiful," wishing she could record and savor the moment in all its artfulness: she wants to take part creatively in the performance and even wishes to preserve it so that she can enjoy it at home.

By introducing the plaza reenactment with the Zapruder film and by showing a performance in black and white and then in color, *The Eternal Frame* suggests that these images will continue to be mediated in an unbounded space, will be forever reshaped by the progression of new visual media: the images will appear eternally, in new frames, like the Kennedy image. *The Eternal Frame*, Mellencamp suggests, reminds the viewer that Kennedy's death was "both a real death and an image death" and that it "enthroned the film image."[49] Whereas the president died, the Kennedy image gained a different kind of power. "To represent," Louis Marin writes, "is to make the dead man come back as if he were present and living."[50] Zapruder's images, as performed by Ant Farm, produce a simulation of this empowerment of the image.

In the moment Kennedy was assassinated, what Christopher Lasch calls "the life of Kennedy's death" began.[51] In years afterward, the president's death was described in sacred terms "as his last and his most important act."[52]

The assassination thus led to what Arthur Neal calls a "sanctification" of the Kennedy image.[53] His death became, Sturken writes, a "trope of America's loss of innocence."[54] Increasingly, the Kennedy image was projected as a symbol of martyrdom and consequently became transformed into a ritual image; Zapruder's images began to aspire to what Hellmann describes as a collective "mythic and religious sensibility."[55]

This transformation, of course, has several implications, some of which are explored in *The Eternal Frame*. The bust hints at the growth of a comprehensive industry of commemoration, the kind of "preservation" Baty describes as following the death of Marilyn Monroe, whose image has been "imprinted and displayed on T-shirts, calendars, postcards, ashtrays, soap dishes, and ceramic mugs."[56] Biological death implies an empowerment of the image that is reflected in a comprehensive production of pictures; in a sense, then, the Kennedy image has been only more intensely circulated since his death—its traveling has gained speed and territory. More central in the second part of *The Eternal Frame*, however, is the question of what the implications are of the sanctification of the Kennedy image for the changing status of Zapruder's images.

Indeed, in simulating what we recognize to be the images Zapruder once recorded, Ant Farm simultaneously creates them and destroys them, and adds something to them that transforms them. In doing so, it performs what Bruno Latour refers to as an "iconoclash": "Icono*clasm* is when we know what is happening in the act of breaking and what the motivations for what appears as a clear project of destruction are; icono*clash*, on the other hand, is when one does not know, one hesitates, one is troubled by an action for which there is no way to know, without further inquiry, whether it is destructive or constructive."[57]

This sense of ambiguity, of performance as an act of exploration, informs *The Eternal Frame*. Throughout its narrative, it exposes the ambiguity of the actors involved and questions its own image play. After being performed as well as projected, it allowed audience members, in the plaza as well as outside a theater in San Francisco, to have their say. It thus repeatedly invites its viewers to work out their own interpretation of what the video says and what it shows as well as what it is.

In producing its own Zapruder film and staging the production as well as the projection, Ant Farm reminds us that Zapruder himself unwittingly created an image of destruction, an iconoclastic image. Iconoclasm, Mitchell writes, "is more than just the destruction of images; it is a 'creative destruction,' in which a secondary image of defacement or annihilation is created at the same moment that the 'target' image is attacked."[58] Zapruder's images are such secondary images. A biological body was destroyed, but the target image not only escaped, but also gained power. In trying to eliminate images from the collective imagination—thinking that the destruction of pictures can extinguish mental images—Belting argues, iconoclasts always ultimately end up destroying bodies or objects.[59] "When the human body, a nation's flag, money, or a public statue is *defaced*," Michael Taussig argues in *Defacement*, "a strange surplus of negative energy is likely to be aroused from within the defaced thing itself."[60] "Image death," the Artist-President insists, entails rebirth: "Because I must function only as an image, I have chosen in my career to begin with the end, and to be born, in a sense, again, even as I was dying."

This paradoxical logic of empowerment is of some consequence, *The Eternal Frame* suggests, for the cultural status of Zapruder's images as well as his film. Nowhere in the video is what Taussig calls a surplus of negative energy addressed more clearly than in a scene in which the actors freeze as if in a still: they perform a single frame, rather than film (fig. 2.2).

FIG. 2.2   Doug Michel and Doug Hall performing the single frame in *The Eternal Frame* (Ant Farm and T. R. Uthco, 1975).

The postcard quality of this still image suggests that Zapruder's footage is, in the words of Mellencamp, "encapsulated as 'art' and replayed for us as image."[61] Vaguely reminiscent of *Life*'s color displays, the "still" reminds us that at the time of *The Eternal Frame*'s making, the public had just seen the film broadcast for the first time. It still existed mainly as still images to many; now it existed as both. "Remembered and re-presented images transcend their positions in relation to specific events," Janis L. Edwards writes in an essay about iconic photographs, "and create larger rhetorical frameworks that revive and reimagine the narratives that constitute cultural myths."[62] This montage of reenactment and quasi still suggests the complex iconicity of Zapruder's images, the multiple bind of images that travel across media. These images are icons of both death and of dying; they evoke the what-has-been of the moment as well as the process of human suffering and shock. Their impact depends on the frame, on the medium in which they appear. Zooming in on the still, the video exposes its overwrought ornamentation, its imagery almost connoting religious kitsch. What turns the Zapruder film into an icon, then, is not its status as an evidentiary image, nor its privileged status in the formation of cultural memory—it is, ultimately, the suffering and destruction the images depict.

In an essay on what is arguably the best-known image of suffering in Western culture, the crucifix, Joseph Koerner describes the paradox that stands at the center of "the great machinery of Christian images." "What to the rest of the world was the ultimate punishment—crucifixion as the most painful, public, and humiliating of deaths reserved for criminals, traitors, and slaves," Koerner observes, "was for Christians the emblem of their God."[63] In an increasingly secularized culture, the "defaced" image, Taussig argues, the image in a "state of *desecration*," is "the closest many of us are going to get to the sacred"—indeed this negative state, he adds, "can come across as more sacred than the 'sacred.'"[64] *The Eternal Frame* suggests that the expressive charge of Zapruder's images unleashes a kind of collective longing, another meditation on death by imaginative recollection.

Importantly, Ant Farm's video neither reduces nor ignores the tragedy of human loss—rather, it distinguishes images from human bodies and thus invites reflection on what finally constitutes cultural memory of a national leader as well as of his assassination. By performing Zapruder's images in a series of reenactments, recording them, and projecting them in shifting styles, the group's performance indeed shows us what Mitchell describes as a symmetry between iconoclasm and idolatry. Acts of creative destruction can create secondary images, he argues, "that are, in their way, forms of idolatry just as potent as the primary idols they seek to displace."[65] The image of destruction can thus become an idol in its own right, and the idolater, paradoxically, the accidental iconoclast. Zapruder took on this double role when he unintentionally recorded an event that would have been remembered very differently without the existence of his film—which, again, would never have been made in the first place if not for the construction of the Kennedy image. Toward the end, Hall, elated and sans makeup, declares that Ant Farm's performance marked the end of his interest in the images as well as his involvement in the fantasy. "We all killed Kennedy," he adds. We return, then, to the observation by McEvilley that what the audience loved in the first act made it insatiable in the second—an insatiability that is, ultimately, destructive.[66] The last image of the video, a final zoom-out from the bust, transforms the analogy between gaze and bullet from keynote into afterthought and implicates the viewer with new urgency.

If quoting entails "a possible way of dealing with 'the past today,'" how is this the case with *The Eternal Frame*?[67] The pun of the video's title refers to the name given to the flame that burns at the grave site where Kennedy's body is laid to rest in Arlington National Cemetery, "the eternal flame"—a symbol proclaiming that the memory of the president lives on. Inspired by the eternal flame at the Tomb of the Unknown Soldier at the Arc de Triomphe in Paris, it was requested by Jackie Kennedy, who had observed the impression the tomb had made on Kennedy during a visit in 1961. Whereas the flame connotes the persistent vision of historical progress that Kennedy so infectiously expressed, *The Eternal Frame* is about images of the past, which burn differently. They appear, as Walter Benjamin put it in his theses on the philosophy of history, with the suddenness of a flashing light.[68] The repetitions of the reenactment remind us that the frame is "eternal" only in the sense that the images always reappear as something new.[69] The Zapruder film enables only a fragmentary vision of past events, a glimpse into the past that Benjamin describes as a ruinous landscape.[70]

In its Zapruder quotation, I suggest, Ant Farm's iconoclash is informed by what Craig Owens observed and described at the end of the seventies as an "allegorical impulse" in the contemporary art of the period.[71] Inspired by Benjamin, who saw quoting as a way to "tear from context, to destroy," Owens suggests that artists "confiscate" images when quoting them and that they add new meanings in the process.[72] In *The Eternal Frame*, Zapruder's images are the mystery, Patricia Mellencamp observes, and "not who killed Kennedy and how, the usual concerns brought to bear on the Zapruder footage."[73] Significantly, Ant Farm's quoting suggests an interventionist strategy rather than the critical distance of the observer in addressing this "mystery." Instead of describing a diagnosis (as, for example, Daniel Boorstin did with his notion of the pseudo-event), Ant Farm sought contamination.[74] It bears mentioning, I think, that the somewhat automatic and commonplace tendency to consider *The Eternal Frame* "a perfect illustration of Baudrillard and simulation, the mediated world we all inhabit"—as Constance M. Lewallen describes it— needs to be amended.[75] As Mellencamp points out, the Baudrilliardian mystic-apocalyptic sits uneasily with the playful criticality of *The Eternal Frame*.[76]

REFRAMING *THE ETERNAL FRAME*

"The Zapruder film, once it enters mass circulation, spreading throughout the habitat of national and international imaginaries, clearly wants something, especially in the sense that it lacks and needs something, namely, an explanatory frame, a context," Mitchell says in an interview.[77] *The Eternal Frame* explores how such a shifting frame will always condition how we see Zapruder's images as they appear in new media. However, any experience of watching the video itself is also determined by shifting acts of framing. I was reminded of this as I watched the video while visiting the exhibition "Ant Farm, 1968–1978" in New Haven on an October afternoon in 2005.

Certainly, as Ernest Larsen points out in a review in the *American Quarterly*, the traveling exhibition, which was curated by Constance M. Lewallen and Steve Seid at the Berkeley Art Museum and Pacific Film Archive in the spring of 2004, thereafter visiting Santa Monica, Philadelphia, Houston, and Karlsruhe before finally ending in New Haven, was "long overdue."[78] When artistic collectives such as Ant Farm are treated in a "marginal way" in video history, this is "indicative of the way in which socially concerned work was simply written out of the art-historical agenda for video set forth in its museumization," Sturken argues.[79] But how does the form's belated inclusion in such an agenda transform *The Eternal Frame*?

Indeed, the video becomes something of a relic in its own right, a treasured object of the art world. Undoubtedly, the exhibition narrative itself led my thoughts in these directions as I visited the show. At the door, I was given a little perforated leaflet that contained some information and small pictures in black and white—collectibles—and was then invited to walk through the gallery and look at various objects and memorabilia. In a small brochure, Dean

Sakomoto, director of exhibitions at the Yale University School of Architecture Gallery, refers to the exhibition's New Haven visit as "fitting and timely," since the gallery was a site for student activism in the sixties and Michels was a student at the Yale School of Architecture. Walking along a wooden wall, I looked at pictures, letters, and posters and soon located a screen permanently showing *The Eternal Frame* underneath a poster announcing the San Francisco screening of an early version of the film. I inevitably came to think that the video ultimately commented on its own framing. Not entirely unlike the Zapruder film, Ant Farm's playful iconoclash was now institutionalized as a historical image, an object to be preserved, and the visitor to the gallery could peruse various objects—pictures, contracts, letters, and, quite spectacularly, the hat worn by Michels during the reenactment in 1975—inside display cases. In a separate room, one could sit in living-room-like seclusion and watch *The Eternal Frame* played on a laptop screen, on a forever loop, in eternal rerun.

Like the Zapruder film, Ant Farm's video is now part of the cultural memory of the assassination. "Whether the loss of memories exists on the scale of a single life or that of an entire nation, the loss of primary documents recorded on videotape threatens our cultural legacy," Deirdre Boyle writes in *Video Preservation*. At the Yale gallery, the screening of *The Eternal Frame* was very much a celebration of this legacy, a response to Boyle's call for the need to salvage "a rapidly deteriorating past."[80] Newly restored, *The Eternal Frame* is now canonized as a revered iconoclash. Indeed, the restoration and commercial distribution of the video as part of a narrative about its restoration occurred not long after the restoration of the Zapruder film. What does this tell us?

Zapruder's images, quoted in an allegorical work about image, memory, and past, were transformed into yet another icon. So in the end, *The Eternal Frame* invites its viewer to address the fragility of material memory. Indeed, preservation is, in a sense, a strategy against iconoclasm, as Dario Gamboni suggests in an essay in which he discusses where to draw the line between neglect and destruction. There are "pictorial and rhetorical equivalences between oblivion and abolition on the one hand and, on the other hand, intentional or unintentional degradation and destruction," Gamboni observes; these "are predicated upon a double equation between material disappearance and oblivion, material preservation and memory."[81] Both Zapruder's and Ant Farm's images are projected within a discourse that corresponds with the heritage industry's obsession with artifacts. Visiting the museum in Dealey Plaza, one can see Zapruder's camera in a glass display case, and at the Ant

Farm exhibition, I gazed at the props, safely placed under glass, that had been used in the making of the group's video.

Memory is not the same as material survival, Gamboni insists, and speaking from an exhibition wall in the fall of 2005, the Artist-President seemed to say the same thing: I exist only if you look at me.[82] Indeed, surrounded by artifacts, the flashing screen finally invited reflection on the museum as a site for experiential art.[83] *The Eternal Frame* had produced its own relics, which were part of the exhibition, and so in this case, the presence of objects contributed to the defining of the film as experience. In an essay, Craig Owens describes what he finds to be a shift in attention from artwork and artist to what he calls the "frame"—the entire network of institutional practices that "define, circumscribe and contain both artistic production and reception," as well as the art world apparatus (handlers, agents, publicists, administrators, and so on). The frame thus understood, Owens holds, increases the spatial and temporal distance between the artist and the visitor.[84] Having watched the video on my television set and on my laptop screen over several years, I was now struck by how the viewing experience had not been transformed by the distance Owens describes. Judging from the exhibition I visited, the canonization of *The Eternal Frame* suggested that the preservation of experiential art cannot escape materiality. Looking at Michels's pink hat, now greyish after years in obscurity, I could not help thinking that even the copy of Jackie's hat had become an icon in its own right. I photographed it, but was not allowed to touch it.

As years pass, our memories of images as well as exhibitions are changed by new experiences, by new images and new exhibitions. A year after my visit in New Haven, on November 12, 2006, the *Las Vegas Review* informed its readers that a wax figure of president George W. Bush had been pushed over by a visitor in Madame Tussauds celebrity waxworks in Las Vegas. The figure was attacked the day before the 2006 Senate elections. "People are always touching them, but this was pretty rare," a representative of the museum told the paper. Among the other wax creations in the exhibition were effigies of John F. Kennedy and George Clooney, the *Review* reported. The article made me think of a visit I had made a few months earlier to the Astrup Fearnley Museum of contemporary art in Oslo, where I had found John F. Kennedy on a ceremonial bed, barefoot and dressed in a dark blue suit. The piece, titled *Now* (2004), was made by Maurizio Cattelan, an Italian artist who lives in New York; in Oslo, it was part of an exhibition of recent American art, "Mo(nu)ments," where it was surrounded by work by Damien Hirst,

Jeff Koons, Matthew Barney, and Andy Warhol. I peered down into the open coffin and looked at the shoeless feet: an obvious reference to holiness, to martyrdom. When I returned home, I found out that *Now* originally had been exhibited at the Carnegie International exhibition in the fall of 2004.[85]

Twenty years after the assassination, Christopher Lasch suggested that "it has been possible to see in Kennedy's death, as in his life, pretty much whatever an observer wanted to see. Both present a rich field for the unchecked play of fantasy."[86] There is always a new "now" for the Kennedy image. To me, the experience of seeing *Now* perhaps inevitably came to be informed by years of watching *The Eternal Frame*. I was tempted to bow down and touch the wax face, just as I had wanted to touch the fabric of Michels's hat in New Haven. In his book about what he calls the "animation fantasy"—a fantasy of statues coming alive—Kenneth Gross describes how, in the courtyard of the J. Paul Getty Museum, he was confronted with a statue of Venus that was flanked by an official sign reading, "You may touch this statue." The statue was a modern copy of an original, hence the invitation; it had been "stripped of the taboos that might grant it a greater aura of seriousness."[87] Contrary to this copy, *Now* seemed to achieve such an aura of seriousness, even if it was hard to say what it consisted in. (Cattelan is widely known for his iconoclastic installations, including *La Nona Ora* [The Ninth Hour], a wax figure of Pope John Paul II in papal costume with a crucifix in his hand that is crushed by a meteorite that has fallen through the roof, as well as numerous embalmed animals.) The question the Kennedy installation seemed to ask of me, half a year after its original exhibition in New York, was, what is the now of *Now*? It was impossible to look at the barefoot figure without thinking that he was nothing but an empty vessel, an image confiscated by yet another allegorist.

Leaning over the coffin, I thought I could see a smirk on the figure's face: indeed, I could not help thinking it was the Artist-President who lay stretched out there, eternally on *lit de parade* yet ever ready to render his ultimate service to the media, which created him and without which he would be nothing. *The Eternal Frame*, then, inevitably steals its way into confrontations with other artworks, as much resonant art does. The wax figure did not evoke sacrifice as much as yet another quasi-ritualistic image death. The image of the president, whether dead or dying, now an allegorical image, hardly made me think about the assassination at all; neither, for that matter, did it strike me as a work that produced nostalgia or anger. If *Now* seemed to insist on anything, it was this secularization of its very own image of martyrdom. The work seemed to me striking in its self-conscious criticality.

Perhaps it was the wax that invited such an interpretation? The wax figure has its own history as a medium; *Now* seemed to comment on that history. Wax has evoked the event of death in both religious and secular imagery. David Freedberg writes about the transition from funerary imagery to public waxworks in *The Power of Images*: in 1611, the sculptor Michel Bourdin "appears to have commercially exploited his wax bust of the assassinated Henry IV by putting a replica on public display," Freedberg explains. Bourdin offended his audience in the process: "The assassination of Henri was still fresh in everyone's memory."[88] Assassinated presidents in wax join a line of royal images of death. Cattelan's figure, however, did not have the kind of auratic power Freedberg goes on to observe in the wax images in his book. Its resemblance was certainly uncanny, but it would be wrong to say that the installation was realistic. Instead, the wax figure drew attention to its materiality, its mediality, to the empty vessel. The "now" of *Now*, in other words, was not so much the now of the fall of 2004, or of the day I visited the Astrup Fearnley Museum a few months later, as it was the now from which the Artist-President addresses us every time *The Eternal Frame* is projected.

Inside the Zapruder Museum

> They were like tourists walking through the rooms of some small private collection, the Zapruder Museum, one item on permanent display, the twenty-some-odd seconds of a home movie, and it runs continuously. // Don DeLillo, *Underworld*

THE EPISODE TAKES UP ONLY THREE TO FOUR of the more than eight hundred pages of Don DeLillo's *Underworld*, yet a reader will never put away the book without remembering it: a painter and artist, Klara Sax, follows a film connoisseur, Miles Lightman, to the apartment of a video artist he knows; a crowd of visitors is sitting on the floor, on folding chairs, and on a sofa in an apartment filled with television sets. From all the screens flicker the images of an amateur film that lasts less than half a minute yet never seems to end. The "rare and strange" event is a screening of a videotaped bootleg copy of the Zapruder film, taking place during what is referred to as a "rooftop summer" evening in New York City in 1974.[1]

This chapter will present a close reading of this episode, a novelistic description of a fictive projection of Zapruder's images. A novel that has sold more than a million copies worldwide, *Underworld* not only reaches masses of readers, it also says something about Zapruder's images that would have been difficult to say in any other form than that of the novel. DeLillo does not merely describe how cultural memory is shaped—he simultaneously contributes to shaping it as well. The most celebrated novelist to fictionalize the events that surround Kennedy's death, DeLillo considers the assassination and its various representations to be "prisms" through which the profound impact of contemporary technologies of mediation on the shaping of cultural memory and human imagination can be seen. Speaking of the assassination in an interview, DeLillo suggested that Kennedy's death no less than "invented" him as a writer; while working on *Libra* (1988), his novel about Lee Harvey Oswald and the events surrounding the assassination, he came to realize that all his previous eight novels "seemed to be collecting around the dark center of the assassination."[2] Several critics have echoed these remarks made by the writer. "Almost all of DeLillo's writing has been in some sense about the assassination," claims N. H. Reeve.[3]

DeLillo's preoccupation with how technology continues to inform self-identity is so strong that it can be regarded as a defining theme in his fiction.[4] Arguably, the image saturation of the twentieth century is of specific significance here; from his first novel, *Americana* (1971), and onward, DeLillo has sought to reflect upon the power that images seem to exert over his characters. In an interview from the year *Underworld* was published, DeLillo comments on this:

> Howard: Why does film stand so conspicuously at the center of your work rather than books?
>
> DeLillo: Because this is the age of images, I suppose, and much that is different about our time can be traced to the fact that we are on film, a reality that did not shape, instruct, and haunt previous cultures. I suppose film gives us a deeply self-conscious sense, but beyond that it's simply such a prevalent fact of contemporary life that I don't think any attempt to understand the way we live and the way we think and the way we feel about ourselves can proceed without a deep consideration of the power of the image.[5]

In this chapter, I will explore how the difference between what Zapruder's images do in *Underworld* and what they do in *Libra* throws light on the film's changing cultural status.

"Exposition," Philippe Hamon writes, "comes into play in both literary and nonliterary works whenever the text shifts over into a *descriptive* dominant." It can vary in length and serves a variety of functions in a narrative: rendering a story legible, jolting the reader, or providing an "illusion of the real."[6] Arguably, Hamon's readings of Balzac and Proust raise the question, how come there are not more readings of DeLillo's books from the perspective of visual description and exposition, given this writer's preoccupation with contemporary visual culture? This chapter seeks only to begin to amend this neglect, by addressing the fiction of a writer whose vision is distinctly shaped by concerns with visuality.

DeLillo is not alone, of course, in writing novels about the assassination or in writing about Zapruder's images in novelistic form. Several crime novels have been inspired by the mythology that gradually came to surround the contested evidentiary status of the Zapruder film and have contributed to its cult status in popular culture.' Novelists have had a keen sense of how the cultural memory of the assassination, its manifold narrativizations in culture, has shaped individual memories of what happened. One of the "epitaphs" of William T. Vollmann's *Thirteen Stories and Thirteen Epitaphs* (1991), "Epitaph for President John F. Kennedy," serves as a good example:

> The extra bullets left darker streaks in Zapruder's movies than any deeds of cracked loyalty that we could explain. They hurtled at you like comets from Enigma, so when Oswald got death, Ruby got life, but he died before he talked. Castro got a breather; you got the privilege of not having to undo yourself; you outlived the vulgarity of survival. I was four years old. When your icon began to shine, the radio was talking to the steering wheel (I remember that, but not what it said) and my mother said   *our President is dead*   and my mother was crying and I looked out the window, crying because my mother was crying, and I saw so many cars creeping slowly among the freeway and everyone in every car was crying.[8]

The narrator's memory of the assassination is shaped by a description of its sensorial impact—he remembers listening to the radio and looking at the response of everyone around him. As a four-year-old, he did not fully understand or take part in what had happened, yet the impact was tremendous—he was afflicted by the sheer mental pain he observed in others. And then there is the reference to the "darker streaks" in Zapruder's footage, the images of which, we gather, the narrator has grown up with, but which would not have been broadcast before he was in his midteens.

It is not always immediately clear what the performativity of Zapruder's images consists of, once transformed by artists and writers. Many of them are attracted by the enigmatic, expressive charge of the images, by their sheer hold on individual and collective memory. No writer has explored how Zapruder's images can travel into the unmapped territories of the unconscious more uncompromisingly than J. G. Ballard. When Nelson Doubleday saw the original print of *The Atrocity Exhibition* before it was to be published in 1970, he ordered the entire press run shredded for fear of the controversy the book would provoke. The author himself describes the novel well in an interview:

> Its landscape is compounded of an enormous number of fictions, the fragments of the dream machine that produces our lifestyle right now. . . . My book deals with the irrational violence of modern society, the side of our culture that could be described as an atrocity exhibition. . . . [It] portrays a doctor who's had a mental breakdown. He has been shocked and numbed by events like the deaths of the Kennedys and Marilyn Monroe. To make sense of the modern world he wants to immerse himself in its most destructive elements.[9]

Ballard's exposition of atrocity, then, is double: through a series of fifteen chapters it represents, as David Pringle observes, both an exteriorization of the mind and a concretization of a collective imaginary.[10] In its radical fragmentation of character, it resembles novels by William S. Burroughs or, more recently, the movies of David Lynch as it seeks to describe the mind of the disturbed doctor whose name changes throughout the narrative (Travis, Travers, Traven, Talbot), a ruinous landscape scattered with images among which we find Zapruder's. The assassination, Ballard suggests, "presides over *The Atrocity Exhibition*, and in many ways the book is directly inspired by [Kennedy's] death, and represents a desperate attempt to make sense of the tragedy."[11] In the book's closing chapter, the assassination is imagined as a remake of Alfred Jarry's "The Crucifixion Considered as an Uphill Bicycle Race," now titled "The Assassination of John Fitzgerald Kennedy Considered as a Downhill Motor Race," a piece described by Kathy Acker as "jagged as broken glass."[12]

This brief glimpse into Ballard's fictional universe serves less as a detour than as an entry into DeLillo's very different exploration of how Zapruder's images shape human imagination, including the unconscious. "A huge volume of sensational and often toxic imagery inundates our minds, much of it fictional in content," Ballard observes in his commentary on *The Atrocity Exhibition*: "What actually happens on the level of our unconscious minds when, within minutes on the same TV screen, a prime minister is assassinated, an actress makes love, an injured child is carried from a car crash?"[13] Whereas we saw in the Introduction how Zapruder's images are projected as traumatic memory in Petersen's *In the Line of Fire*, and in Brown's *Elm Street* as distorted memory, Ballard's novel explores what happens when Zapruder's images travel into the mental landscape of a disturbed mind, where they are transformed into surreal images.

In *Underworld*, Klara Sax, visiting a Manhattan loft, witnesses how the Zapruder film ceases to be "the Zapruder film" before her very eyes and becomes something new. But what exactly? The art event enables Sax to meditate on some of the central preoccupations of the novel: death, visuality, and memory. The film is, in Sax's spontaneous words, "powerfully open." This immediate response as well as her later thoughts about the images, that the film carries "a kind of inner life," brings her to think that the images show a "crude living likeness of the mind's own technology."[14] What she sees makes her think less about the Kennedy assassination than about death as a fact of human existence.

In *Libra*, Zapruder's footage is emblematic of the epistemological crisis that develops during the ongoing forensic analysis of evidence from the assassination; for Nicholas Branch, the retired senior CIA analyst hired to write a secret history of the assassination, the film is more than anything "a major emblem of uncertainty and chaos," with its "blurs, patches and shadows"; he "has abandoned his life to understanding that moment in Dallas, the seven seconds that broke the back of the American century," but he is "stuck."[15] The film not only resists the kind of interpretation that Branch attempts, but also comes to do so to the degree that it symbolizes that very resistance. With *Underworld*, however, DeLillo wishes to take us elsewhere. For Sax, the strange, "secret" history of the film exists somewhere in the periphery of the event of actually watching it: "She knew she'd hear from Miles at dinner about the secret manipulation of history, or attempts at such, or how the experts could not seem to produce a clear print of the movie, or whatever."[16] Sax is more alert to other aspects of watching Zapruder's footage than is Branch. Where Branch thinks of the Zapruder film as a series of frames that form a larger whole, Sax is caught up in and almost exhilarated by projection, by an experience that fills her with something like awe.

Indeed, *Underworld* describes several visual events that are no less than epiphanic for its characters. There are several "visionary moments," to borrow Paul Maltby's words, when characters experience "that flash of insight or sudden revelation which critically raises the level of spiritual or self-awareness."[17] Sax's visit to the Zapruder installation is such a moment. It reflects how the projection of Zapruder's images in an art installation does something to a spectator that is very different from what they do under the poring gaze of either Branch in *Libra* or John Connally in the November 25, 1966, issue of *Life*. *Libra* and *Underworld* can thus be said to form a trajectory, to explore the transformation of Zapruder's footage from evidentiary to aesthetic image.

In an interview with Adam Begley in 1993, DeLillo returned to the subject of the Zapruder film:

> Kennedy was shot on film, Oswald was shot on TV. Does this mean anything? Maybe only that Oswald's death became instantly repeatable. It belonged to everyone. The Zapruder film, the film of Kennedy's death, was sold and hoarded and doled out very selectively. It was exclusive footage. So that the social differences continued to pertain, the hierarchy held fast—you could watch Oswald die while you ate a TV dinner, and he was still dying by the time you went to bed, but if you wanted to see the Zapruder film you had to be very important or you had to wait until the 1970s when I believe it was shown once on television.[18]

In *Underworld*—published four years after this interview appeared in the *Paris Review*—Klara visits the Zapruder art installation the summer before Gerald Rivera's broadcast of a copy of the Zapruder film in 1975. This moment was, of course, carefully chosen by DeLillo; it accounts for the fact that the fictional screening has "an edge of special intensity."[19] The novel describes a viewer's response to a film that is on the verge of being broadcast to masses of people, but that still, at the moment of projection, retains the cultish quality ascribed to images that seem in a sense to be secret, concealed, and therefore exclusive.

Today, the majority of readers who pick up DeLillo's novel will in some way be familiar with Zapruder's images. Knowing this, the author focuses more on the impact of the images than on the images themselves. This is achieved through a very particular deployment of ekphrastic description. As the Zapruder film is projected, the audience members, confronted with the unspeakable, struggle to find words to respond to what they see—Miles Lightman spontaneously displays a sense of the sublime as he reverently exclaims, "It's outside language."[20] "Wary of their own anticipation," those who attend feel "lucky," but they also know "a kind of floating fear" of the images they are finally about to see that they only vaguely know—from memories of reproductions, from conversations—and then, suddenly, the film is projected:

The footage started rolling in one room but not the others and it was filled with slurs and jostles, it was totally jostled footage, a home movie shot with a Super 8, and the limousine came down the street, muddied by sunglint, and the head dipped out of the frame and reappeared and then the force of the shot that killed him, unexpectedly, the headshot, and people in the room went ohh, and then the next ohh, and five seconds later the room at the back went ohh, the same release of breath every time, like blurts of disbelief, and a woman seated on the floor spun away and covered her face because it was completely new, you see, suppressed all these years, this was the famous headshot and they had to contend with the impact—aside from the fact that this was the President being shot, past the outer limits of this fact they had to contend with the impact that any high-velocity bullet of a certain lethal engineering will make on any human head, and the sheering of tissue and braincase was a terrible revelation.[21]

The gaze shifts from screen to audience and back again in this dazzling multi-perspective passage. The single long sentence echoes the single long shot and creates a correspondence in duration: it takes about as long to read it as it takes to project the Zapruder film. Indeed, the very visceral and visual event itself stands out as the ekphrastic "object," not merely the images flashing on the many screens that fill the apartment.[22] The focus shifts from projection to spectatorship; looking at others looking is a vital part of the experience, as is listening to the response of others. Significantly, the excerpt—like the other few pages devoted to the event in the novel—never spills entirely over into the descriptive in the way that, for example, the verbal text of *Life*'s imagetexts do, in spite of the fact that the words here are unaccompanied by images, a reflection of how the tensions between showing and telling can be accommodated by literary narrative. The images are not described because the reader already knows them; when reading, we feel as if we are seeing them anyway. This absence of an extended pause to allow for a description of Zapruder's footage in any detail also corresponds to the aesthetics of the ongoing loop, which suggests that the film always begins again before there is time to let it all sink in, let alone describe it; many of Sax's thoughts about the images present themselves after she views them. A full description of the footage can thus be said to constantly threaten to foreground the absence of what is evoked: the film's images. Instead, an ekphrastic tension shapes the passage, forces it to linger on the moment of projection, to make the reader wait for waiting's sake—for something she will literally not see.

It is not surprising that several critical readings of a novel that boasts the most memorable Eisenstein moment in fiction, and an invented one at that—the projection of the unknown movie *Unterwelt*—adopt concepts from film theory in order to analyze the visuality of DeLillo's style in the novel. Philip Nel suggests that the language in *Underworld* is "a kind of performance art that functions in apparently opposite ways," and he makes use of Eisensteinian terminology (montage, juxtaposition) to demonstrate how DeLillo thereby "interrupts" the reading experience.[23] Similarly, Mark Osteen applies Eisenstein in his reading of several episodes in *Underworld* and considers its montage "counterhistory."[24] Even if one reads DeLillo's Eisenstein through Eisenstein's glasses, however, this does not necessarily imply that the video projection should be approached in the same way. The loft screening, typical of the avant-garde scene in midseventies New York, arguably sites its own reappropriation as only an art event can do. It can thus plausibly be considered an expression of the same impulse that informs Ant Farm's video, what Craig Owens described at the end of that decade as an "allegorical impulse."[25]

What kind of projection is it that Sax and Lightman are so stunned by? A video copy of the Zapruder film runs continuously, at "normal speed on some sets, slow motion on others," thus making its reappropriation hypervisible, drawing attention to it in typically postmodern fashion.[26] The distinct theatricality of the event is that of the mixed-media performance, which, according to Andy Lavender, is defined by its "intrinsic plurality effect in representation"—"different things are happening in different ways at once."[27] The visitors to the apartment find themselves to be both actors and audience as they look at the screens and steal glimpses at one another's responses. The wall of television sets, "a kind of game board of diagonals and verticals and so on, interlocking tarots of elemental fate, or synchronous footage running in an X pattern," makes Zapruder's images appear in a distinct way.[28] Unlike the linear, frame-by-frame presentation that seems to invite a microscopic gaze or forensic search, the TV wall with its moving lines is simultaneously a comment on its own mode of visualization as well as on the moment of death that it keeps projecting. The synchronization of the screens invites recognition of fleeting patterns; an *X* calls up several calligraphic denotations, of which the alphabetical-mathematical ("the *x* in the equation") serves only as a beginning. The *X* shares a ripping or tearing quality with the *Z*. A flashing *X* of identical screens thus becomes an emblem of fusion and diffusion, two lines meeting and separating at their midpoints and then reflecting back on the two kinds of passages we are confronted with: that of 8 mm film to television screen, and the passage from life to death, both of which entail a crossing from one form into another.

The result is a double-edged "aesthetics of transition," a crossing of aesthetic boundaries in a confusion of genres.[29] The loop can be considered what Owens calls "the epitome of counter-narrative," since it "arrests narrative in place, substituting a principle of syntagmatic disjunction for one of diegetic combination," and "superinduces a vertical or paradigmatic reading of correspondences upon a horizontal or syntagmatic chain of events."[30] With reference to Owens, Josh Cohen recognizes an "allegorical aesthetic" in postmodern American writing, defined by how images are "shot through with a surfeit of meanings" and thus generate infinite interpretations.[31] Certainly, *Underworld* can be said to express such a counternarrative impulse in the sense that it represents an alternative to the past described in historical narratives. DeLillo has referred to language as "a form of counterhistory" that "transforms the past," an "agent of redemption, the thing that delivers us, paradoxically, from history's flat, thin, tight and relentless designs, its arrangement of stark pages."[32] If allegory, as Owens claimed, is characterized by "its capacity to rescue from historical oblivion that which threatens to disappear," then *Underworld*, like the projection it describes, is motivated by an allegorical impulse.[33] "The prospect of recovering a nearly lost language, the idiom and scrappy slang of the postwar period, the writer's own lifetime but misted, much of it, in deep distance—what manias of anticipated pleasure this can summon," DeLillo writes.[34]

The loft, in the words of *Underworld*'s narrator, is like a "Zapruder museum," an exposition "with one item on permanent display."[35] To Sax, watching the film is an exercise not in the Branchian semiotics of *Libra*, where signs either mediate truth or fail to do so, but rather in something quite different. The installation opens up the twin problematics of death and redescription through its brief play with moving signs. Death "is always only represented," as Sarah Webster Goodwin and Elisabeth Bronfen put it; "there is no knowing death, no experiencing it and then returning to write about it, no intrinsic grounds for authority in the discourse surrounding it."[36] This "revelation" also implies that the event of the assassination has always been and remains "enacted with a sense of what will be its own representation."[37] Far from having experienced the real event of Kennedy's death, of course, or any definitive documentation of it, Klara Sax has nevertheless very much had a real experience in her confrontation with staged simulation. She feels as if she can sense human mortality in a new way. In a description of her response to the projection, she finds that she has to contend with the impact that "any high-velocity bullet of a certain lethal engineering" will make on "any human head, and the sheering of tissue and braincase"—note the significance of that small word "any"—and this insight represents for her "a terrible revelation."[38]

By describing the allegorical artist at work, DeLillo here poses as the ek-phrastic artist. The novelist cannot move beyond the restrictions of the medium, but he can make a reader feel as if such a thing is in fact happening: the Zapruder film becomes not only DeLillo's invention, but also that of the reader-viewer, through the evocation of the absent image. The summer night in 1974 ultimately thus resonates fittingly within the larger framework that is *Underworld*. This is, after all, a novel in which a *Life* reproduction of Brue-gel's painting *The Triumph of Death* floats from the upper stands of Yankee Stadium and into the hands of J. Edgar Hoover, and in which one of the characters, Nick Shay, is haunted by memories—involuntary mental images—of having shot a childhood friend by accident. And it is also, significantly, a novel in which images of the road shootings committed by the "Texas Highway Killer" light up television sets in every living room. In all these instances, I would argue, the Zapruder film hints at its own presence, its "triumph of death" always haunting the collective unconscious. "From the will to preserve the traces of something that was dead, or about to die, emerged allegory," Owens writes; it can involve a transformation "into a memento mori."[39] If DeLillo's fiction is "collecting around the dark center of the assassination," as the writer has suggested, *Underworld*'s dark center is its Zapruder projection, the *punctum* of the novel, a memento mori in the eyes of Klara Sax.[40]

FOUR

No Hugging, No Learning

There had to have been a second spitter. Behind the bushes on the gravelly road. // Jerry Seinfeld, "The Boyfriend"

JERRY SEINFELD IS TALKING TO HIS FRIENDS Elaine Benes (Julia Louis-Dreyfus) and Cosmo Kramer (Michael Richards) about a new friendship he has struck up with Keith Hernandez (making a cameo appearance), and at the mention of the baseball legend's name, Kramer recoils; simultaneously, a wild-eyed and exasperated Newman (Wayne Knight) appears in the open door to the apartment. "I hate Keith Hernandez!" exclaims Kramer.[1] Foaming with contempt, Newman adds: "I despise him!" Then the two begin to spin a wild tale. On June 14, 1987, they attended a baseball game at Shea Stadium, where the Mets lost against the Philadelphia Phillies. After the game, Kramer and Newman waited outside the stadium in the parking lot in order to confront Hernandez, who, according to Newman, "opened the door to a five-run Phillies night and cost the Mets the game." As Hernandez exited, the three passed one another and Newman shouted, "Nice game, pretty boy!" "Then, a second later," Newman says, "something happened that changed us in a very deep and profound way from that day forward." "What was it?" Elaine inquires. "He spit on us," says Kramer. The dialogue then goes on to introduce one of the subplots of "The Boyfriend," an hour-long episode of the sitcom *Seinfeld* that parodies how Zapruder's images shaped the style and the narrative of Oliver Stone's *JFK*.

In this chapter, I will address how the Zapruder quotations in "The Boy-friend" can be said to perform what Linda Hutcheon calls a "stylistic confrontation."[2] Quoting thus represents a kind of doubling that exposes the logic of a particular kind of storytelling, that of the docudrama. Unlike the allegorical doubling of Ant Farm's midseventies video, the metapictorial play in *Seinfeld* is directed at how a genre depicts a particular vision of history. "The Boy-friend" invites the audience to laugh at the visual rhetoric of a contemporary morality play and simultaneously comments on its own identity as an antididactic situation comedy. In the process, it provides, in the words of Geoffrey O'Brien, "a brief and reliable pleasure"—always a primary goal for a sitcom.[3]

In an essay published in the spring of 1987, Ronald Berman admits to missing the satirical American comedy of the past. "Comedy has many desires, and not all of them are respectable," he insists, and bemoans contemporary comedy for being "full of advice about hot social issues." "Sitcoms in the eighties often tell us how to run our lives," he claims.[4] Indeed, from the moment it premiered, on July 5, 1989, and throughout its nine seasons, *Seinfeld*, whether it was the kind of show Berman called for or not, broke with what he saw as the dominance of comedy informed by cultural politics. Focusing on the many trivialities of everyday life, *Seinfeld* was the product of a meeting of the minds of two stand-up comedians, Jerry Seinfeld and Larry David, who set out to make a television show that would be as funny as it would be adamantly uninstructive. "The crucial guideline," O'Brien writes of the show, "is that the characters do not learn from experience and never move beyond what they intrinsically and eternally are."[5] The self-proclaimed "show about nothing," *Seinfeld* was not as much about nothing, however, as about advocating nothing, David Marc suggests. It is about "details," and is thus about "nothing" in the sense that it is not concept driven and does not address big social or political issues explicitly.[6]

The show could thus be considered antithetical to the "melding of historical fact and dramatic form" that is docudrama, in which "coherence and narrative structure emerge, and fragments of memory are made whole."[7] Never about the major events of historical narrative, *Seinfeld*'s "plot formula," Amy McWilliams argues, played with the traditional and expected story arc, and in particular with the "problem/resolution format."[8] An episode of *Seinfeld* seldom resolved toward the end, and if there was some sort of resolution, it was ironic; as a result, the comedy was, in the words of Larry Charles, one of the show's supervising producers, "very dark." "The idea that you would have an unhappy ending . . . this really shook the foundation of the sitcom genre."[9]

Seinfeld never succumbed, O'Brien observes, "to the feel-good impulse that is the last resort of American movies and TV shows."[10] Its form, in other words, was suited perfectly for a parody of the docudrama, which often aims to offer "closure" through a revision of an authoritative narrativization of historical trauma.[11]

THE SPITTING PLOT

When Kramer and Newman begin their story of what happened that "fateful day" in Shea Stadium, images appear on the screen that instantly remind the viewer of the Zapruder film, in composition as well as texture. One man opens an umbrella and another hides behind a bush in front of a fence on what is a Seinfeldian take on the "grassy knoll" in Dealey Plaza. Then we see a man filming with an 8 mm camera, supported by a woman, recording the event from an angle corresponding to Zapruder's in 1963. The scene illustrates well Michael Dunne's observation that the jokes in *Seinfeld* "rely on cultural allusion, generic familiarity, and self-referentiality to connect the present example with its presumed intertexts." One such familiar cultural narrative is the Zapruder film, Dunne suggests, and the quotation is thus a form of "intertextual encounter."[12] Whereas both Ant Farm's video and "The Boyfriend" stage such encounters, the Warren Commission's report or *Life*, for example, present Zapruder's images as what Dunne calls "mimetic text."[13] In spite of this distinction, however, Dunne neglects the complexity involved when traveling images enter into what he calls the intertextual encyclopedia—and consequently he does not explore the full range of implications of the parody in the episode. In suggesting that the allusion in "The Boyfriend" is to Zapruder's original film, and that the parody is loosely directed at assassination mythology, he does not fully appreciate that the episode in fact recalls a very specific rhetorical situation in which Zapruder's images appear—namely, a courtroom projection of the film in Stone's *JFK*, which was running in theaters when "The Boyfriend" was broadcast.

In the DVD commentary to the episode, Tom Cherones, the director of "The Boyfriend," explains that it was intended to be a parody of *JFK*.[14] By parodying how Zapruder's cinematography shaped *JFK*'s style and, more significantly, how the images perform particular narrative functions in the movie's plot, *Seinfeld* addresses both a genre and a mode and simultaneously manages to illustrate how cemented Zapruder's images have become in the collective imaginary. Since there is no mention of the assassination, of Zapruder, or of

Stone's film, the parody depended entirely on its ability to evoke the imagery and echo the dialogue of *JFK*. The DVD, however, historicizes this parody by exposing the quotations in its bonus material.

Exhaustively analyzed and debated, Stone's film tells the story of how Louisiana district attorney Jim Garrison (Kevin Costner) came to charge Clay Shaw (Tommy Lee Jones), a New Orleans businessman, with being part of a conspiracy to kill Kennedy and brought him to trial.[15] The movie is characterized by its expressive editing and extensive montage. And although *JFK* is highly controversial for its juxtaposition of fake and authentic footage, its narrative structure is, in fact, very traditional. As David Bordwell suggests, the "disjunctive techniques are situated within an orthodox plot," and the movie develops what he calls "work" and "romance" plotlines in a "sturdy six-part structure."[16] In his quest for truth, Garrison neglects his family; his reconciliation with his wife, Liz Garrison (Sissy Spacek), and children toward the end of the film, during the trial against Shaw, is a triumph of the nuclear family, all the more controversial for the movie's depiction of its villains as a motley crew of homosexuals eagerly plotting the assassination.[17]

Seinfeld's parody revolves around Stone's use of Zapruder's images. "It's as if not just the event represented in the Zapruder film, but its grainy, out of focus, jumpy, and fragmentary character becomes the fundamental tone structure of Oliver Stone's cinematography," W. J. T. Mitchell suggests.[18] Similarly, that very structure informs "The Boyfriend." Stone stuck fake splices into his fictional footage in order to make it look authentic, Bordwell observes.[19] Likewise, in quoting Stone's fake footage, the *Seinfeld* team heavily treated its own film of the "spitting incident" in order to make the fake seem authentic.[20] Indeed, every detail in *Seinfeld*'s Zapruder quotation refers in some way to Stone's movie; for example, the umbrella man alludes not only to an open umbrella visible in the foreground of the Zapruder film, but also to its prominent placement in Stone's depiction. A central feature of Stone's narrative, the theory that the umbrella-carrying man near a road sign was involved in the assassination, is developed in Jim Marrs's book *Crossfire*, and has become one of the myths that has taken on its own life in popular culture.[21] A strange occurrence in a sun-bathed plaza, the umbrella has been the source of much speculation by conspiracy theorists, who have questioned whether it was used to give signals in a crossfire or was indeed a disguised weapon. The phrase "umbrella man" is thus now part of the peculiar phenomenon that is the assassination-myth lexicon (along with "grassy knoll," "picket fence," and so on). Stone intercuts fake footage of the umbrella man in black and white with real footage and adds several visualizations of eyewitness testimony, often making it difficult for the viewer to distinguish what is simulated from what is not.

In *Seinfeld*, the umbrella man is Tom Leopold, whom Jason Alexander (George Constanza in the series) refers to in the audio commentary as the writing team's "*JFK* consultant." Leopold saw Stone's film and came up with the idea to make a parody of it. A "JFK buff," Alexander explains, Leopold "knew the conspiracy theories and everything about the Zapruder film." In the reconstruction, then, he poses as one of the "conspirators" behind and within the parody. Leopold's inside-joke cameo reflects the playfulness of *Seinfeld*'s parody. Similarly, the filming man in *Seinfeld* echoes Stone's fake footage of Zapruder, through which he becomes a semimythological character in *JFK*'s narrative, existing mysteriously and fundamentally on the periphery of the story he so heavily came to shape.

The climactic moment of Newman and Kramer's recollection, however, comes with what corresponds to the head-wound shot in the Zapruder film (fig. 4.1).

FIG. 4.1   Michael Richards's head being thrown back and to the left by the "magic loogie" in the *Seinfeld* episode "The Boyfriend" (Tom Cherones, 1992).

Kramer's head is thrown violently backward, and his unruly hair clearly resembles the blood spray from Kennedy's head in the contested frame 313 of the Zapruder film, the frame that caused *Life* so much worry when producing the imagetext of its November 25, 1966, issue. That worry—as well as the shock produced by Geraldo Rivera's scandalous exposé—seems distant, since the very movements that once traumatized an audience are met with laughter when Kramer's long and spastic body falls over from the impact of a gob of spit. His contorting body is instantly comical, and yet the moment of impact must be considered the episode's riskiest quotation of Zapruder's images.

To a viewer who has not seen Stone's film, the story of "the second spitter" could potentially be considered to be in poor taste—an easy laugh at the expense of a tragedy now decades in the past. The audience laughs at the sheer absurdity of a story in which spittle takes the place of bullet; however, the makers of *Seinfeld* could not be certain of this response. Rick Ludwin, an NBC executive, points out in a bonus segment on the DVD release of the episode that "the audience howled to such an extent that the laughs had to be shortened in editing." According to Alexander, the *JFK* sequence produced "one of the longest prolonged laughs for a live audience."[22] "But it occurred to me that if a comedy show is able to wring comedy out of what is clearly a national tragedy," Ludwin adds, "this show had risen to another level."[23] However, *Seinfeld* did not make national tragedy laughable so much as it mimicked the narrativization of national tragedy in popular culture. What was quoted is not Zapruder's images of the assassination, but their performative function in Stone's depiction of the Shaw trial. In *JFK*, frame 313 of the Zapruder film appears only in the courtroom scene toward the movie's end, but then, in the words of Vera Dika, in "obsessive repetition."[24]

"BACK, AND TO THE LEFT"

In *JFK*, Louisiana DA Garrison manages to subpoena the film and project it to a packed courtroom ten times on February 13, 1969. The curtains are drawn as Stone dwells on the very act of projection: we see the projector, we hear it—a strategy that adds to our sense of being present in the room. "Cinema is a particularly powerful tool in the incitement of desire and the fantasy of history precisely because of the classic ways in which it invites us to view the past as if we were there," Marita Sturken writes.[25] Stone mythologizes the only authorized public projection of the Zapruder film during the years of

Life's ownership by presenting Garrison's expository agency as heroic. Just as the courtroom is transformed into a theater, the theater in which *JFK* is projected is transformed into a courtroom: Garrison addresses not only the jury and his audience in New Orleans, but also the viewers of the film. To tie Shaw to a conspiracy, he needs to prove that there was more than one assassin in Dealey Plaza; the Zapruder film is presented as evidence that Oswald could not have acted alone. The jury and the audience gasp at the sight of Kennedy's head being blown open. After the projection, Garrison asks his visibly shaken listeners: "A picture speaks a thousand words, doesn't it?" In a reconstruction, he then goes on to use the Zapruder film to criticize the conclusions of the Warren Commission that Oswald fired three bullets. One bullet missed, Garrison claims, since fragments from it hurt a bystander in Dealey Plaza; another caused Kennedy's fatal head wound. That left one bullet to account "for the seven wounds on Connally and Kennedy," a bullet that exited all wounds and came out "in almost pristine condition." Costner's district attorney traces the unlikely trajectory of the bullet, its "U-turn" and its "pause midair," and concludes, "That's some bullet."

The climax of Garrison's address depends heavily on repetition. In a series of five projections of the Zapruder film, we see Kennedy's head exploding five times as Garrison describes the president's upper body as moving "back, and to the left." He goes on to argue that the assassination was a coup d'état in which Earl Warren and Lyndon B. Johnson were "accomplices after the fact." As Bordwell argues, the visual narration during this final phase of the trial "validates Garrison's account by putting his hypothesis on the same visual level as the prologue" of *JFK*, a montage that consists exclusively of documentary footage. During the trial, however, Stone's narrative more aggressively juxtaposes fake and real footage. In addition, the trial resolves the film's two plotlines: several times, Garrison's eyes meet those of his wife, who is transformed by the projection as well, realizing that her husband's neglect of his family has, in fact, been a sacrifice for a great cause.[26] The projection saves the marriage of the film's protagonist. Garrison sought to try his case in the legal system but lost; in Stone's narrative, however, he is given a second chance to try his case in movie theaters, and succeeds better as a character portrayed by Costner than he did in real life. Ironically, the effect of his appeal, once it was performed by a famous actor in the realm of popular culture, was the legislation that became the JFK Act.[27] After Garrison's closing speech, *JFK* invites its viewers to join in his quest for truth and in advocating the opening of all government files concerning the assassination.

Not only do Zapruder's images shape the style of Stone's movie, then, they also structure its narrative arc, which reaches its definitive climax in this 1969 screening. Both the real Garrison and Costner's Garrison project the Zapruder film in order to render what has been called "the magic bullet theory" absurd; in *Seinfeld*, however, it is Costner's Garrison who is caricatured, not Garrison. It is the pathos with which Garrison's argument is delivered rather than the argument as such that is the subject of parody in *Seinfeld*. Newman recalls how the spit "ricocheted" off Kramer and then hit him; Jerry then interrupts with a monologue that breaks with the conversational tone of the show and adopts one that is more legalistic and echoes that of Costner's Garrison: "Unfortunately, the immutable laws of physics contradict the whole premise of your account. Allow me to reconstruct . . . as I have heard this story a number of times. Newman, Kramer, if you'll indulge me." He directs the two out on the floor for a reconstruction (fig. 4.2).

With a golf club, he traces the trajectory of the spit after it hit Kramer: "The spit then proceeds to ricochet off the temple, striking Newman between the third and the fourth ribs. The spit then came off the rib, made a right turn, hit Newman in the right wrist, causing him to drop his baseball cap. The spit then splashed off the wrist, pauses—midair, mind you—makes a left turn, and lands on Newman's left thigh. That is one magic loogie." The fact that Wayne Knight (Newman) also played one of the lawyers on Garrison's team in *JFK* foregrounded and added to the comic effect of *Seinfeld's* parody (fig. 4.3).

The Zapruder-like images change function seamlessly as they gradually come to visually support Jerry's theory of a second spitter, his "magic loogie theory." Initially, the quotation enables the viewer to distinguish past from present, since the 8 mm texture evokes the mental images of the characters and we see how the event is remembered (by Newman and Kramer) and imagined (by Seinfeld and Elaine) in a flashback typical of visual narration in movies as well as in television shows. But the parody becomes more clearly targeted at Stone's narrative when the images perform a rhetorical function in Jerry's reconstruction of the spitting and we see Kramer's "head shot" again and again:

Jerry [*asks Kramer*]: What happened to your head when you got hit?
Kramer: Well, my head went back and to the left. [*images of the hit*]
Jerry: Say that again.
Kramer: Back and to the left. [*images of the hit*]

FIG. 4.2   Jerry Seinfeld parodying Kevin Costner's Jim Garrison in the *Seinfeld* episode "The Boyfriend" (Tom Cherones, 1992).

FIG. 4.3   Jim Garrison (Kevin Costner) argues against the "single bullet theory" in *JFK* (Oliver Stone, 1991).

Jerry [*with pointed finger, directed to Elaine*]: Back and to the left. Back and to the left.

Elaine: What are you saying?

Jerry: I'm saying that the spit could not have come from behind. There had to have been a second spitter. Behind the bushes on the gravelly road. If the spitter was behind you as you claim, that would have caused your head to pitch forward.

The insistency of the repetition is depicted for dramatic effect in Stone's film, but for comic effect in *Seinfeld*. Hutcheon describes parody as a form of imitation "characterized by ironic inversion," a "repetition with critical distance."[28] *Seinfeld*'s insistent repetition of repetition exposes Stone's visual rhetoric by rendering it overwrought; furthermore, it caricatures the gravitas of Costner's mythologization of Garrison.

Like Dunne, McWilliams observes that *Seinfeld*'s parody generally depends on the viewer's awareness of genre.[29] Shane Gunster claims that *Seinfeld*'s "alienation effect" is "vaguely reminiscent" of Bertolt Brecht's in that it "uses interrogative dialogue and absurd situations to force the audience into a confrontation with objects, experiences, and social conventions that have been stripped of their normalizing context."[30] "To great comic effect," Gunster argues, the show reveals, through its juxtaposition, "the underlying absurdity of that which had previously been taken for granted." As Jerry's living room, normally a scene for conversations about "nothing," is transformed into a scene for a mock-courtroom drama, our memory of, as well as any future encounter with, Stone's film is transformed in the process. The parody itself becomes part of the intertextual encyclopedia.

The brainchild of two stand-up comedians, *Seinfeld* is normally thought of as a predominantly verbal comedy show. In "The Boyfriend," Jerry invokes the assassination-myth lexicon (a spit that "ricochets," "the bushes behind the gravelly road") that infuses the dialogue of *JFK*. Arguably, however, the effect of the parody depends highly on the interplay of verbal and physical comedy and therefore on its Zapruder quotation. Jerry's pointing and gesturing is significant, but even more so is Richards's fall. In quoting the gestures of a dying president, he invites associations to a tradition of physical comedy that can be traced back to silent movies and vaudeville theatre. The violence of the impact of the bullet is transformed into the kind of violence that befalls an unfortunate character who endlessly tumbles over in physical gags.

In the DVD commentary to "The Boyfriend," Richards explains how he "was always battling not to fall into caricature," since his comedy was defined by the physical. The repetition of the impact of the spit is an interruption in that it insists on the doubling of texts, in that its laughter depends on its allusion to the target of parody. Dan Harries describes parody as a "discursive mode"; central to this mode are a number of "disrupting" techniques.[31] Although Richards's "gestic theater" hardly can be said to "alienate" in the sense that Walter Benjamin describes, it certainly interrupts context in the way that it clearly calls attention to the act of quotation. The effect is that *Seinfeld* distinguishes itself as antirealistic through its use of what Benjamin called the "quotable gesture."[32]

What is mystery and tragedy in *JFK* is transformed into comedy in "The Boyfriend." The point of *Seinfeld*'s play, however, is not so much to ridicule or criticize Hollywood history or Stone's expressive style as it is to distinguish itself from both. It is the distance, Hutcheon insists, that enables repetition to mark difference rather than similarity. This happens "not always at the expense of the parodied text," since "conventions as well as individual works can be parodied." The function of parody is not "disrespect" but "ironic difference," and the two are not necessarily the same.[33] When finally Hernandez meets Kramer and Newman toward the end of "The Boyfriend," he is allowed to share his own memory of what happened: "I was walking up the ramp, I was upset about the game, that's when you called me 'pretty boy.' It ticked me off. I was turning around to say something, and as I turned around, I saw Roger McDowell behind the bushes over by that gravelly road. He was talking to someone, and they were pointing at you. I tried to scream out, but it was too late. It was already on its way." Maybe this happened, Kramer suggests, "because we were sitting in the right-field stands, cursing at [McDowell] in the bullpen all day." "He must have caught a glimpse of us when I poured that beer over his head," adds Newman. And the mystery of the second spitter, who turns out to have been the only spitter, is finally solved.

In a book about what he calls the "critical intertextuality" of *The Simpsons*, Jonathan Gray argues that the series is able to "mock, make us laugh, and teach all at once" because of "television's oft-underappreciated complexities." Gray thus calls *The Simpsons* an "anti-fairytale" because of the way in which its heroes do not "improve or better their worlds."[34] "No hugging, no learning": such was Larry David's well-known dictate for *Seinfeld*.[35] These antididactic sentiments make a parody of Stone's cinematic vision into a perfect expression of identity for the show's makers. *Seinfeld*, John Docker suggests, "continuously presents an absurd mirror image of other television programs."[36] In "The Boyfriend," it is a motion picture that is caught in that mirror image. The quasi incident of "The Boyfriend" ends with a quasi resolve. Where *JFK* ends with an appeal to future generations, and with a "hug," as its much-criticized romantic subplot ends harmoniously and Garrison and wife leave the courthouse in an embrace, *Seinfeld* ends as Kramer and Newman leave the apartment with Hernandez to help him move his furniture. Whereas *JFK* is naive, *Seinfeld* is all irony.

The DVD release of "The Boyfriend" historicizes the broadcast's allusions by making them explicit, by teaching parody, as it were. What was once a gesture for the initiated, exclusively for those familiar with the intertextual encyclopedia, is transformed into an all-inclusive gesture. All one has to do is buy the set, watch the bonus material, and sit back as the jokes are explained. Ultimately, "The Boyfriend" thus illustrates how Zapruder's images, when quoted, can allude to other distinct quotations and to specific mediations, invented or real—but it also says quite a lot about how far images of trauma can travel. Indeed, performed in one of the most popular television shows ever made, the images reached a new audience and were transformed yet again, into another legend of popular culture.

FIVE

Pleasing to the Eye

The film of Kennedy's assassination is the Sistine Chapel of our era. //
J. G. Ballard

A COPY OF THE ZAPRUDER FILM IS PROJECTED, and then large color prints
of individual frames are exhibited in the room. Reproductions of Andy Warhol's silk print *Orange Marilyn* (1964) and Alfred Stieglitz's photograph *The
Steerage* (1907) are then shown, the latter of which is compared with frame
182 of the Zapruder film. "The colors are beautiful," Steve Johnson observes
about the frame. "The ever-familiar hues of the tragedy—the pink of the First
Lady's outfit, the red of the wounds, the green of the grass, the bluish-black
of the Presidential limousine—would not have been better if selected by Warhol or Matisse."[1]

The setting for this scene is not a gallery, but a courtroom in Washington,
D.C., in May 1999. Johnson, an appraiser hired by Zapruder's heirs—who
are, at this point, owners of Abraham Zapruder's camera-original footage—is
arguing that the film is worth thirty million dollars. Johnson's audience, an
arbitration panel consisting of three judges appointed by the U.S. government, have seen numerous affidavits filed and are nearing a decision that will
establish a market value for the film. Arguing against Johnson and a team
of lawyers is an opposing team appointed by the U.S. government, which is
about to purchase the film in accordance with a federal law from 1992 requir-
ing all assassination-related documents to become governmental property

and to be stored in a collection at the National Archives. This legal taking is a case of eminent domain, and the panel's job is to decide on fair compensation for the film's owners.

In this chapter, I will argue that this governmental taking of the Zapruder film must be considered a definitive expression of its transformed cultural status. In previous chapters, I have addressed how Zapruder's images can be said to have traveled through a range of different discourses and cultural spheres and thus can be described as traveling images. As we have seen, in spite of their increasing epistemological uncertainty, their dispersion in culture makes them more "durable" as aesthetic and allegorical images.[2] This, in turn, affected the evaluation of the original film when it finally became public property in 1999.

After Time Inc. denied Geraldo Rivera the right to broadcast Robert Groden's copy of the Zapruder film in 1975 but ABC nevertheless did so, Time reversed its decision and allowed the broadcast without fee after the fact. A little more than a month later, Time transferred the copyrights and the Zapruder film to Abraham Zapruder's family (he had died in 1970). Shortly afterward, the National Archives agreed to store it.[3] The burden of ownership had become greater than its privileges. However, neither the film nor the copyrights had shifted hands for the last time.

After the controversy of Stone's movie, a bill passed by Congress became the first step toward the appointing of the Assassination Records Review Board to oversee the release of all classified federal records about the assassination and the investigations into it. At the termination of the House Select Committee on Assassinations in 1979, a number of files remained in closed storage. Stone's picture, which was seen by sixty million moviegoers in the United States and was followed by an outburst of press articles and television segments, created considerable pressure to open these files.[4] In the fall of 1992, the President John F. Kennedy Assassination Records Collection Act of 1992, widely referred to as the JFK Act, was enacted. It was "an unprecedented piece of legislation," Richard Trask writes, since it "mandated the gathering and opening to public access of all records which related to the death of President Kennedy by all government agencies."[5] An independent governmental agency, the Assassination Records Review Board, was established to oversee implementation, work that would take years.[6] During the period that the board was at work, a struggle between competing interests ensued. At the heart of the conflict was the Zapruder film's troubled identity as both assassination record and commercial property. Not long after the act was passed, Zapruder's family sought the return of the original film, which had been in storage at the National Archives since 1978.[7] The Review Board quickly began trying to find out whether it could acquire the film through the act and, if so, how just compensation to the owners could be determined. It was during this period also that Zapruder's family started planning a commercial release of the camera-original film.[8]

A COLLECTOR'S ITEM FOR ALL AMERICANS

Image of an Assassination: A New Look at the Zapruder Film (1998), directed and produced by Howard D. Motyl, tells two distinct stories: that of the Zapruder film and that of its digital restoration.[9] Its expository discourse is defined by this double gesture; not only the film but also its restoration—and, ultimately, the DVD release—is rendered unique. Embedded in this logic is a conflation of the cultural status of the original film and the mass-produced DVD. The uniqueness of the first is strategically used to argue for the uniqueness of the second in a paradoxical and problematic rhetoric of exposition.

The two stories are framed in a way that is typical of the DVD as a medium and reflect how profoundly home video has changed with the advent of DVD. Derek Kompare argues that the progression of visual technology represents not merely "enhancements" of media but rather "reconceptions," "profoundly altering our relationship with dominant media institutions and with media culture in general." In the case of DVDs, bonus material can "amplify various elements of their central text, thus producing new media experiences."[10] *Image of an Assassination*'s central feature is a fairly traditional four-part documentary that narrates the story of the film with voice-over, interviews, and film clips in chapters titled "Capturing the Image," "Sale of the Image," "Public Screenings," and, finally, "Renewing the Image," which describes how the film, through a process of duplication, scanning, reanimation, and motion stabilization, is guaranteed eternal life through the use of digital technology. Dust and scratches on the original film were digitally removed in yet another strategy to "enhance" the images. The DVD also offers a navigable menu that invites the viewer to peruse the Zapruder film in four different versions ("close-up frame," "full frame," "medium frame," and "wide frame"). Watching *Image of an Assassination* on DVD, then, is very different from watching it as a television documentary. Unlike the singular event of the broadcast, the DVD makes instant access to projection ad infinitum possible. It is an example of what Kompare calls "publication as an alternative means of television distribution and reception," in which the DVD as "collectible object" fosters "a new commodity relationship between television and viewers."[11]

Image of an Assassination conflates the uniqueness of Zapruder's original film with its own uniqueness as mass-produced collectible object; it simultaneously evokes a democratic ideal of making the images publicly available and seeks to render the event of projection revelatory. It most directly does so in how it frames its own release through promotional strategies that are fundamental in shaping its distribution and reception. In what follows, I will turn away from the narrative of the DVD itself and explore the imagetext of its cover as an expository discourse, arguing that this "frames" both the proliferation and the projection of the images. When I use the verb "frame" in this chapter, I thus imply that the events described have been framed in a way that implies an awareness of their shared circumstances, an awareness that informs agency and intention: "Framing," writes Jonathan Culler, "is something we do."[12]

Indeed, the clearest expression of the paradoxical rhetoric that informs *Image of an Assassination* is a statement on its back cover, describing the release as "a collector's item for all Americans!" (fig 5.1).

The oxymoronic phrase characterizes the DVD as an exceptional commodity while promoting its public availability; arguably, the exclamation mark brings to it a sensationalist ring. It summarizes the producer's wish to have his cake and eat it too by inviting commemoration as simultaneously fetishization and collective experience. In effect, the text masks commercial interest by invoking ideals of democracy. Buying this film, the cover suggests, will allow the purchaser to share in the experience of owning an exceptional object.

By combining portraits of Kennedy, frames from the Zapruder film, and a roll of film, the cover suggests that it contains the story of the images and the camera-original footage and that it addresses the historical event of the death of a national leader. Kennedy's face smiles from the spine when the disc is shelved, suggesting that this is a film not merely about a film, but also about a cultural memory the buyer can take share in—in the form of a "commemorative DVD." The cover proclaims the release unique in this respect, since it captures history in a new and revelatory way: the prospective buyer is promised "a never-before-seen version of president Kennedy's assassination!"—an invitation made speculative by yet another misplaced exclamation point. One of the enhanced versions, the cover furthermore promises, is "64 percent wider than has ever been seen before."[13]

FIG. 5.1   Cover, *Image of an Assassination* (1998).

In what he calls "the age of biocybernetic reproduction," W. J. T. Mitchell argues that the relation of the copy to the original is reversed, so that the copy can be said to have more aura than the original.[14] The citations on the DVD cover—from Richard Trask, the author of several books on the photographic record of the assassination; from *Life*; and from Anna Nelson, a member of the Assassination Records Review Board—lend authority to the DVD's expository agency and, in sum, deliver a description of the Zapruder footage as both a symbolic and an evidentiary image: *Image of an Assassination* is doubly unique.

What is implied in the improvement in quality that the cover promises, one might ask? How does it transform the viewing experience? If the versions do not contain new crucial information, then what kind of commemoration does this disc envision? What should motivate the repeated watching it invites and stages? In addition to containing an index of chapters, the image-text of the insert to *Image of an Assassination* repeats the imagery and the citations on the cover and adds in uppercase, "DVD makes ultimate use of new technology!" In its aggressively optimistic tone, this promotional discourse is performative. It does not merely describe an object; its gesture of showing and telling is instructive. Even if it is subtler than the cover copy, the narrative of the DVD very much delivers the same performance. The progression of visual technology transformed the original film, and the DVD tells the story of how this happened—and takes share in its aura. These strategic expositions are again framed, I argue, by events that coincided with its production.

When *Life* returned the Zapruder film to his heirs in 1975, Abraham Zapruder's widow and two children formed a corporation, the LMH Company, to control the film.[15] On April 24, 1997, the Assassination Records Review Board voted that the government would take possession of the film on August 1, 1998, and that the Justice Department would negotiate "fair and just compensation" for it.[16] That very summer—only weeks before the transfer of the film—the release of *Image of an Assassination* began to circulate as a news story. It was originally slated for a late-summer release, but its publisher, MPI Home Video, moved up the date to mid-July.[17] Promotional material was widely distributed to media outlets, video stores, schools, and libraries, referring to the film as "a must." As Richard Trask suggests, the release seemed to "effectively upstage the Assassination Records Review Board in its quest for public ownership and public access of the film, while at the same time making a profit."[18]

The point here is not to criticize Zapruder's family or MPI Home Video, but rather to explore how the release of the DVD and the negotiations in Washington informed each other and reflected a contested concept of value that is significant for the transformation of the film's cultural status. Mitchell's distinction between image and picture is illuminating in this respect. In Mitchell's terminology, the "image" is the intellectual property that "escapes the materiality of the picture when it is copied," and the "picture" is "the image plus the support." The picture, then, is "the appearance of the immaterial image in a material medium."[19] Several critics have pointed out the peculiarity of the government not seeking to take over the copyright, only the film, thereby settling for presiding over materiality rather than intellectual property.[20] The LMH Company probably believed that the copyright would be included in the government's taking, and it therefore sought to control the film's distribution to the public, in the form of a DVD, while it still could.[21] The fact that the film was no longer considered primarily criminal evidence, but rather a cultural artifact, required a very different form of evaluation when the appraisers were establishing a market value.

As Arjun Appadurai argues, value is "embodied in commodities that are exchanged," and a focus on "the things that are exchanged" instead of on "the forms or functions of exchange" enables us to see that "what creates the link between exchange and value is *politics*, construed broadly." Commodities, in Appadurai's striking conceit, have "social lives."[22] Both Zapruder's camera-original film and *Image of an Assassination* are, in Mitchell's words, "bearers" of Zapruder's images. Their shared uniqueness results in a paradoxical double fetishization that informs their social lives. Images acquire cultural value because they have the capacity to "change the way we think and see and dream," Mitchell observes.[23] It was the ability to recognize this power of Zapruder's images, I argue in what follows, that enabled the Zapruder family's legal team to convince the arbitration panel in Washington, D.C., to make the camera-original film the most expensive photographic artifact in the world.

THE ATROCITY EXPOSITION

In an issue of the *Art Newspaper* that came out the summer after *Image of an Assassination* was released, J. G. Ballard was invited to choose seven images that had been of specific importance to him. Alongside works by, among others, Salvador Dalí and Francis Bacon, Ballard mentioned frame 224 from the Zapruder film, which, he suggested, is "the Sistine Chapel of our era."[24] Ballard's observation may seem provocative, but in fact, it echoes how the film increasingly came to be described as something like a work of art as the government went into negotiations to take it. In a hearing in the spring of 1997, Art Simon was invited by the Assassination Records Review Board to reflect on the Zapruder film's status as an assassination record and to comment on whether it should be taken as such. Simon said that it was an essential record not because of its evidentiary value, but because it had "become the dominant visual point of view of the event" and had to be considered a "secular relic." "Individuals and nations hold on to such relics," he argued, concluding that the film should go into public ownership.[25]

Ironically, the Zapruder family's lawyers might very well have noted Simon's argument as much as the board did (the hearings were broadcast on C-SPAN). In arguing for the camera-original film's value during the negotiations with the government, they echoed the film professor's sentiments. As the Zapruder film was being prepared for commercial release and the camera-original film was being taken by the government, the negotiations over compensation showed the parties to be still far apart in their valuations. Sources differ concerning how much the government offered, but the amount was somewhere between one million and three million dollars; the Zapruder family, however, demanded thirty million.[26] Zapruder's son, Henry, expressed frustration with the government in an interview with the *Washington Post* on June 13, 1998: "My own view of the matter is that the main stumbling block is in getting the government to face up to the hard question of how much the film is really worth," [Zapruder] said. "If they knew that, we could come to terms. If they drive this case to litigation, we will get a fair-market valuation that will be much higher than what we are willing to settle for. We are trying to make a contribution."[27]

When the negotiations seemed to be leading nowhere, the family hired Robert S. Bennett, a well-known Washington lawyer, to represent their position. In the fall of 1998, a federal arbitration panel consisting of three judges, Kenneth Feinberg, Walter Dellinger, and Arlin Adams, was appointed, with the agreement that a monetary award would not exceed thirty million dollars and that the process would be completed by June 1999.[28]

In May 1999, the panel reached a conclusion after evaluating testimonies and appraisals in support of arguments from both sides. It is evident from various accounts of the negotiations that Bennett's strategy was to address the concept of value in a way strikingly different from that used by the government's legal team.[29] None of the teams chose to focus on the evidentiary status of the film.[30] The government based its assessment on the premise that the Zapruder film is unique as a historical record, as a cultural memory; comparing it to the Declaration of Independence and to Lincoln's handwritten "House Divided" speech, which had sold in 1992 for $1.5 million, John Staszyn, an appraiser, argued that the assassination was a less significant historical event than Lincoln's speech and that the film could be valued at $1 million.[31] Its value was to be decided on the basis of what it shows, not how it shows it.

"In general use appraisal can refer to both the assessment of the documentation in relation to its *monetary* (or *fair market* or *intrinsic*) value, or to its *archival* value (historical, informational, research) in relation to the society supporting the archival activity, now and in the future," writes Sam Kula—and these two approaches "should, of course, relate to each other."[32] The archival value of the Zapruder film was addressed in 1994 when it was one of the 25 films selected by the librarian of Congress for the National Film Registry, which at the end of 2006 consisted of 450 titles.[33] As Kula observes, however, fair-market value is "extremely difficult" to establish, since concepts of "research value," "historical value," and "cultural value"—criteria often referred to in appraisals—are "largely subjective."[34] In an early appraisal report for the Civil Division of the U.S. Department of Justice, dated February 5, 1997, C.M.M. Associates lists several "appreciating" and "depreciating" factors, and distinguishes between a "fair market value" of $752,306 and a "full market value" of $13,932,707.[35] Reading the report, one is struck by how it struggles to approach the question of value, since it has to address not only how a culture values a material object, but also how it values a series of images. The lack of precedent was also a problem. How does one translate a concept of "cultural value" into "monetary value" when appraising the Zapruder film? An image, Mitchell suggests, can become "the focus of both over- and underestimation," and thus has "some form of 'surplus value,'" but to translate such a value into monetary compensation for a pictorial object is a complicated calculation.[36] The "surplus value" of Zapruder's images is tremendous, and it enables them to exert a manifold and complex power. How does one evaluate images that, in the words of David Lubin, have "grabbed hold of imaginations across the world, affecting the way that vast numbers of viewers have reconceived power, love, conflict, and history"?[37]

While Staszyn recognized the value of the film as a visual record of history, he not only ignored the ways in which written manuscripts differ from films as visual artifacts, but also neglected to address the impact Lubin describes. This was a strategic perspective that he argued for in affidavits, in which he denied any consideration of the film's aesthetic properties. "This 26-second spool of film does not belong in any market encompassing Fine Arts," he insisted. "Turning a tragedy into a monetary source has negative aspects."[38] However, as Lubin points out, the film acquired a commodity status when Zapruder sold it in 1963 and has maintained it ever since.[39] Bennett's team made any argument against such a status look futile. A turning point in the negotiations came when Bennett brought out a baseball he had bought in a store for ten dollars and asked an appraiser hired by the government to explain how an identical baseball, which, though in far worse shape, had sold at auction for three million dollars "because it had collided with the bat of Mark McGwire," could be worth more than the Zapruder film.[40] The value of the Zapruder film, Bennett argued after having projected a copy of the film and exhibited stills from it, had to be located "not only in its rarity but also in formal attributes such as color and composition, and the sheer emotional impact of its subject matter."[41] The compensation, then, had to reflect how Zapruder's images not only shape memories and postmemories, but are also widely considered to be simultaneously difficult yet irresistible to look at.

In an essay, David Lee Strauss remembers how, as a child, he once came upon a picture folder at the public library marked "Atrocities," which contained photographs from Nazi concentration camps. Strauss recalls coming back to the photographs again and again, finding that he was drawn to them even if he did not understand what they referred to. He examined them, stared at them, imagined them with his eyes closed. "My attraction to these images was not prurient or political," he concludes, "but religious."[42] Strauss's urge might have been what Susan Sontag calls a "despised impulse" to look at atrocity, one that she traces in writings by Plato, Edmund Burke, and Georges Bataille, observing that in Bataille, it entails a particular kind of religious experience.[43] Indeed, Simon's description of the Zapruder film as a "secular relic" suggests that individuals and collectives can discover a range of meanings in its images and return to them for a variety of reasons—as previous chapters in this book have suggested. However, to discuss whether the film qualifies as a work of art is, I argue, to raise the wrong questions. What is of interest here is that Zapruder's images can be described very much as a work of art, as Lubin and John Beck observe, and that it is finally through this form of description as a discursive act that the camera-original film is defined as a relic.[44] The performance of Bennett's team illustrates the significance of "the key role played by appraisers in assessing monetary value" and, in effect, the impact of the cultural status of the appraiser.[45] Several of the appraisers in Washington, D.C., had experience working at Sotheby's and Christie's.

In mixing legalistic and aesthetic discourse in a thought-provoking way, Bennett's team carried out its arguments in what can best be considered, once again, as ekphrastic descriptions. Ekphrasis here implies not so much an evocation of an absent image, however, as a rhetorical description that not only renders the image vividly, but also, as has often been the case in the history of art, ascribes value to it. Thus, Sylvia Leonard Wolf and Steve Johnson, appraisers hired by Bennett, appealed precisely to what Sontag calls the "despised impulse" in describing Zapruder's images as sublime. Johnson described the images as an art appreciator might, referring to them as "haunting" and "beautiful," and suggested that an object comparable to the film was Leonardo da Vinci's Codex Leicester, a manuscript that documents his experiments with water, which was bought by Bill Gates in 1994 for $30.8 million.[46] Whereas such a comparison was motivated solely by speculation concerning what Kula calls "comparative market value," other arguments were based on comparative analyses.[47] Wolf stated that the Zapruder film was like *Orange*

Marilyn, which sold at Sotheby's in 1999 for $17.6 million, in that it shares "the additional element of fascination with violence and tragedy." The film's frames are "pleasing to the eye," she argued, its colors "rich and vibrant."[48] What Wolf calls the "additional element" is, in fact, an interpretation of the film's "surplus value," one of the ways in which one can address the expressive charge of the images.

Values, writes Kula, "are not found in records, but rather in theories of value of societal significance which archivists bring to records."[49] "When it comes to objects like celluloid film or battered baseballs," Mary Panzer reflects in her account of the hearings, "the main value seems to lie in the associations that they arouse in the observer, and the desires that those associations kindle."[50] When the panel, in its majority decision, arrived at a $16 million figure, it was convinced by how Bennett had translated currencies, and how he had proposed that the value of the pictorial object corresponds to the very different value of the images.

Paradoxically, the government bought an object that it cannot exhibit but must merely store. The camera-original film is defined as unique because of aesthetic properties that will, in fact, never again be made visible by a projection of it, since it has to be stored in a cold, dry, dark vault if it is physically to survive.[51] As we approached a new millennium, then, Zapruder's camera original, now the world's most expensive photographic artifact, was unexhibitable, but was nevertheless canonized as an aesthetic object; simultaneously, its images could be screened in constant replay, in the realm of home video.

In her affidavit for the Zapruder family, Beth Gates Warren, formerly an appraiser at Sotheby's, found it plausible that the Zapruder film could travel the world, that "a selection of images from the film could be enlarged and displayed in a tasteful, artistic manner," supported by a "lavishly illustrated catalog" that "might include interviews with people close to the event, such as Walter Cronkite and Dan Rather."[52] Indeed, as I demonstrate in the next two chapters, Warren's remarks were not at all far-fetched, but rather reflected how Zapruder's images, now widely recognized as aesthetic images, could be projected in the same sphere as, and consequently framed similarly to, the fine arts.

SIX
Death in Dallas

And now I'll sing a song,
and picture the assassination
of Kennedy the president //
Jozo Karamatic, "Smrt u Dalasu" ("Death in Dallas")

TWO OR THREE PEOPLE ARE SEATED ON THE FLOOR, four on a bench in the back, and a couple lean against one of the black walls. They have all drawn aside a curtain and stepped into a small, dark room where a video projection provides the only light. The images are all too familiar. Once again, Kennedy smilingly waves to the Dallas crowds from the motorcade, unaware that the moment of his impending death—the very moment the audience is awaiting—is only seconds away. However, Zapruder's images are not accompanied by the usual mélange of breathless radio and television reports from the day of the assassination or by an authoritative voice-over, as is often the case in documentaries. Neither is it repeated in a continuous multiscreen loop. There is no district attorney delivering his closing argument. Instead, the only sound is that of a plaintive Balkan folk ballad, "Smrt u Dalasu," the lyrics of which are translated somewhat awkwardly into English couplets in the subtitles. Performed by Jozo Karamatic, who strums a *gusle*, an ancient, one-string, bowed instrument as he sings, the song recalls the epic oral tradition of conveying news by singing it and comes to profoundly shape the experience of watching the newsreel-like montage.

As one of the visitors to the Whitney Museum of American Art in New York City on July 16, 2003, I found my way into the space where this striking juxtaposition of image and sound, Zoran Naskovski's *Death in Dallas* (2000), was projected. The installation was part of the exhibition "The American Effect: Global Perspectives on the United States, 1990–2003," curated by Lawrence Rinder. I took extensive notes, knowing that the projection was a singular event; I knew that if I were ever to see Naskovski's work again, it would be part of a different museum exhibition—or alternatively, it would be projected on my television screen at home, if I could get hold of a DVD copy. In any event, the experience would then be transformed. In an age characterized by extensive mediatization, there is much disagreement whether the preservation of installation and performance art—expressions markedly defined by a situational mode—is desirable or even possible.[1] This chapter explores how my interpretation of Naskovski's installation is informed not only by my reading of the work, but also by how I experienced its situatedness within a specific museum discourse. This perspective enables me to be both the subject and object of framing in analyzing *Death in Dallas*: I took part in its framing within a situation, and in turn, I frame it by describing and interpreting the event in my own words. Such a strategy will inform the next chapter as well.

My encounters with two other works of art, Chris Burden's *America's Darker Moments* (1994) and Andy Warhol's *Flash: November 22, 1963* (1968) also influenced my interpretation of Naskovski's installation. I argue that the interplay between these works of art—the way they can be said to frame and be framed by one another—invites critical reflection on their inevitable circulation in the "unbounded cultural space" into which Kennedy projected his "image."[2] As will be evident, Zapruder's images have come to be exhibited not only according to the same institutional practices used to display the artworks by Burden, Warhol, and Naskovski, but also in the very same spaces—and thus have been framed according to a similar poetics of exposition.

PICTURING THE ASSASSINATION

Death in Dallas is profoundly informed by a double word-image tension. The visitor to the installation simultaneously listens and reads while watching the collage of images. For the English-speaking visitor, the effect is a strange, contradictory sensation of both recognition and a lack of it. Even if it had been recorded mere days after the assassination and released on seven-inch vinyl, the chanted song would sound like something "a thousand years old," as J. Hoberman writes in a review, to an overwhelming majority of the audience in New York.³ This juxtaposition of collage and folk epic, Kelly Vance suggests, can seem "eerie."⁴ Torn out of their original context, the images produce a new narrative situation; the effect is that the assassination seems to have taken place "before images could be recorded," in the words of Gary Shteyngart.⁵ The sound of vinyl adds to this sense of being transported to a past that comes to seem uncannily distant.

Furthermore, the sensorial collision between what we see and what we hear in *Death in Dallas* invites reflection on the shifting circumstances under which media and memory have continued to inform each other. Although now conditioned by audiovisual recording technology, our sense of memory and the past was once shaped by oral transmission, by a kind of creative preservation of pastness that depended on the ability to carve out in syllabic sound verbal images so memorable that they would continue to travel from mouth to ear. Images have always traveled.

Indeed, Naskovski's most effective interplay of sound and image comes during its initial quotation of the Zapruder film. Edited into the collage, the shot to Kennedy's head is repeated, and a scratch in the record is timed to startlingly add to the effect. The effect of Naskovski's repetition, however, is very dissimilar to that used in Stone's *JFK*. A trivial accident, the scratch nevertheless instantly suggests the possibility of endless, unwanted repetition, the danger that the oral narrative will halt and remain stuck in stagnation, the needle caught in the vinyl groove. The juxtaposition lucidly illustrates the fixation with and incessant repetition of the moment of fatal impact. As Kathrin Becker observes, this manipulation suggests that neither sound nor image merely illustrates the other in *Death in Dallas*.⁶ Naskovski transforms the moment of impact, adds something to make it new, gives it a visceral effect. This and similar moments are a disruption; it is difficult to say which jostles the other, word or image. In Naskovski's hands, one of the bystanders in the plaza becomes a puppet on a string, the figure's bodily movements repeated so that it seems to be dancing to Karamatic's song. By disarmingly blurring the boundaries between footage and choreography, the scene hints that any narrativization is, in a sense, theatrical.

The translation of Karamatic's lyrics evokes time travel and cultural relocation; the odd phrasing reacquaints the viewer with Kennedy's death "through foreign eyes and vernacular," as Shteyngart puts it.⁷ The translation sticks loosely to the decasyllabic meter of the original; several inversions and alliterations add to its archaic feel. Some 160 lines long, the song is incredibly rich in detail. It correctly names both a nurse and a doctor who cared for the dying Kennedy at Parkland Hospital. The image-word relationship is thus complicated by the narration of the song, which has several elements characteristic of an epic. In the opening apostrophe, Karamatic addresses his instrument much as an epic poet would address his muse:

> Oh my gusle, my instrument of old,
> By modern times you will suffer not,
> For gusle gentle tunes
> Became our national lore.

Simultaneously, a filmic narrative of national lore is introduced as the title flashes across the screen. Against black-and-white images from Kennedy's funeral, the title, sharply picked out in red, hints at the bloodshed to follow, at imagery both verbal and visual (fig. 6.1).

FIG. 6.1 The opening titles of *Death in Dallas* by Zoran Naskovski (2001). Used with permission of the artist.

The verse frequently recalls romantic balladry; for example, Karamatic dwells on an image of blood-drenched roses, of "petals in blood." In spilling red across the screen, the title is proleptic. The evocative verbal imagery is ekphrastic, clearly meant to produce a collage of mental images in the listener that is every bit as strong as the images appearing on-screen. In *Death in Dallas*, verbal and visual depictions thus form a contested relationship as death is pictured in a doubly descriptive mode: "I'll sing a song and picture the assassination," Karamatic sings as images of the event flash across the screen. This juxtaposition of verbal and visual images places the formation of cultural memory in a historical continuum. The news event inevitably enters contemporary folklore and becomes every bit as myth-infused as it would have been in ancient times.

In the extensive montage of found footage, selections from several print publications appear, including *Life*'s imagetext and various covers of the *New York Daily News*, *Time*, and the *Nation*. Images from the courtroom projection of the Zapruder film in *JFK* are included; we see the projector as the faint sounds of video projection can be heard in the installation space. We are watching the projection of a projection of a projection. The arresting montage increasingly addresses the iconoclasms of modern myth and fame: photographs from the Kennedy autopsy at the Bethesda Naval Hospital are intercut with images of Marilyn Monroe and then with a still of the cover of Seymour Hersh's self-proclaimed "myth-debunking" book about Kennedy, *The Dark Side of Camelot* (1997)—a chain of images that exposes the pathological zeal with which bodies both biological and symbolic are cut open, exposed.

Karamatic's voice and the subtitled lyrics add more layers to this already densely layered imagetext. As the narrative proceeds, the cumulative effect of the imagery of Camelot—family pictures from summers in Hyannisport, footage of children playing on the beach, a young and slender Kennedy smoking a cigar, Jackie playfully taking pictures of her posing husband—is indeed a sense of an epoch. The words, however, often describe something the images, familiar as most of them are, suddenly seem to have concealed all these years. Behind Jackie Kennedy's dignified composure, for example, there is "her heart frozen still and harder than stone" (fig. 6.2).

As Eleanor Hartley observes, the translated lyrics are "full of pathos and sincerity."[8] Ultimately, for all the textual play, the effect of seeing these images as if through a new prism is to see human grief with fresh eyes. Naskovski's installation reminds the visitor that Zapruder's images are images of trauma, not only of immense physical pain, but also of the kind of pain brought about

HER HEART FROZEN STILL AND
HARDER THAN STONE.

FIG. 6.2 Jacqueline Kennedy in Zoran Naskovski's *Death in Dallas* (2001). Used with permission of the artist.

by loss—a nation's loss of a leader, a wife's loss of a husband. Seated on a bench in the back of the installation space, scribbling in my notebook, I had to steal a glimpse at the woman sitting next to me, who burst into tears and continued to cry, silently, until the projection was finished.

"Phonography," Michael Chanan writes in his history of the recording industry, "wrested the voice from the throat and embedded it, like an echo, in a mechanical memory."[9] *Death in Dallas* can be said to explore the sound of that echo. Significantly, it was not the found footage—most of it has been numbingly rerun over the years—that triggered this response, but rather the sound track, the "found audio" of *Death in Dallas*.[10] Naskovski came upon Karamatic's record in a flea market in Belgrade. Indeed, the entrance to the installation space at the Whitney seemed to insist on the significance of the music, since the cover of Karamatic's single was on display. A caption described *Death in Dallas* as an "installation with album cover and video projection." The sleeve, then, is also an element in this mixed-media work. On the cover is a picture of Karamatic lifting the gusle and glancing down at the visitor, who has yet to draw the curtain and enter, insisting that it is *his* imagery that inspired *Death in Dallas*—not the footage (fig. 6.3).

FIG. 6.3 The record sleeve of Jozo Karamatic's "Smrt u Dalasu" (1963), which appears in Zoran Naskovski's installation. Used with permission of the artist.

As Bill Horrigan observes, gusle players were once "chroniclers of unwritten history": they spread news of an event before newsreels and bulletins took over that function.[11] When a sign next to the record warned that the work "contains violent imagery and may not be suitable for children," I nevertheless suspected that it referred to the footage—to Zapruder's picturing, not Karamatic's.

A few months later, *Death in Dallas* was exhibited at the Osterreichische Galerie in Vienna as part of an exhibition simply called "Trauer" ("Mourning"). For visitors to the gallery, Naskovski's installation was thus inevitably framed as a lament. As part of an exhibition titled "Urban Collisions: Zivilisatorische

Konflikte im Medium Video," at the Neuer Berliner Kunstverein in Berlin ear-lier that year, however, it had been one of several video works to question the possibility of art "to inspire alternative structures of thought."[12] In each of these new framings, whether intended to invoke grief or metacritique, *Death in Dallas* was transformed by the image environment in which it appeared: it quotes and transforms Zapruder's images and thus reframes the film, but was in turn reframed itself. "The experience of *Death in Dallas*," Ed Osborn writes, "is an extended moment of cultural vertigo, one in which a distinctly national memory is read through the filter of a remote society and reinscribed as part of a larger and more ambiguous set of world histories."[13] As Horrigan points out, Karamatic is "variously mournful, reportorial, and skeptical," and this shifting quality to his narrative makes it aptly reframable for the curator as well as the museum visitor.

DREAM MACHINE

Instead of simply acknowledging this as an obvious fact of curatorial practice, I am going to dwell on its implications. Indeed, once out of the secluded space of Naskovski's installation, I noticed how its meanings began to be negotiated by the other artworks exhibited. If it was a meditation on grief and the shift-ing formations of cultural memory, how did this correspond thematically to "The American Effect"? If an exhibition is an utterance within the museum as part of a larger discourse, what kind of utterance was "The American Effect"? To *National Review* critic Steven Vincent, the show continued a Whitney tra-dition of "combining contemporary art with fatuous political sentiments."[14] To *Village Voice* critic Kim Levin, it was not "just an important exhibition," but also, "at a moment when Uncle Sam seems to be morphing into Godz-illa," a "necessary one."[15] Given such responses, the questions the exhibition raised, rather than the answers it poses, Jane C. Desmond suggests in a re-view in *American Quarterly*, may be said to have produced "the most intrigu-ing results" of the show.[16] In various newspaper interviews as well as in the exhibition catalogue, Lawrence Rinder, the curator of the show, explains how "The American Effect" surveyed a range of artworks that broadly address the implications of U.S. influence. The show was the first at the Whitney to fea-ture primarily work done outside the United States. One intention was to confront visitors with visions and opinions from the outside; in his catalogue essay, Rinder points out that only 14 percent of U.S. citizens hold passports.[17] "Hatred and fascination," Shteyngart observed, were thus "the two disparate strains" that ran through the exhibition.[18] "The American Effect" was to explore U.S. global relations through art's interaction with discourses outside the museum.

This implied that the show addressed current issues, among which were the global repercussions of the terrorist attacks on the city that the Whitney is located in. "Mr. Rinder can be accused of trying to cover too many bases, and the show has weak spots," wrote Grace Glueck in the *New York Times* on the exhibition's opening day (July 4, 2003). "Still, much of it seems relevant in the lingering aftershock of 9/11," she added.[19] Even though it had been made years earlier, the Japanese artist Makoto Aida's model *Picture of an Air Raid on New York City* (1996), which depicts in horror what its title promises, created much controversy. Aida's work entered a dialectical relationship with one by the Congolese artist Bodys Isek Kingelez, whose *New Manhattan City 3021* (2001–2002), a large sculptural model of a futuristic downtown Manhattan, simultaneously evokes persistence and fragility as well as the possibility of redemption through reconstruction. Aida's model, the *New York Times* columnist Frank Rich suggested in a commentary, was "jolting in the context of this moment and this show"—a new kind of "culture war," he argued, had sprung from the events of September 11, one being fought over "the future, aesthetic and otherwise, of ground zero."[20] Displayed together, the works by Aida and Kingelez raised the inevitable questions of icon and iconoclasm that the attacks on the World Trade Center had provoked, and did so only half a dozen miles away from the site where it happened, what Desmond in her review calls the "shadow exhibit" of "The American Effect."[21]

Rich was certainly not alone in noting how many works evoked President George W. Bush as imperialist icon; several seemed to insist on being read against the background of the Iraq War, which was in its early phase that July, a mere four months after the invasion on March 20.[22] July had begun with a declaration by Bush that U.S. troops would remain in Iraq. Walking around the floor where "The American Effect" was exhibited, I overheard several conversations, some of which were heated, about the terrorist attacks as well as the invasion; many of them had been provoked by the exhibition.

In all this upheaval, images of Kennedy created an upsurge of nostalgic sentiment, as Cattelan's *Now* would at the Carnegie International exhibition the following fall. Naskovski's installation was not the only one to include Kennedy imagery. One of the most popular installations at "The American Effect," *Dream Machine*, by the Russian artist Sergei Bugaev, invited visitors to lie down on a titanium sheet covered with carpets woven with images of

Kennedy and Martin Luther King, Jr. Other elements in the installation were several folkloric Russian items, ambivalently suggesting both cultural exchange and cultural imperialism. Bugaev, who had been trained as a psychotherapist, invited visitors to lie down and sleep and then take notes on their dreams when they awoke. Shteyngart, who was born in Russia, described in his review how he had lain down on the carpet only to find that his Russian identity had been "subsumed" by that of his adopted country.[23]

Indeed, *Dream Machine* aptly illustrates the global reach of the Kennedy image and also suggests that the collage of found footage in *Death in Dallas*—including Zapruder's images, whether appearing as stills or moving images—has entered a global unconscious. Exhibited as part of "The American Effect" and alongside Bugaev's work, Zapruder's images, as they appeared in Naskovski's installation, thus invited visitors and critics to recognize a grief that was being projected as universal and timeless, indeed as a factor of the human condition. The images produced a welcome sense of universal loss. Whereas several of the other artworks criticized the United States as an imperialist power and a global hegemon, *Death in Dallas* was considered an exception, a work that invited reconciliation—including among the critics who visited the show. Vincent, who described how he was offended by several of the exhibited works, applauded Naskovski's installation as the show's only "outstanding piece," arguing that it was "elegiacal" and "utterly sincere" and "dares to suggest that Americans suffer sorrows and tragedies like the rest of humanity"—a point, he added, "that 'The American Effect' seems to forget."[24] Although much more positive toward the exhibition as a whole, Charles Giuliano likewise suggested that Naskovski's piece represented a contrast to instances of "propagandistic art that has difficulty transcending mere illustration and cartooning," a problem, he found, that pervaded "much of the work in the exhibition."[25] While the show received mixed reviews, all critics referred to Naskovski's installation as a success. To Desmond, the work "creates a situation that evokes a double vision—eliciting our own memories of [the assassination], and pairing them with a newly introduced knowledge of others mourning elsewhere and otherwise." *Death in Dallas*, she argues, "resituates America in a wider global context in a visceral and conceptually evocative way."[26]

Mixed as my response to the works exhibited in "The American Effect" was, I nevertheless was struck by the feeling that the most poignant was indeed the one that quoted Zapruder's images. It was also the one that most attracted my professional interest. However, the responses of other critics suggest it was not my admittedly sharpened attention to the work that led me to single it out. I shared with Shteyngart the impression that Naskovski's installation "tempered" the irony of the other works exhibited.[27] Perhaps, however, I was also guilty (like Shteyngart) of "fetishizing" a sense of foreignness, something, Desmond suggests in her review, that the Whitney invited—for indeed, "the dichotomy of insider and outsider" is a problematic one, and one that "The American Effect" perhaps did not so much problematize as enforce.[28] The fact remains, however, that it was this sense of "foreignness"— of being, like most of the artists exhibited, born in another country—that led me to think something about Zapruder's images that I had not thought before. Wandering among the fifty artworks from thirty countries on six continents, I had to think that Zapruder's images had indeed come to roam the global "dream machine." The second thought I had, as I walked out of the exhibition, was that the images now seemed to appear chiefly within the spheres of popular culture and, increasingly, the art world. Beth Gates Warren's sentiments—set out in an affidavit for the Zapruder family during the compensation negotiations in Washington—that the images could form a traveling exhibition inevitably came to mind.[29]

MIRRORS AND WINDOWS

As with any new show that creates a buzz, "The American Effect" attracted large crowds of visitors during the first couple of weeks. I spent quite some time during my visit either waiting in line or looking at art over the shoulders of others. After I had had enough of bumping into neighbors, I fled the exhibition and, on one of the other floors of the Whitney, came upon Chris Burden's *America's Darker Moments* (1994), a piece I did not know at the time. Burden's piece is a model, a glass display of painted tin, wood, glass, mirrors, Plexiglas, and fluorescent lights, shaped (intentionally, no doubt) like a pentagon. It is divided into five departments, each showing a historical scenario, a frozen moment of which the model gives a bird-eye's view: the Hiroshima bombing, the My Lai massacre, the Kent State shootings, the Emmett Till lynching—and the Kennedy assassination. Clearly, the American effect was on display both inside and outside Rinder's exhibition at the Whitney.

The Kennedy section, which inevitably evoked the toylike models the FBI had made for the Warren Commission, had all the iconographical elements intact: the school book depository with a big clock on top of it, the picket fence, and Zapruder filming. Among the small tin figures were also a mother holding a child, waving bystanders, a seated man taking photographs, and a man curiously either running or falling over. At the center of it all, a neck-clutching Kennedy was seated in the Lincoln, about to be struck by a bullet in the head. The familiar tumultuous scenario was now played out in miniature with what resembled toy figures. As Holland Cotter points out, the tableaux suggest "that the facts of history are mere playthings—of gods, politicians and, of course, of artists."[30] "All the toys one commonly sees are essentially a microcosm of the adult world," Roland Barthes writes in his book about modern popular mythology.[31] And in one of several brief texts spurred by the publication of a history of toys, Walter Benjamin suggests that a child's tireless repetition in playing with toys constitutes the very activity of playing, not a "doing as if" but a "doing the same thing over and over again."[32] *America's Darker Moments* reflects the prescience of both these observations. Not only does the lilliputian Dealey Plaza allude to several reconstruction models; the sense of repetition is all the stronger for the mirrors that divide the five sections of Burden's model, reflecting its "dark moments" and, in effect, repeating them, demonstrating their unendedness in human and cultural memory.

One of the pleasures of walking around art galleries is the specific connotative domino effect that sometimes arises, in which encounters with artwork after artwork intensify or modify an initial impression or thought. "We see one display while recalling or imagining how that art could be installed differently," David Carrier observes.[33] Exhibited at the Whitney that summer was also Andy Warhol's *Nine Jackies* (1964). I stopped briefly in front of the prints, all of which I had seen before, struck by how still they seemed after Naskovski's projection: still, in the sense of both movement and sound. It is "futile," John Beck suggests, "to try and see *into* a Warhol silkscreen," since his work tends to "expose the impossibility of 'deep' reading."[34] That day, it seemed to me, Warhol's Jackies concealed exactly what Naskovski's Jackie had exposed, her heart "frozen still and harder than stone." Like Doug Michels in drag in *The Eternal Frame*, the print evoked an image, not a person. "What is prescient about Warhol's assassination work," Art Simon writes, "is his recognition as early as December 1963 that, despite media claims to the contrary, the superabundant imaging of these events could have a distinctly alienating effect."[35] In the book documenting the Warhol retrospective at the Museum of Modern Art (MOMA) in 1989, Kynaston McShine suggests that it was in his treatment of the assassination "that Warhol's use of repetition and serial imagery became something more than a simple aesthetic device." The "inescapable repetition" of the assassination "had itself become a part of everyone's consciousness of that time," McShine writes.[36]

The concept of repetition, of course, is significant to any interpretation of Warhol's art. Hal Foster suggests that the Freudian notion of repetition as restorative—that one can repeat the traumatic event in a confrontation and, in Foster's words, "integrate it into a psychic economy, a symbolic order"— does not quite describe Warhol's art; it not only reproduces but also produces traumatic effects, he argues.[37] According to Peggy Phelan, Warhol inhabits a "double space in the production of his work, and thereby rehearses the spectator's performance of observation of it," so the art, in effect, becomes "theatrical and performative" through this interaction. In his many prints of Marilyn Monroe, Phelan posits, Warhol thematizes "how the image performs after the death of its subject, how it remains alive long after its inspiration is dead."[38]

A few days before my visit to the Whitney, I had studied Warhol's *Flash: November 22, 1963* (1968), a portfolio of eleven silk-screened prints bound together by a cover, as in a book. A slipcase was ceremoniously brought to my desk at the New York Public Library, which held one of the two hundred copies of the work.[39] I carefully unwrapped the portfolio, frequently glancing at the librarian seated at the desk by the door, who had worryingly advised caution. The accompanying teletype text of *Flash*, assembled by Philip Greer, consists of wire-service and newspaper accounts of events surrounding the assassination; it is yet another assassination imagetext. Six prints contain images of Kennedy, the rest allude in different ways to Oswald and Jackie; one is a faint reproduction of the presidential seal. As Simon observes, the prints differ from the Jackie portraits in their diverse imagery: superimposition results in a kind of repetition of visual elements within the individual panels.[40]

My encounter with *Flash* was different from that of my many other experiences of looking at Warhol's art. It was tactile and somehow, in effect, seemed more exclusive. There was an intimacy to the situation that caught me off guard. Except for the librarian, I was alone with the prints. Lifting each picture as if I were turning pages, going back and forth in the series as if to recall its semblance of a narrative, I clearly had entered the double space described by Phelan: seated at my desk in the Spencer Collection, I saw Warhol's visual art as "theatrical and performative." In "Getting the Warhol We Deserve," Douglas Crimp argues that the retrospective exhibition of Warhol's paintings at MOMA in 1989 "seemed dedicated, as if once and for all, to the idea of 'Warhol as Art History,' as the title of one of the catalog essays forth-rightly put it."[41] To Crimp, this implied a "constricting of Warhol's cultural complexity." Perhaps, he suggests, what has been called "a lasting Warhol effect has been to make possible expansive approaches to contemporary art more generally, or at least to those contemporary art practices that insist on their articulation with broader social practices."[42] Crimp thus claims the right to make of Warhol's art "the art I need and the art I deserve," an art that to him "disdains and defies the coherence and stability of all sexual identity."[43]

Whether I needed or deserved "my Warhol," I do not know, but the encounter in the reading room differed from that in the gallery in decisive ways, precisely because the changed setting and mode of looking invited a consideration of my own framing. Being able to look at the prints in the order I chose, and to look again, created a new form of repetition; to engage with the work as a book produced a deepened sense of interactivity. Simultaneously banal and poignant, one of the prints shows the sniper's window in the book depository. Seemingly lifted from some publication, it singles out the window Oswald fired from with a gigantic arrow. In its original, pre-Warhol form, the arrow presumably was meant to indicate: "This is where he fired from." In Warhol's reproduction, however, the arrow signals something else: it reenacts the pointing gesture in order to expose the window as a vantage point of visualization and reenactment. This, the print says, is the window to which we return.

Four months after my visit to New York, in late November 2003, I found myself standing in Dealey Plaza, looking up at Oswald's window and thinking about Warhol's print. I had walked around the plaza and looked at the pervasive reenactments and visualizations going on; I had climbed Zapruder's concrete pillar. Now I was standing outside the building that houses a museum "dealing with the life, times, death, and legacy of John F. Kennedy with a focus on the impact of his death on the nation and the world," as its website put it.

The Sixth Floor Museum stages a rich variety of exhibitions, all of them "utterances" within its discourse of addressing the impact of Kennedy's life and, in particular, his death on the world. In 2002, an art gallery opened on the seventh floor of the building; in March 2003, the *New York Times* reported that it would open with a show of Warhol's prints of Jackie Kennedy. "Viewing the images," Stephen Kinzer wrote, "visitors stand one flight above the spot on the sixth floor from which the shots were fired." After making a few phone calls, Kinzer learned from the directors of several other museums that the exhibition was "part of a trend toward finding unusual places to display modern art"—Tom Sokolowski, the director of the Andy Warhol Museum, suggested that the prints would have "a very different kind of resonance when they're shown in that building in Dallas."[44]

"There is something irresistible in the pairing of the Kennedy assassination and Andy Warhol," John Beck writes, "and not just because of Warhol's prompt and sustained response to the event."[45] From Dealey Plaza, Warhol's prints traveled to Pittsburgh in late October 2003, where the Andy Warhol Museum staged an exhibition, "November 22, 1963: Image, Memory, Myth," to "coincide with" the fortieth anniversary of the assassination.[46] The exhibition, organized in collaboration with the Sixth Floor Museum, displayed photographs, broadcast and media coverage, home movies, eyewitness testimonies, evidence, investigation reports, and large-scale photographic reproductions of the crime scene. Video monitors screened footage in the gallery. "Visitors will also be encouraged to explore the concept of memory, particularly 'flash bulb' memories—deep, vivid experiences of highly emotional events such as the JFK assassination," the press release suggested. Among the works exhibited in Pittsburgh were not only the Jackies that had recently been exhibited in Dealey Plaza, but also *Flash: November 22, 1963*, Naskovski's *Death in Dallas*—and the Zapruder film. Warhol's window, then, points to a comprehensive visualization that ultimately comes to involve the print itself as an exhibit.

It seems likely that the appraisal reports that resulted in the Zapruder film becoming the highest-priced photographic artifact in the world not only reflected a transformation of the film's status, but also contributed to it. What the implications of this are for how we will continue to encounter Zapruder's images, however, is an open question. When images travel, they both change and are changed by the variety of discourses they "pass through" in the process. "The conflation of the aesthetic merits of Zapruder's 26 seconds of 8mm film and Andy Warhol's silkscreens does indicate how far the categorical boundaries separating art and other forms of visual information have broken down since the 1960s," Beck observes. "Both the Zapruder film and Warhol carry a considerable share for that breakdown."[47] When framed next to one another, the footage, the prints, and the video installation display an expository poetics that is rapidly transforming the institution of the museum.[48] An analysis of how Zapruder's images travel enables the critic to reflect on this ongoing transformation of the gallery space, the places where the images are projected, and the shifting framing strategies involved. As these chapters have illustrated, cultural expressions that quote Zapruder's images can be read, at least in part, as metacritical commentaries on these developments as well as contributions to them. In its many framings, Naskovski's installation serves as a striking example of this, suggesting that images have always traveled, long before the first history painting was made, long before the first camera was invented—and, indeed, long before Zapruder fought his sense of vertigo and climbed on his perch to record the death of a president.

SEVEN

Oswald's Window

It's history. People should be able to have that view. // Jeff West, the former executive director of the Sixth Floor Museum at Dealey Plaza

"WE'RE NOW GOING TO GO INTO THE KENNEDY MUSEUM and talk to the curator," the Artist-President says, waving to a small group of bystanders from the stairs to the Dal-Tex Building in Dealey Plaza. Flanked by his wife, he enters what was a Kennedy museum in 1975. As he walks into the lobby, several visitors turn to look, and many are puzzled by what they see. There is much muttering. The Artist-President walks over to the front desk, turns to the scattered crowds of guests, and addresses them: "I want to thank you all for coming to the Kennedy museum. And I also want you all to know as you watch the history of my life . . ." Unsurprisingly, that is as far as he gets before an attendant asks him to leave. "It's good worthwhile work you're doing here," the Artist-President amicably responds, as if addressing a group of campaign workers on a bizarre election tour. Then he turns around and walks out, and the video cuts to the Zapruder film, which introduces Ant Farm's Dealey Plaza reenactment in *The Eternal Frame*.

Dealey Plaza is defined by the ongoing and conflicting interpretations and narrations of a diversity of groups, including television networks, independent researchers, tourists, and artists, all of which have continued to swarm the site—and the museum that has permanently settled there. All these groups participate in a particular kind of "secular ritual," in a "public drama," in David Chaney's words. Social life, Chaney observes, "has become more self-consciously staged as something to be looked at."[1] By including a brief and quickly aborted visit to a Kennedy museum in *The Eternal Frame*, Ant Farm not only foresaw how Dealey Plaza would be the site of a struggle for the authority to define and reenact a civic trauma, but also hinted at the powerful ways in which museums tend to govern and direct such processes through their discourses. Their guerilla reenactment serves as a deliberately irreverent contrast to the sanctioned version, a seemingly impromptu visit that many thought inappropriate and possibly disrespectful.

The commercial museum Doug Hall and Doug Michels were asked to leave in 1975 was in operation from 1970 to 1981. Today, a new museum resides on the sixth floor of the former Texas School Book Depository building at 414 Elm Street, the Sixth Floor Museum at Dealey Plaza. Soon after the government purchased Zapruder's camera-original film, the Zapruder family stated that it would begin "actively pursuing" copyright transfer; in 2000, the Sixth Floor Museum became the copyright holder and also became responsible for how the images are projected within the museum's discourse. The building from which Oswald shot, then, now houses the institution that holds the copyright, but the very place Zapruder shot from, to which visitors continue to return, remains outside its expository space.

Whereas a guide for sale in a gift store on the museum's ground floor advises visitors to begin their tour of the site with a visit to the museum, I chose not to heed this advice and instead walked around the plaza first, observing the pressure to visualize that I describe in the introduction.[2] In her review of "The American Effect," Jane C. Desmond describes how she left that exhibition and took the subway to Ground Zero, only to find that the site itself had gone through a profound "museumification," with its displays of photos and texts, with which visitors engaged in a "contemplative and searching" way. "These attempts at visual interpretation, along with visceral reactions to the physical space and to the occasional symbolic fragment," Desmond observes, "were deeply engaging in ways that so few of the Whitney works were." If the comparison is unfair, Desmond holds, it is because places such as the former World Trade Center site, with their combination of memorialization and pilgrimage, are likely to "always overshadow any art exhibition."[3] Indeed, the site of trauma can be transformed into a communal expository space, a powerful meeting place in which memory and postmemory are shared. As James Young points out, the ritual of remembering together at such sites is something that in itself becomes an event to remember.[4] It is thus that private photography comes to define the ways in which what Chaney calls public drama plays out.[5]

Arriving in Dealey Plaza, I had felt, while walking around and putting off my museum visit, that the entire site had been transformed into an expository space, with its showing and telling, its reenactments and simulations. However, this ongoing "public drama" was complicated by the struggle for cultural authority that Ant Farm dramatizes in its video. As I paid and took the elevator to the sixth floor, the questions I kept asking myself concerned the relationship between different forms of "insides" and "outsides." Would the pressure to visualize and to simulate that was so strongly felt in the plaza be equally strong inside the museum?

"BEING THERE"

Dealey Plaza was created in the mid-1930s by George B. Dealey, a civic leader and the publisher of the *Dallas Morning News*, and was soon widely referred to as "the front door of Dallas," a symbol of civic pride.[6] In 1962, the Texas School Book Depository Company leased space in the building at 411 Elm Street, which had been a commercial building for years. By the end of the following year, the plaza had been transformed into a murder site. For years, city planners did not know what to do with it. It continued to stir up painful memories, not only of Kennedy's death, but also of how the city was increasingly associated with the assassination. The book depository company moved out in 1970, after which the building shifted hands a couple of times; one potential buyer requested, but was denied, a permit to tear it down. In 1977, Dallas County bought and restored it, turning it into an administration building. Today, floors two through five house county administration offices, whereas the museum resides on the ground floor and the two top floors.

During the first two decades after the assassination, formal ceremonies marked anniversaries, but in 1983, the Kennedy family officially stated that they preferred that remembrances take place on May 29, Kennedy's birthday, in the future. In the late eighties, plans were nevertheless made to open an exhibit in the old depository building. Since hordes of visitors kept flocking to the plaza in the years that followed the assassination, Dallas County recognized the need for a meeting place for those who wanted to learn more about what had happened there.[7] With financial support from the National Endowment for the Humanities, the Dallas County Historical Commission finally recommended that a public exhibition space be included on the site. The private, nonprofit Sixth Floor Museum opened in 1989, with the stated ambition to "chronicle the assassination and Kennedy's legacy" and "preserve" the site. Four years later, the site was ceremoniously declared a National Historic Landmark District on the day of the thirtieth anniversary of Kennedy's death.

This sweeping ambition—to narrate life, death, and legacy—is both understandable and problematic. The idea of chronicling Kennedy's life and addressing his legacy on the site where he was shot to death may indeed seem morbid. However, this strategy seems to have been the only way to address the event of the assassination without building a death museum. Indeed, the identity problem of the museum in Dealey Plaza derives from the fact that U.S. culture is sensitive to the institutionalization of a commemoration of death. Conover Hunt, who was involved in creating the museum and worked as a project director and chief curator there in its early years, has addressed these challenges several times. "Sites in America are battlegrounds for different points of view" and "platforms for debate," she points out. Significantly, she observes, it was the public—not Dallas or Texas leaders—that insistently turned Dealey Plaza into "sacred ground" and "associated it with the culture of hope and key elements of American patriotism." Community leaders were only following up on the demands of the public when they decided to preserve the site and offer educational information there. Hunt observes what she finds to be a difference in the way sites are preserved in the United States, where preservation "seems tied to interpretation," and in Europe, "where buildings are preserved all the time but not necessarily interpreted."[8] In her guide to the site and in *JFK for a New Generation*, a book written for those born years after the assassination, Hunt repeatedly calls for a "foundation of understanding" for those who want to "interpret JFK and his legacy dispassionately and according to their own unique vision." Dealey Plaza, Hunt posits, presents the perfect frame for such individual interpretation, for a comprehensive construction of postmemory. It is one of the places people visit to "experience history firsthand." Sites such as Dealey Plaza offer a "physical context for past events," Hunt holds, if they are preserved or restored accurately.[9]

The Sixth Floor Museum's various narratives raise several questions concerning the meaning of "preservation." The word has been used in the museum's promotion to refer to both the material and the immaterial, both the physical and the metaphysical. The ambition is to preserve objects, a site, and the memory of a president's life and death. In her narrative of the assassination written for new generations, "Being There: November 22, 1963," Hunt asks the reader to join her "on a journey back in time and to another place" and introduces a second-person-singular narrator who observes, responds to, and interprets what happens in Dealey Plaza. This narrative agent places herself next to Zapruder in the plaza, so she comes to share his perspective of what happens.[10] From this vantage point, Hunt's "you" is instructed to "focus on the limousine" as stills from the Zapruder film accompany the text toward a narrative climax of shots ringing out in the plaza.[11] A graphic verbal description of the fatal shot is illustrated with a blow-up of frame 313, which shows Kennedy's head exploding; the imagetext, which recalls *Life*'s narrative of the event in its November 29, 1963, issue, seeks to transport its reader back to the site at the moment of death by describing a traumatic experience in impossible detail.

What is actually described is, in reality, the visual record of the event. The second-person singular and the present tense add to a sense of "being there." Unlike Zapruder, whose traumatic response the narrative's "you" observes ("tears stream down his face"), the "you" is resolute and quickly gets to her car to listen to the radio reports of what has happened, then goes home to turn on the television, "seeking further information about the horrible tragedy that you saw with your own eyes."[12] By overwhelming her reader-narrator with sensorial impressions and endowing her with supernatural gifts of observation that remain fully intact during the trauma, Hunt creates an agent whose ability to narrate is not fractured by witnessing a murder. Instead, the "you" of her narrative registers data in a somewhat machinelike manner, more like Zapruder's camera than Zapruder. The implications are clear: the preservation of memory happens through a narrativization that makes the event vivid, that creates a sense of "being there."

The Sixth Floor Museum's permanent exhibition, "John F. Kennedy and the Memory of a Nation," ultimately aims to achieve the same effect, but replaces Zapruder's perspective with that of the assassin in order to use its location to full effect. This becomes evident only gradually because its narrative is split between its double mission of narrating life, legacy, and death. In what has become a traditional museological narrative strategy, the exhibition invites you to wander around and look at various displays while listening to an audio guide.[13] As you arrive on the sixth floor, the narrative opens by framing the presidency in cultural history with music, books, and movie posters from the early sixties. Indeed, the brevity of the Kennedy presidency is reflected in the brief survey of its key events. A film about the Kennedy years, *The*

Presidency, lasts some six minutes; a number of photographs and panel texts address the civil rights movement, Kennedy's social programs, the Bay of Pigs and the Cuban missile crisis, and the space race as well as the "style" of the Kennedy White House.

The exhibition then turns to the assassination. It first details the events of the trip to Dallas and then the Dealey Plaza shooting, in panels, including enlarged frames from the Zapruder film, photographs, and two films. Every now and then, the voice-over is replaced by eyewitness descriptions and news reports, turning parts of the walk into a genuinely polyphonic experience. Exhibits show various objects, photographs, and films, reflecting the ambition to evoke memory by preserving historical objects. The visitor is given space to look, think, and formulate her own thoughts. During the ten-minute film showing how the world responded to Kennedy's death, we hear only music. Then, panels and objects, including forensic evidence, give an unbiased account of the controversies surrounding the investigations of the assassination. Among the exhibited objects is a replica of Zapruder's camera, the original being stored in the National Archives. In this section, a miniature Dealey Plaza made by the FBI and used by the Warren Commission in its various reconstructions is also on display.

Indeed, many of the artifacts and displays could have been exhibited elsewhere. In Boston, for example, where Kennedy was born, the John F. Kennedy Presidential Library and Museum addresses his life and legacy by offering a "you are there" experience that includes Kennedy's own voice in self-guided exhibits. As Cynthia Brandimarte observes in an otherwise positive review of the Sixth Floor Museum's permanent exhibition, one might question the very idea of an exhibition at Dealey Plaza.[14] However, the museum deploys its location strategically when it comes to describe the moment of Kennedy's death. Understandably, it is the exhibits that are specific to the space—the views onto Dealey Plaza and the window Oswald shot from—that tend to be crowded.

PRESERVING THE VANTAGE POINT

Indeed, the view of the plaza is displayed very much like the exhibits elsewhere on the sixth floor, with small captions that describe what the visitor is seeing through the windows. No one walking through the exhibition on the sixth floor will be surprised by this. As Chaney points out, one of the effects of the advent of amateur photography is that we have become used to "seeing as though what we are seeing is framed in a pictorial space."[15] As the visitor looks out over the plaza, her sense of "being there," where it happened, produces a sense of having been there when it happened. The view is supposed to do the trick that Zapruder's images did for Hunt's narrative. The perspective, however, is different. Even though the view is from one of the neighboring windows, the museum narrative's "you" inevitably places herself in the position of the assassin—not that of the bystander or the witness. While narrating the significant events of Kennedy's life and those surrounding his death, the museum also invites the visitor to imagine what it was like to shoot the president.

Ironically, however, the exact view from the window Oswald shot from is inaccessible to the visitor. In what is called "an accurate re-creation," the area around the window is sealed off behind Plexiglas and has been made to look as it did in 1963, with stacks of book boxes covering the wooden floor. During my visit in 2003, I found that a police photograph from the day of the assassination had been placed by the exhibit to attest to the realism of the display. Next to the corner, the original window was on display in a glass frame; a caption informed the visitor that it had been stashed away for years, but had been reinstalled and unveiled on President's Day, February 21, 1995, at a ceremony attended by elected officials and members of the Dallas County Historical Commission. (The window was later sold to an anonymous bidder at auction on eBay for a little more than three million dollars).[16] On the plane to Dallas, I had read in my *Lonely Planet* guide that the corner window was the "most evocative exhibit." No one, the book claims, "can fail to get choked up at the view: the same vista suspected sniper Lee Harvey Oswald had on that fateful day."[17]

Indeed, the exhibition invites its visitor, its "you," to function as a narrative agent in a construction of individual memory, but its poetics of preservation is compromised by its display of the corner window. The area surrounding the window is mythologized by its inaccessibility, giving the visitor a contradictory sense of being invited both to share Oswald's perspective and to look at him from the outside. It is thus here, by the corner window, that the exhibition narrative in effect is subsumed by its framing and transformed by the museum's site-specific discursiveness. This paradoxical attempt to make Oswald's view both exclusive and accessible reached new heights with the installation of a web camera in 1999. On June 24 of that year, the *Dallas Morning News* reported that "thanks to the internet, history buffs, assassination theorists and the just plain curious can see what Oswald is alleged to have seen as the Kennedy motorcade rumbled toward him."[18] Jeff West, the executive director of the museum from 1994 to 2004, told the paper that EarthCam had offered to install a webcam at no cost and maintain it. Thus, a rotating camera now provides images of a mostly uneventful plaza night and day. "For the generations that didn't grow up with computer technology, yes, this might seem a little odd," West told the *Jewish World Review*. "But for younger generations who are growing up with computers and the Web—believe me, this is really no big deal." Senator Edward Kennedy, John F. Kennedy's last surviving brother, told the same publication that he saw it differently: "Those who guided the original creation of the Sixth Floor Museum made a substantial effort to prevent the exploitation and commercialization of President Kennedy's death, and their efforts were a great credit to the people of Dallas. It is unfortunate that their accomplishment is now being undermined in this insensitive and tasteless manner." "It's what it is," West responded. "We couldn't have people walking up to the window, because we wanted to preserve the area around the window just as it was in 1963. . . . It's history. People should be able to have that view."[19]

What does having such a view entail? How is the image "history"? Indeed, the specificity of concepts such as "history" and "preservation" is reduced in these remarks to serve a tautological rhetoric of expansive visualization. For what is the role of this image in the museum's poetics of preservation? How is memory preserved by the webcam's constant feed of images to an audience that is defined by not being present on-site? The installation reflects how the pressure to visualize is far more than merely the by-product of a collective need to commemorate a tragic event; rather, it conditions such commemoration. Like Zapruder's images, Oswald's view is concealed and then exposed on a large scale; the mythologization of one vantage point contributed to creating interest in the other. Indeed, EarthCam launched the webcam shortly before the U.S. government was expected to announce the verdict regarding its acquisition of the Zapruder film. In a press release dated June 24, 1999, the company stressed the "exclusive" view from the window and compared the uniqueness of this "vantage point" with that of the Zapruder film. "We've already had 4 million hits on the Web page that has the camera shot," West observed a month later.[20]

As a conclusion to a tour of its permanent exhibition, the Sixth Floor Museum features a ten-minute film, *The Legacy*, narrated by Walter Cronkite. It ends on a note of dignified remembrance rather than mourning, on what was achieved rather than what was lost. But the visitor who leaves the museum is unlikely to remember this film, which resembles numerous others, as vividly as the corner exhibit. Indeed, the exhibited window, the sealed-off corner, and the webcam installation trouble the museum's mission of preservation as commemoration. A spectacular exhibit, "The Corner Window" problematizes the museum's various narratives of transformation through confrontation. One such narrative was the exhibition "Loss and Renewal: Transforming Tragic Sites," which opened November 20, 2001, two days before another assassination anniversary and only a couple of months after the terrorist attacks on September 11. The exhibition, which lasted through December 2002, reflected the museum's wish to create an exhibition that, in the words of one reviewer, "captured the tumult of emotions immediately following 9/11 and attempted to put it into a historical perspective."[21] Large display cases contained text, pictures, film, and objects devoted to six sites: Ford's Theater, where Abraham Lincoln was assassinated; Pearl Harbor; Dealey Plaza; the Lorraine Motel, where Martin Luther King was assassinated; the Murrah Federal Building, the site of the Oklahoma City bombing; and the World Trade Center. Intended to be therapeutic and inclusive, "Loss and Renewal" invited visitors to write down their thoughts and immediate response.

"The human need to commemorate must first overcome the impulse to hide, deny, or even destroy sites of tragedy," a short narrative titled "Loss" told visitors to the museum's website, www.jfk.org. Another brief text, "Renewal," claimed that a nation's spirit is renewed by acknowledging loss. As "one voice," the narrative says, "we honor our dead and pay tribute to our heroes. And thus renewal begins." The preservation of tragic sites is significant in this process, the text stated: "For many years after an event, renewal comes daily to those who return to the site of tragedy to pause, reflect, and remember the moments that altered our nation's history." Renewal happens, in other words, in spaces such as the Sixth Floor Museum. But what, a visitor to Dealey Plaza might ask, does such a renewal consist of?

In an essay published in *American History* in December 2003, Jeff West observes that museum professionals and historians "now readily recognize the importance of preserving sites that have difficult and emotional associations." In comparing the attack on the World Trade Center with the assassination in Dealey Plaza, he suggests that there was a widespread sense that "something would be done to preserve the memory of this horrific event."[22] The idea of working through rather than forgetting or denying, expressed by West as well as Hunt, may be a noble one. But to stage and institutionalize a process of "renewal" is a daunting project, and in the Sixth Floor Museum's narratives, the concept remains as abstract as "preservation" or "history."

In *Regarding the Pain of Others*, Susan Sontag asks why the United States does not have a Museum of the History of Slavery, something comparable to the Holocaust Memorial Museum in Washington, D.C., and concludes that it is because such an institution would "acknowledge that the evil was *here*"—it would threaten a "national consensus on American history as a history of progress."[23] Indeed, a "national consensus" is precisely what West calls for. Pointing out that two-thirds of the visitors to the museum in Dealey Plaza were born after the assassination, he claims that the museum should provide "for a national, emotional catharsis."[24] West does not explain what would be entailed by this catharsis, which is indeed a problematic concept to invoke, but by stressing that it is felt by a national collective, he echoes the web narrative's reference to a national spirit. "The massive revival of American patriotism that followed the tragedy in New York—we had a similar experience after Kennedy was assassinated," Hunt observes. "It was one of those trigger points that unified the nation in grief. It reminded many people what it means to be an American. I think that will certainly form a part of the interpretation in the future in New York."[25]

The point here, of course, is not so much to criticize Hunt or West as it is to critically address the expository discourse their institution gives expression to. That discourse joins concepts such as trauma, memory, and renewal with concepts of catharsis and national spirit. In *Writing History, Writing Trauma*, Dominick LaCapra warns against conflating the concepts of loss and absence when addressing trauma; he situates the first concept on a historical and the latter on a transhistorical level. Absence, in this sense, "is not an event and does not imply tenses"; losses, however, "are specific and involve particular events"—there is a danger, consequently, in situating loss on a transhistorical level, since it "cannot be adequately addressed" when "enveloped in an overly generalized discourse of absence, including the absence of ultimate metaphysical foundations."[26] Indeed, the poetics of remembrance outlined by West and the museum falls prey to this conflation by advocating a "renewal" and "catharsis" that involves an entire nation by way of simulation-as-preservation, a collective joined by looking at webcam images of the site of trauma.

"Memory is, achingly, the only relation we can have with the dead," Sontag writes, but adds, "Perhaps too much value is assigned to memory, not enough to thinking."[27] The construction of national identity takes place in part through collectively remembered events, and such events are often characterized by rupture.[28] Remembering is thus an ethical act; "it has ethical value in and of itself," in Sontag's words.[29] In aiming to evoke the event for "new generations," the Sixth Floor Museum faces a problem because it is not addressing an experience shared by those visitors. For it is difficult to see how the webcam images preserve either memory or the site—or invite the construction of postmemory—as much as they document the compulsive visualization that the very installation of the camera ultimately expresses.

THE ASSASSINATION THEME PARK

The museum in Dealey Plaza is troubled by the pressure to visualize, which has come to shape its discourse. Its poetics of preservation is contested not merely because of that pressure, however, but also because the museum's "mission" has been clouded by the institution's increasingly transforming self-definition. The preservation of the historic site as described by Hunt in her book suggests that a visitor's sense of "being there" depends on the site's claim to historical authenticity. Indeed, several preservationists objected strongly to the installation of an elevator that enables visitors to get directly to the sixth floor.[30] In the spring of 2003, a few months before I came to Dallas, the Sixth Floor Museum announced that the two top floors, after a $2.4 million renovation, had been "sealed to ensure constant temperature and humidity."[31] West pointed out that the idea was to keep it "intact," to preserve "the warehouse feel for the space."[32] It was also in 2003 that the museum proposed to restore the entire site "to its 1963 historic integrity." Approximately $3 million was sought to fund the restoration, which has not been realized.[33] The museum, it would seem, sought to transform the entire site into an exhibit.

"The concept of a preserved landscape," Tadhg O'Keeffe writes, "is clearly a contradiction in terms, since a landscape sealed at a particular moment stops being the landscape that it was and becomes a new landscape."[34] Whereas the original intention of the Sixth Floor Museum was to focus on how the place could be preserved in order to offer a particular kind of spatial practice, it increasingly seems to accommodate the place to new and very different practices. The landscape, available on computer screens across the globe, seems likely to instill in the visitor what Joshua Meyrowitz years before the advent of the web camera called "no sense of place."[35] If a poetics of exposition centers on the significance of "being there," it cannot center on "being elsewhere" without being transformed.

Whereas the museum in Dealey Plaza ultimately has contributed to transforming the site into something like an assassination theme park, it has done so in part because its functions have long since exceeded those expressed in its original mission. The gift store on the first floor sells a range of commodities that transform the building itself into an assassination icon, its image printed on caps and T-shirts. When I visited, I could put a quarter into a machine and receive a small commemorative coin, a keepsake to help me remember the visit. This apparatus conditions the site's ability to offer its visitors an intended renewal or catharsis if it helps transform them into "memory tourists." Further contributing to this sense of conflation is the fact that the seventh floor of the building not only functions as a gallery, but also is available for rent, for corporate dinners and receptions, of which there have been many. "Guests," the *New York Times* informed its readers, "are free to wander down the open staircase and view the artifacts of the assassination."[36] "It's about opening these places for communal activities," West told the paper.

In describing what he calls the "semiotics of tourism," Jonathan Culler suggests that tourism represents a "reduction of cultures to signs." "The paradox, the dilemma of authenticity," according to Culler, "is that to be experienced as authentic it must be marked as authentic, but when it is marked as authentic it is mediated, a sign of itself, and hence lacks the authenticity of what is truly unspoiled, untouched by mediating cultural codes."[37] There is no solution to this problem for preservationists and city planners, whether in Dealey Plaza or elsewhere, only different strategies with which to meet it. In 1992, Michael Sorkin observed the growth of what he called an "ageographical city" in the United States; the structure of such a city, he claimed, "is a lot like television," characterized by "a conceptual grid of boundless reach." Such a place is ultimately one of simulations, "the city as theme park," a place where "the preservation of the physical remnants of the historical city has superseded attention to the human ecologies that produced and inhabit them."[38] Theming, Mark Gottdiener argues, blurs the line between production and consumption.[39] "It seems to me we are losing sight of what parts of culture cannot be turned into a theme," Sorkin has argued more recently. He identifies the theming of tragedy specifically as a "danger represented by the theme park," a site distinguished by the fact that it enjoys a "freedom to make use of historical forms and artifacts."[40] Dealey Plaza has become a self-enclosed area within a cityscape, dedicated to a comprehensive assassination simulation that exceeds the physical borders of the site; the conceptual grid that informs it is that of the Internet. Once the "door of Dallas," Dealey Plaza is now everywhere, only a click away, where live images "preserve" the memory of historical trauma.

Like Zapruder's images, Oswald's view spurs a culture of reenactment that is ultimately uncontrollable. Together with the two vantage points—that of Zapruder's perch and Oswald's window—the *X* mark in the street where Kennedy was shot in the head marks a triadic configuration of extensive assassination simulation. In part an effect of decades of visualization as reenactment, the view from the window arguably had already begun to produce fantasies and projections in 1964 when *Life* covered a page with a photograph taken from the "sniper's nest" and described the FBI reenactments that were done there for the Warren Commission (fig. 7.1).

On November 22, 2004, Traffic Management Limited, a Scottish company, released a video game, *JFK Reloaded*, which put the player in the role of Oswald: from the sniper's perch, one aims and fires at the motorcade. The website marketed the game with a tagline: "You are looking through the eyes of Oswald. Can you prove it was possible?"[41] To win the prize, a player had to reenact history perfectly and create the perfect assassination simulation, since the score depended on how closely a player's shooting matched the findings of the Warren Commission report. It is the player's familiarity with Zapruder's footage, Tracy Fullerton argues, that makes the player prepared and almost intuitively ready to play.[42] Its imagery gives any reenactment a touch of déjà vu. *JFK Reloaded*, then, invites its player not only to imagine the assassination but also to create it, to narrate it by reenacting it in a simulation. After finishing, the player gets a multiperspective replay that allows for zooming in and out; the player can select the location from which to study a reconstruction of the assassination attempt: from Zapruder's perch, from the grassy knoll, from the presidential limousine.

Kirk Ewing, the creator of the game, suggested, upon its release, that *JFK Reloaded* was a new kind of "docu-game," an "interactive entertainment" that would bring "history to life" and "stimulate a younger generation of players to take an interest in this fascinating episode of American history."[43] The game, according to Ewing, was intended to lay conspiracy theories to rest for good. It was supposed to be educational. But of course, *JFK Reloaded* was immediately controversial. Ted Kennedy commented through his spokesman that the concept was "despicable," and Douglas Lowenstein, the president of the Entertainment Software Association, was quick to insist that the product was "neither entertainment nor a video game as normally understood."[44] Joseph Lieberman was "sickened" by the game. Christy Glaubke, of Children NOW,

ASSASSINATION: THE TRAIL TO A VERDICT

Vol. 57, No. 14   Oct. 2, 1964

RE-ENACTMENT. The cross hairs of a gun sight zero in on a car simulating the presidential limousine at the assassination scene. At right, FBI man takes sightings with killer's rifle from sixth-floor window Oswald used. On floor below another agent briefs Warren panel.

FIG. 7.1   *Life* invites the reader to see what Oswald saw. *Life*, October 2, 1964, 40.

was quick to dismiss any educational merits: "I would think the only [lesson it teaches] is how to be an assassin," she commented.[45]

Different in most respects from the museum in its framing of the event, *JFK Reloaded* nevertheless is similar in inviting us to project the assassination from Oswald's perspective. Both invite a "you" to reenact the assassination creatively by projecting it visually. If Hunt's verbal narrative were to use the corner window literally as its framing device in a similar manner, she would have to instruct her narrative agent explicitly to take on the role of assassin. *JFK Reloaded* was so contested upon its release as much from skepticism about its value as a "documentary game" as about its narrative strategy. Critics did not address specifically the dubious ethics of framing its simulation as a competition, but rather worried about its game narrativization.

Indeed, in its virtual aesthetics, *JFK Reloaded* most resembles a 3-D simulation by Dale Myers that was projected in the ABC documentary *Beyond Conspiracy*, which was hosted by Peter Jennings and broadcast on ABC as part of the fortieth anniversary of the assassination.[46] In introducing the television special, Jennings insists that he will present "stunning technology which will make it clear precisely what happened."[47] Myers, a freelance computer animator, won an Emmy in 2004 for his animation, on which he spent years. He made use of maps and blueprints and worked with a computer software package, LightWave 3D, in rephotographing the assassination as recorded by Zapruder's camera. This enabled him, in the words of Jennings, to "leave the place where Zapruder was filming and see the shooting from any point of view." In the documentary, Myers explains, in a frame-by-frame analysis, that what has been called a single-bullet theory is "a single-bullet fact." Having re-created Zapruder's images, Myers's presentation traces the bullet from Governor Connally's entry wound back through Kennedy's upper body and up to Oswald's window, where we finally see the plaza from the assassin's perspective (fig. 7.2).

Myers's painstakingly detailed animation introduces a new chapter in using Zapruder's images for state-of-the-art exposition. Like Robert Groden arguing for the value of his "enhancements," Myers promised that he would resurrect the Zapruder film as an evidentiary image, even as he explained that "none of the final animation frames will exactly match any given frame of the Zapruder film."

The introduction of webcam technology into Oswald's window and the 3-D triangulation of various animated reenactments do not so much suggest a "closing of the case" or the end of an epistemological crisis as reflect the

FIG.7.2   A 3-D simulation of the view from Oswald's window by Dale Myers for *Beyond Conspiracy* (2003), produced by Peter Jennings.

fact that Zapruder's images will continue to shape how new forms of visual technology reframe the assassination. One simulation bleeds into the next as Zapruder's images of a motorcade in Dealey Plaza travel into new virtual models. The pressure to visualize has come to shape a triadic visualization in a pervasive aesthetic of "the vantage point." From such a perspective, the existence of *JFK Reloaded* should come as no surprise to anyone who has visited the plaza or dipped into assassination culture. As Fullerton observes, the immediately negative response to *JFK Reloaded* could thus have been in response to the fact that it is a game simulation. Ian Bogost, an assistant professor at the Georgia Institute of Technology, told the *Washington Post* that *JFK Reloaded* could create a frame for understanding, since not unlike Stone's movie, it "explicitly positioned itself to try to explain what actually took place." The negative reaction thus came from a prejudiced notion that "video games can never take on a serious topic," he held.[48]

Whereas the assassination is considered a fitting motif for some cultural forms, for others it is clearly not   but such things depend on changing cultural climates. When *Image of an Assassination* made Zapruder's images available on the home-video market, the controversy revolved less around its specific expository mode or its promotion than around the fact that it was being released for such a market at all.[49] Documentary games, Joost Raessens argues, do not strive for historic objectivity, but they nevertheless reach for something more substantial than merely the subjective impressions of the artists who make them. "Whereas the documentary film has always tried to find stylistic as well as narrative ways to address spectators," he writes, "gamers are immersed into experience and reenact historical events in interactive ways."[50] Certainly, the moviegoer is invited to take on Oswald's perspective several times in Stone's movie. Deploying a shifting focalization in describing the assassination, DeLillo allows the reader to look at the motorcade through Oswald's eyes in *Libra*—a novel that stirred controversy for that reason. If it is the use of an assassin's perspective that automatically triggers outrage, then the museum's webcam installation should meet with the same response as the movie, the novel, and the video game.

When I visited Dallas, *JFK Reloaded* was yet to be released. Leaving the Sixth Floor Museum and going back to my hotel room, I thought about my arrival in the city. Curious about how the site would look, I had hurried down to Dealey Plaza to find it practically empty. The experience was both ordinary and exceptional. The site seemed to me to be defined by its practicality. A parklike juncture, its basic function was to organize traffic efficiently. But it also seemed to me tremendously powerful, precisely because the persistent and widespread imaging of the site had already done the job of making it so.

After sitting down for a while on the grass, I got up and walked the area surrounding the plaza. Two blocks away, I came upon a thirty-foot-high white concrete square that seemed to somehow float above ground; it was lifted by what seemed to me impossibly thin pillars. Upon closer inspection, I understood that this was an effect that its designer, Philip Johnson, had sought to achieve. The Kennedy Memorial, dedicated in 1970, was empty when I walked over to look at it, as it would mostly be when I walked by it in the days that followed. Entering, I found that its room was roofless; a black granite plate rested in the middle with Kennedy's name inscribed on it. Etymologically, the word "cenotaph"—a monument erected in honor of someone whose remains are elsewhere—derives from Greek and means "empty tomb." A cenotaph was traditionally built because a body was lost—for example, at sea or at war. However, the empty tomb of the Kennedy Memorial also suggested to me another kind of displacement. Commemoration goes on elsewhere, at a burial site where a flame burns in the president's memory. In the nearby plaza, I had to think, the eagerness to record and picture had come to overshadow collective remembrance. And in the museum, the ambition to narrate the life, death, and legacy of Kennedy seemed compromised by several changes that had transformed the institution in the years leading up to the fortieth anniversary. With its web camera installed, the isolated, unavailable corner exhibit in the museum seemed almost symbolic of this conflation, since it denied what it promised: to fulfill the understandable desire to stand there and reflect upon what could have been going through the assassin's mind.

EIGHT
Traveling Images

Let the atrocious images haunt us. // Susan Sontag, *Regarding the Pain of Others*

IN SLOW MOTION, A LIMOUSINE GUARDED by two policemen on motor-cycles arrives at a park in Los Angeles, and out of the car steps Bill Gates (Steve Sires). An opening title suggests that we are in Los Angeles, and that what we are going to see took place on December 2, 1999; the sound track, consisting of a fragmentary mix of journalese, hints that a "tragedy" is about to ensue. Carrying a large cardboard check, Gates smilingly walks to a podium, waving to the crowd that has gathered. Suddenly, a gunshot hits his shoulder, and he falls to his knees; then another shot hits him in the head, and we see a spray of blood before he falls back. A member of the audience jumps onto the stage, turns around, and points to the top of the opposite building. Newspaper headlines then begin to flash across the screen, reporting what we gather is a series of events that followed immediately after the Gates assassination, including "Assassin Killed by Lone Rookie Cop," and "Gunman: Clues to Motive May Have Died With Him."

Thus begins Brian Flemming's *Nothing So Strange* (2004), a story of the assassination of Bill Gates and, more significantly, of the culture that grows out of the event. The film quickly goes on to introduce David James (David James), who is putting the finishing touches on a scale model of the assassination site. While carefully placing small figurines in his model, he tells us that after having lost his job, he has spent the most of the last months investigating Gates's death. James goes on to narrate what happened while moving his tin figures around: Gates arrived in MacArthur Park, the assassin fired two shots from the top of the Park Plaza Hotel before fleeing the building—and "that's when the mystery begins for us," he explains. For the unemployed James, a copresident of the newly founded organization Citizens for Truth, studying and analyzing the events that surrounded the assassination has become a full-time job. A policeman, he explains, was shot to death on the fifth floor of the hotel moments after Gates was assassinated; shortly afterward, the "alleged assassin" was killed by the police in the basement of the hotel. *Nothing So Strange* goes on to describe conspiracy theories, various meticulous reenactments and high-tech simulations, and the many foreseen and unforeseen ramifications of these events—all with clear reference to the culture that has come to surround the Kennedy assassination. Tellingly, the last words of the film are "We'll never know what happened." A minor hit on the festival circuit (Slamdance, South by Southwest, the Berlin Film Festival), *Nothing So Strange* is an independent moviemaker's attempt to explore the social, cultural, and political implications of the assassination of a contemporary icon, especially how such an event spurs the formation of a subculture. Typically, the film was met with positive reviews by critics and with outrage in parts of the U.S. news media.[1]

Anyone who sees Flemming's movie will recognize how its opening images quote the Zapruder film, and several critics remarked on the resemblance. More than anything, the quotation reflects the persistent presence of the images as we approach the fiftieth anniversary of both the assassination and the footage. As the previous chapters make clear, *Nothing So Strange* is far from unique in this respect. On March 17, 2010, Erykah Badu and a small crew shot a controversial video for her song "Window Seat" in Dealey Plaza; during the performance, the singer stripped naked in front of grassy knoll bystanders on the very spot where Kennedy was shot in the head. Reactions ranged from "groans to yawns," the *Dallas Morning News* reported.[2] Shot in faded colors that evoke those of the Zapruder film, the video shows the baffled response of visitors to the plaza as Badu pretends to be shot and falls down on the asphalt near the *X* mark in the street. In gaining what can be described as cultural prominence, Zapruder's footage is today quoted in allegories across the vast terrains of contemporary visual culture in a way that makes its transformation into an aesthetic image evident. The film is also surrounded by a mythology that is persistent enough to produce a steady stream of stories about the film's making and its contested history. In March 2002, the Donmar Warehouse in London premiered Keith Reddin's stage play *Frame 312*, a story about a secretary at Time Inc. who has secretly held Zapruder's camera-original film in her possession for decades. Not only do several scenes show the early projections in *Life*'s offices, but the entire production can also be said to revolve around and be structured by a series of screenings of the film.[3] One cannot help wondering what Zapruder would have said if someone told him in 1963 that the events surrounding his footage would form the plot of a play in a theatre in Covent Garden almost forty years later.

All these recent phenomena suggest that Zapruder's images are still on the journey that I set out to explore in *Zaprudered*. A visit to YouTube shows that the images flourish there in the age of Google. It is only fitting, then, that my book takes its title from William Gibson's novel *Pattern Recognition*, in which mysterious segments of footage, posted on a website, continue to haunt its characters, producing a culture of "footageheads," "followers of the footage" who "comprise the first true freemasonry of the new century" and meet regularly online in a "footage fetish forum." In a striking passage, Gibson describes its proliferation: "The footage has a way of cutting across boundaries, transgressing the accustomed order of things . . . Fragments, having been endlessly collated, broken down, reassembled, by whole armies of the most fanatical investigators, have yielded no period and no particular narrative direction. Zaprudered into surreal dimensions of purest speculation, ghost-narratives have emerged and taken on shadowy but determined lives of their own."[4]

I could have described here the many ways in which Gibson's story—the footage haunts Cayce Pollard to the point that she is led to chase after it— brings to mind the story of the Zapruder film. Instead, I would like to pause to note that forty years after the assassination, the proper name that came to designate Zapruder's 8 mm film has been transformed, without any warning or explanation from the narrator or the novelist, into a verb. What does it mean to "zapruder"? The word seems to leave questions of agency unresolved. It refers less to something one does than to something that has been done. It suggests that a cultural transformation has taken place, one that it is easier to observe than to describe, much less understand. Images that were once descriptive, anchored in what they showed, have loosened their chains and set out on unending journeys that continue to perplex and fascinate beholders.

This book departs from earlier writings of cultural critique of the Zapruder footage in its range, scope, and overall methodology. Its findings, I believe, would have been impossible with an approach that did not grapple with what I have described as the unruly object domain of traveling images. The transformation of Zapruder's footage into an aesthetic image is observable only through a critical engagement with how the images travel across media. The ramifications of *Zaprudered* thus extend beyond its attempt to describe and understand one phenomenon in contemporary visual culture. It therefore seems appropriate to briefly explore what new questions its findings raise and address how the journey of Zapruder's images may suggest something about how we can look at more recent, and indeed future, images that travel.

In Clint Eastwood's *Flags of Our Fathers* (2006), Joe Rosenthal's photograph of U.S. troops raising the flag atop Mount Suribachi, one of the most enduring pictures of the twentieth century, is exposed as a traveling image. "Raising the Flag on Iwo Jima" (1945) became an iconic symbol of victory, and Eastwood's movie explores in part the burdens imposed on the soldiers that were captured in, and in a sense remained captured by, the image. Rosenthal's picture raises several questions concerning the staging of historical photographs. Many considered the practice controversial because it produced rather than documented a symbolic event. This, of course, was nothing new. Many of the canonical images of early war photography, Sontag observes in *Regarding the Pain of Others*, were staged. In a number of Mathew Brady's Civil War photographs, some of the recently dead at Gettysburg were rearranged and displaced.[5] Brady and Rosenthal were professional photographers with a keen sense for the enduring image. Abraham Zapruder, however, was one of the first amateurs to accidentally catch on film, and create an enduring image of, an event that was staged to be photographed by professionals. As W. J. T. Mitchell observes, the film was in a sense a reappropriation from the beginning, since the motorcade was a staged "photo-op."[6] The Zapruder film can thus be said to raise several questions that are essential in the image wars of contemporary visual culture, since amateurs increasingly tend to record the defining images of events—and since events are staged in order to be extensively recorded and projected.

The terror attacks in Manhattan on September 11, 2001, are widely recognized to have been such an event. The time that passed between the impact of the first and the second plane was long enough for thousands of cameras, wielded by professionals as well as amateurs, to be turned on the World Trade Center (WTC). "Iconoclasm in this instance was rendered as an icon in its own right," Mitchell writes, "an image of horror that has imprinted itself in the memory of the entire world."[7] Indeed, as was the case with the assassination and Zapruder's footage of it, the attacks would eventually produce their very own privileged footage—and an expository discourse in which a transfer of heroism was embedded.

Not long after the attacks, it was widely reported that the only footage of the first strike on the WTC had been recorded by Jules Naudet, a French filmmaker, while he, along with his brother Gedeon, was making a documentary film about a rookie New York firefighter. On the morning of September 11, Jules Naudet had only been practicing his filming technique, since he had less experience than his brother; he was filming firefighters' response to a gas leak several blocks north of the WTC and happened to turn his camera on the first plane as it crashed into the North Tower. He hurried to the scene and managed to get the only footage from inside the crumbling building. His brother found his way to the site moments later and continued to film from the outside. When the first tower fell, each brother realized that the other might very well be dead, but both remained dedicated to filming.

Soon, critics were led to compare Jules Naudet's footage with the Zapruder film. It "may become the Zapruder tape of 9/11," *People* magazine suggested.[8] Naudet's record, accidentally shot by someone who was then a semiprofessional, bears the mark of authenticity; it is "raw footage." The Naudet brothers, realizing immediately what kind of record they were sitting on, hired the William Morris Agency to sort out the pitfalls and possibilities surrounding the footage. The brothers decided to remain dedicated to their original vision and made a documentary about the firefighters instead of hastily selling their footage to the highest bidder.[9] When they struck a deal with CBS, the network bought the rights for one million dollars for just two broadcasts; the brothers retained copyright and creative control of the project. The result was *9/11*, the most critically acclaimed documentary to surface after the attacks.[10]

The film was recognized as an antidote to what the novelist Philip Roth, in an interview with the British newspaper the *Independent*, described as the "kitschification of 3,000 people's deaths," a stream of documentaries from which *9/11* distinguishes itself in many ways.[11] The brothers sought to take charge and define the expository discourse in which their unique footage appeared, to control how their images traveled. Unlike Zapruder, who contractually obligated *Life* to act according to "good taste," the Naudets themselves actively sought to govern the display of their footage in a way that would have been impossible for the Dallas dressmaker. Many journalists also observed that the brothers donated a portion of the proceeds to the Uniformed Firefighters Association Scholarship Fund, as would Paramount

Home Entertainment, which eventually released a videocassette and a DVD, and Blockbuster, which offered it for purchase or rental. Similarly, Zapruder let it be known in 1963 that he would donate the first $25,000 from Time Inc. to the widow of the police officer, J. D. Tippit, who had been killed by Oswald after trying to stop him.[12]

Unlike *Life*'s early Zapruder narratives, *9/11* presents a transfer not of witnessing, but of heroism; like *Life*'s later Zapruder narratives, it finally comes to direct attention to the footage itself and, in the process, render the filmmaker heroic. Whereas *Life* adopted and accommodated the eyewitness account in 1963, *9/11* ultimately comes to elevate the act of witnessing it describes. To observe this, one has to—as in the case of *Life*'s imagetexts—analyze how the footage itself is put on display in the narrative, how the images travel into a very particular kind of expository discourse. Again, the aim is less to criticize the Naudets than it is to analyze how their images come to appear exceptional according to the prevailing logic of a distinct mode of display; in the end, their footage is as unique as viewers and critics want it to be.

The first words uttered by Jules Naudet in *9/11* are "They say that there is always a witness for history. I guess that day we were chosen to be witness." In their gravity and economy, these twenty words invite several interpretations; significantly, they are uttered with the benefit of hindsight, and they are themselves interpretative. They propose, in part, that the spectator consider *9/11* a testimonial. They certainly address the exceptional role of the filmmaker, in terms not entirely unlike those used by Dan Rather in his memoir, where he describes the reporter as someone who "will sometimes walk closer to the flames, so he may use the light."[13] What is considered remarkable is not only the actions depicted in the documentary, but also the videotape itself as a testimony to those actions. Consequently, the film takes on a split or double function, and it cannot stop remarking on this "doubleness."

Moments after Jules Naudet's remarks, James Hanlon, the former firefighter who was involved in the production of *9/11* and is featured as one of the narrators, compares the exceptional heroism of the rescue workers with that of the footage of the event: "On that day, guys from my firehouse, my best friends, were some of the firefighters in Tower 1 after the plane hit. What they did that day, what everyone there did, was remarkable. And almost as remarkable: it was captured on videotape. Inside the tower. Beginning to end."[14] The tagline-like passage asserts the exceptional position of the footage about to be seen, the uniqueness of the expository object. The word "captured" suggests closure: the event was captured, and we are about to see it. We are invited "inside the tower."

The footage becomes the physical and symbolic evidence of the professional impulse of the filmmakers, of their fateful presence. Jules Naudet's awareness of the power of his "eyewitness account" presents this professional impulse as a "gift" to a "seer." It transports not only the gift's recipients, but also filmmaking itself into a mythic sphere where concepts such as "the elect" and "redeemer nation" already belong quite nicely. The gift of vision is thrust upon the elect. The filmmakers describe their presence at the site as a matter of fate rather than chance or professional impulse. We are not encouraged to ponder the exceptional footage as much as to accept it as providence. In his summary of the year in television for *America*, James Martin concludes that it was difficult not to think that the Naudet brothers "were somehow meant to be there: Witnesses for the rest of the world, offering a glimpse of the valor of the rescue workers, the sorrow of those who died and the tragedy of terrorism."[15] Similarly, James Poniewozik wrote in *Time* magazine that the brothers "who shot tirelessly" became "more like the firefighters they so admired than they could have imagined."[16] Clearly, what we are witnessing when we read these words is a transfer of heroism.

The documentary *9/11* was originally intended to be an account of the day-to-day trials of becoming a firefighter. But what it became is as much a documentary about the trials of filmmaking. Indeed, one of *9/11*'s most central and compelling themes is the significance of seeing, of bearing witness, and of documenting "history." Vision serves as a complex metaphor in the film and carries multiple meanings. To see through a lens while filming is to see future projections of an ongoing event—to see the future construction of the past—and as spectators watching the film, we sense the weight of that, of the dizzying implications of that exceptional gaze for our sense of shared memory. We know, inevitably, that these are images we will come to see again and again.

Indeed, the ability to foresee the editing process—the ultimate shaping of a narrative—even at the moment of recording, is characteristic of the professional impulse that *9/11* describes. The recording moment itself becomes an exceptional visual event, a series of lightning-fast decisions motivated by a particular notion of looking. Today, cultural authority—the ability to stage expository agency and define cultural memory—resides with people who recognize that they have produced a traveling image and who can act correspondingly. The story of how *9/11* came to be—which it itself narrates so compellingly—serves as a striking contrast to that told on September 7, 2003, in the *New York Times*, when the paper reported that a videotape of the

terror attacks on the World Trade Center two years earlier had recently surfaced. A Czech immigrant construction worker, Pavel Hlava, had intended to
make a video postcard to send home and had accidentally filmed both planes
crashing into the towers from the passenger seat of a sport-utility vehicle in
Brooklyn. Almost two weeks had passed that September before Hlava realized that he had actually captured the first plane on video, and

> even then, Mr. Hlava, who speaks almost no English, did not realize that he
> had some of the rarest footage collected of the World Trade Center disaster.
> His is the only videotape known to have recorded both planes on impact,
> and only the second image of any kind showing the first strike. The tape—a
> kind of accidentally haunting artifact—has surfaced publicly only now, on
> the eve of the second anniversary of the attacks, after following the most
> tortuous and improbable of paths, from an insular circle of Czech-American
> working-class friends and drinking buddies.[17]

A copy of the tape was reported to have been traded by a friend of Hlava's wife
to another Czech immigrant for "a bar tab at a pub in Ridgewood, Queens."
Hlava and his brother Josef, who had been with him in the car, had tried to
sell the tape, both in New York and in the Czech Republic, "but with little
sophistication about the news media and no understanding of the tape's significance, the brothers had no success."[18]

As a recent immigrant's story, Hlava's is perhaps not so different from
those that abound from earlier times. The cultural logic that transforms his
videotape into a "haunting artifact" is familiar to those who have grown up
knowing such a logic, but foreign to those who are struggling to come to
terms with the realities of a different culture. Zapruder, the Naudet brothers, and Hlava were all immigrants, but Hlava distinguished himself from
the other three in not understanding that what he had in his hands was an
image that could travel.[19] The reporter refers to Hlava's lack of "sophistication" about the news media as well as his limited knowledge of the English
language (he "speaks almost no English") and specific cultural codes (he "did
not realize that he had some of the rarest footage collected"). Indeed, this lack
of understanding of the "significance" of the tape is what makes the story
entertaining, almost comical. Not only had the tape "bounced around in Mr.
Hlava's apartment in Ridgewood," but it had also almost been erased when
Hlava "noticed that his son was playing around with the video camera and
erasing the tape."[20]

How can we characterize the "significance," in the words of the *Times*, of this tape? On the one hand, the paper reports, it was hoped that Hlava's images would help federal investigators who were studying the collapse of the towers: it was an evidentiary image. But it was the economic value of the tape, unrecognized until recently by Hlava, that defined its significance as a commodity, and it was Hlava's unawareness of this significance that seemed to astonish and amuse the reporter. Eventually, a freelance news photographer, Walter Karling, became aware of the tape and brought it to the *Times*; presumably, it was also he who brought attention to the story. Karling claimed that he was acting as Hlava's "agent," and warned ABC television, which was scheduled to show the tape, not to do so, since the network would be violating copyright.

The point here is not to suggest that these are stories of naivety and cynicism, of innocence and calculation, but rather to observe how images travel only if they are recognized for their ability to do so. Like Zapruder's images, those shot by Naudet and Hlava urge us to pay diligent attention to how and why they are made to appear a certain way. "An image is a sight which has been recreated or reproduced," John Berger wrote in 1972. "It is an appearance, or a set of appearances, which has been detached from the place and time in which it first made its appearance and preserved—for a few moments or a few centuries. . . . Every image embodies a way of seeing."[21] "Harrowing photographs do not inevitably lose their power to shock," Susan Sontag observes in *Regarding the Pain of Others*, "but they are not much help if the task is to understand. Narratives can make us understand. Photographs do something else: they haunt us."[22] Like the photographs Sontag writes about, these pieces of footage are always framed, in the several meanings of the word that this book has explored. Looking at traveling images, then, entails a critical analysis of acts of framing, of different ways of seeing.

As this book has amply demonstrated, the fact that Dealey Plaza was meant to serve as a backdrop for a presidential photo op has profoundly shaped not only the visual record of the assassination, but also the site of death and its ongoing commemoration. Indeed, the World Trade Center site, different as it is from Dealey Plaza, has become the site of a cultural struggle that in several respects echoes the ongoing one in Dallas. Like the assassination, the terror attacks were yet another example of what Hayden White calls a "modernist event," one that seems to resist "inherited categories and conventions for assigning meanings to events."[23] This produces a manifold cultural narrativization that is anything but uniform. Traveling images enter a variety of competing discourses that they both transform and are transformed by. It is worth noting that what Jane C. Desmond describes as the WTC site's "museumification" is ad hoc and loosely organized.[24] It remains to be seen whether the site will produce its own pressure to visualize and what the ramifications will be; there are several indications, however, that the durable images of the event, its iconic pictures, have been recognized as aesthetic images remarkably early—almost instantly. As with the Zapruder film, this status engenders a particular way of remembering that is defined by certain ways of looking at and projecting images.

Indeed, the fact that the WTC site would eventually house or produce some sort of expository space was recognized immediately after the attacks, and the ensuing search for objects for display was defined by how the images of the event that were felt to be most "durable" or "lasting" depicted it. In January 2002, the *New York Times* reported that "with a level of discretion bordering on secrecy, a group of architects, museum experts, city officials and others" were gathering pieces of the World Trade Center that were being "set aside for possible future exhibits," "raw material for museum exhibitions and a memorial that do not yet exist."[25] Within a couple of weeks of the attacks, a committee consisting of three architects and an art consultant had made a list of what to search for in the debris. The fact that an art consultant was involved reflects an important recognition of how fresh images of catastrophe now are valued for their aesthetic properties—even by official institutions. The heavily photographed fragments of the facades of the towers, resembling (as the *Times* and many others observed) a Gothic cathedral, were recognized by the committee as objects that had to be saved. A picture of these ruins figures on the cover of the DVD release of *9/11*. This traveling image thus shaped early attempts to narrativize the event, not only in documentary narratives, but in future acts of commemoration yet unforeseen. It has become one of the emblematic images of the ruinous event.[26]

The 2002 article in the *Times* illustrates how early a cultural struggle came to define the site of destruction. It describes how Mark Wagner, a Manhattan architect and member of the committee, was taking snapshots of possible items for preservation when a group of firefighters interrupted him and said, "This is a grave site. Our brothers are out there." This activity not only provoked on-site controversy but also raised "a host of unfamiliar questions," the *Times* wrote, one of which was: "Among the many people and institutions already asking for, literally, a piece of the trade center, which should have access to the artifacts?"[27] The struggle that has played out between private and public interests, between the news media and various institutions in Dealey Plaza, has also been evident in Manhattan, not least in the ongoing debates about how the entire site is to be reconstructed, what kind of architecture, what kind of poetics of commemoration, and so on.

It seems that the kind of expository discourse that Zapruder's images have traveled into in recent years is gaining prominence. "As art has been redefined during a century of modernism as whatever is destined to be enshrined in some kind of museum," Sontag writes, "so it is now the destiny of many photographic troves to be exhibited and preserved in museum-like institutions": "Among such archives of horror, the photographs of genocide have undergone the greatest institutional development. The point of creating public repositories for these and other relics is to ensure that the crimes they depict will continue to figure in people's consciousness. This is called remembering, but in fact it is a good deal more than that."[28] The way in which Zapruder's images now appear coextensively within museological discourses that no longer distinguish strongly between footage and art is far from unique or controversial. Several gallery exhibitions that began to pop up after the events of September 11 produced modes of display that were motivated by a wish to differ from the existing alternatives, which were mainly created by the mass media. These illustrate how traveling images tend to trouble any initial poetics of exposition by inevitably transforming the modes in which they are displayed.

Two such exhibitions opened in SoHo shortly after the attacks, both with photographs mostly taken in Manhattan on September 11 and in the immediate aftermath: "Here Is New York," organized by Michael Shulan and friends, in Prince Street in late September 2001, and three weeks later in Wooster Street, "The September 11 Photo Project," organized by Michael Feldschuh, a hobby photographer and SoHo resident. Both exhibitions were tremendously successful in every way that they could be: they spontaneously enabled the local community to respond collectively to a recent disaster in a way that was felt to be meaningful, they were seen by thousands of visitors—and reviews were great. Books based on the exhibitions became best sellers, and these distinguished themselves from similar books in significant ways. Instead of relying on emotional narratives and interpretations from pundits or celebrities, they cling to the silence of the gallery—they do not try to distract the spectator or tell her what to think.[29] The introductions to the books are reminiscent of leaflets handed to someone about to enter a gallery room; they are there for one's perusal while watching, if so desired, and strive in their own way to be unobtrusive. The websites seek to extend this sense of a viewer being a visitor; on the *September 11 Photo Project* site, images of gallery walls with pictures enable one to scrutinize single images by clicking on and enlarging them, as if walking up close to a photo in a gallery.

It is significant, however, that both projects eventually turned into something quite different from what they had started as. This reflects, I would argue, the confrontation of any attempt to display images of trauma with inevitable reframing processes that alter the original expression and function of exposition fundamentally. Both New York exhibitions developed into national tours, and in addition, "Here Is New York" went to London, Paris, and Tokyo. By May 2002, the *Here Is New York* website had had 260 million hits.[30] "The September 11 Photo Project" and "Here Is New York" had been transformed into much more than exhibitions. They had developed into ongoing multimedia phenomena for which we have yet scarcely found names or critical concepts—and it all started with a disaster being photographed. When "Here Is New York" arrived at the Corcoran Gallery of Art in Washington, D.C., the organizing idea was not the original organizing idea, the moment was not the original moment, the place was not Manhattan immediately after the attacks, and the public was not New Yorkers. The images have begun to travel across media, to appear nationally and globally, haunting a new dream machine.

Is this important? The introductions to the books express clearly that the original exhibitions depended, to an unusually strong degree, on the gallery sites that were chosen. Both Feldschuh and Shulan stress that all submitted photographs were accepted; the anonymity of all submissions ensured that professionals were not distinguished from amateurs. The exhibitions were to be as inclusive as possible; Shulan explicitly points out that "Here Is New York" was not to be an art exhibition in the conventional sense and that, in fact, the ambition of the organizers was to distinguish their mode of display from that of the dominant media. The integrity of the project, Feldschuh insists, depended on the fact that its pictures belong to an expository discourse that differs from that of galleries or art museums, television or newspapers. However, selections from "Here Is New York" were exhibited at the Museum of Modern Art in Manhattan before they went to the Corcoran or to Paris; reviews in the mainstream media were instrumental in drawing thousands of visitors worldwide.

One can only conclude that in spite of the introductions to the books, the organizers felt that the collection could be removed to different sites—it was judged the appropriate thing to do. The point here is not that I disagree with that decision, but that these considerations are relevant for how visitors experienced the exhibitions differently. A review of "Here Is New York" at the Corcoran, in which 1,200 of the then 7,000 pictures were exhibited, reflects on the museological discourse the pictures now appear in:

> It's not really an art show, though because it's made of pictures, and on view at the Corcoran, the viewer may be tempted to consider it as such. Art thoughts do arise. . . . Art museums are elitist. They openly discriminate. They're supposed to pick and choose, to dodge the meretricious, to show the wheat and shun the chaff. The Corcoran these days takes this duty lightly, but even there the weighty art-museum context (the guards, the fluted columns, the bronze lions at the door) asks us to perceive what makes art good or bad. If you do so here you miss the point. . . . What is vastly more important is the simple act of witnessing, which all these pictures share.[31]

The act of witnessing thus understood is a continual and collective process, amended and extended by the reappearance of previously circulated images and the sudden surfacing of new ones. In the winter of 2010, the Associated Press reported that yet another group of photos from the World Trade Center terror attack had been released.[32] ABC News had obtained the images after it filed a Freedom of Information Act request with the National Institute of Standards and Technology, which investigated the collapse of the towers. Taken from a police helicopter carrying the only photographer allowed in the air space near the towers on the day of the attack, they were described by Jan Seidler Ramirez, the chief curator of the National September 11 Memorial and Museum, as "some of the most exceptional images in the world" of the event.[33] The ongoing narrativization of the terror attacks, it seems, continues to be troubled by a rhetoric of exceptionalism that continues to produce new "defining images."

Even if they differ greatly from pictures taken by both amateurs and professionals in New York on September 11, 2001, Zapruder's images have nevertheless produced chains of visual events that we must analyze in order to address what happens when contemporary catastrophe is photographed, filmed, and, eventually, remembered on a large scale. The images that become "durable"—those that travel—are not merely records of what happened, but are also agents in the sense that they shape cultural and, inevitably, human memory of events. Addressing the shaping of memory in the present moment, then, means analyzing how these images travel, how they are made to appear, how they shape new museological practices and a contemporary poetics of remembrance. "The Zapruder film is impossible to conceive without the mass production and consumption of moving images by non-professionals with access to sophisticated amateur image making technology," writes John Beck.[34] Today, with the radically increased accessibility of portable visual technology, anyone can become tomorrow's "accidental witness" or "accidental iconoclast"; the mobile phone has become the most powerful visual and aural medium by being instantly accessible to a tremendous number of people in the Western world. At present, it is not difficult to imagine how a presidential assassination, caught in a thirty-second clip on a cell phone, would circulate extensively in a matter of minutes and end up defining the cultural memory of the event.

According to Dan Gillmor, these changes imply a significant power shift. Whereas the national news media were able to appropriate the visual record of amateurs such as Zapruder into their own narratives in 1963, they have lost this position, argues Gillmor, who observes the growth of what he calls "grassroots journalism" and "citizen-generated media," a radical democratization in news making.[35] One of Gillmor's examples is a photograph taken during the terrorist bombings in London on July 7, 2005, which instantly began to spread. However, he does not name the photographer, who was Adam Stacey, "by no means a professional photographer," Newsweek reported the day after the bombings, but merely someone "who happened to be on the subway train that was hit in a tunnel outside the Kings Cross tube station."[36] Within hours, the image had appeared in a variety of places, including picturephoning.com, Wikipedia, Sky News, the Associated Press, the BBC, and the Guardian; in reflecting upon this, several commentators echoed Gillmor's observations, first published in 2004. Several incidents over the last few years suggest that "grassroots journalism" has the capacity to shape global conflicts on an unprecedented scale and that traveling images are increasingly troublesome for regimes that seek to control information carefully. When Neda Agha-Soltan was killed in Tehran during the 2009 Iranian election protests and her death was captured on video by bystanders and broadcast on the Internet, it led Krista Mahr to describe the murder as "probably the most widely witnessed death in human history."[37] Agha-Soltan's death was instantly recognized as an icon of protest as the images circulated around the globe.

Whether the extensive production and circulation of amateur photography reflects a democratization of the media is a question that will continue to be raised in the next years. Although wide bandwidth can help an image travel quickly, it cannot ensure that an image will, in fact, travel; there has to be someone who wants to keep looking. As I have shown, the transformation of Zapruder's footage into mythic images was shaped by the ways in which they were concealed and exposed, again and again, in the first decade after the assassination. Indeed, no images travel like those that are not meant to be seen, those we are to turn away from, those we should not have been exposed to in the first place: they are forbidden. The shifting performativity of such conflicted images reflects how it becomes instrumental to address what Miriam Hansen has called "media aesthetics."[38]

In the second chapter, I explored how Ant Farm's video *The Eternal Frame* can be considered what Bruno Latour calls an iconoclash—it reenacts how a public image was transformed by bodily death and how the image of the moment of death became iconic and contributed to a sanctification.[39] Perhaps somewhat unexpectedly, the group's reenactment in Dealey Plaza came to mind when I read about the execution of Saddam Hussein and a number of events that followed it in late 2006 and early 2007. On the first day of the new year, the *New York Times* reported that a new video of the hanging had surfaced, shot by a guard or a witness using a cell-phone camera; no national American television organization had allowed "the moment of the drop" to be shown.[40] It was widely available, however, on the Internet, and a few days later, the same paper informed readers that as a consequence of the circulation of the video of the hanging, Hussein's "public image in the Arab world, formerly that of a convicted dictator," had "undergone a resurgence of admiration and awe."[41] In Morocco and Palestine, demonstrators carried photographs of Hussein through the streets, and in Beirut, activists marched behind a symbolic coffin; in Libya, a statue depicting Hussein on the gallows was to be erected. It was the grainy images of the graphic video that had created this response, according to the *Times*, not least because one could hear the sounds of Shiite militiamen harassing Hussein as he went to his death. The images of the execution, then, produced widespread image production and, by the logic of iconoclasm, empowered the Hussein image.

It is difficult to foresee the effects of any widespread projection of images, but as the journey of Zapruder's images suggest, putting them away, concealing them, is not only not a solution—it is not an option. It is also, as Sontag argues in *Regarding the Pain of Others*, irresponsible. Several important exhibitions in recent years suggest that a gallery might be the place where the implications of both looking and turning away can be addressed and debated.

Indeed, Bruno Latour's concept of iconoclash grew out of such an exhibition, "Iconoclash: Beyond the Image Wars in Science, Religion, and Art," at the ZKM Center for Art and Media in Karlsruhe, Germany, held from May 4 to August 4, 2002. According to Latour, one of the motivating ideas behind the exhibition was to invite visitors to consider the following questions:

> Why have images attracted so much hatred?
> Why do they always return again, no matter how strongly one wants to get rid of them?
> Why have the iconoclasts' hammers always seemed to strike *sideways*, destroying something *else* that seems, after the fact, to matter immensely?
> How is it possible to go *beyond* this cycle of fascination, repulsion, destruction, atonement, that is generated by the forbidden-image worship?[42]

Another institution that explored the expository discourse from within is the Williams College Museum of Art in Williamstown, Massachusetts. In the early months of 2006, the museum housed an exhibition titled "Beautiful Suffering: Photography and the Traffic in Pain."[43] In a book that documents the exhibition, but that differs from the traditional catalogue in its unflinching self-reflection, the curators describe how they ambitiously intended "not only to avoid the dangers of anesthetized viewing and exploitative voyeurism but also to thematize them."[44] A dominant concept for expressing concern about the depiction of suffering, Mark Reinhardt points out in an essay in the book, is that of "aestheticization." Yet, he argues, the concept and the anxieties that underwrite it "ultimately prove to be about the very nature of photographic representation itself."[45] The exhibition, Mieke Bal writes in another essay in the book, was "not didactic" but "philosophical," since it exposed "thoughts without ending, problems without solutions, questions viscerally absorbed and not answered on the spot." As an exhibition, the show was "conceived as an instance of critical visual reflection."[46]

Projection might serve as a powerful critique of strategies of withholding images. Images of trauma inevitably enter a contested terrain and become weapons and tools in image wars, small as well as great. A central insight of *Zaprudered* is that to address these processes critically, we should study not only images, but also how they appear, what words accompany them—and what we do *not* see, hear, or read. With reference to the reluctance of U.S. media to present photographs of individual victims of the Iraq War, Reinhardt observes how "as a response to suffering, the refusal to picture may pose the most basic problems of all."[47] Perhaps the most important aspect of a cultural history of the Zapruder film is that it instructs us to keep in mind the fundamentally shifting quality that is bound to characterize traveling images. The photographs from Abu Ghraib, Reinhardt posits, "intimate the elasticity of photographic meaning, the importance of circulation or display, and the related opportunities of reframing."[48] "Let the atrocious images haunt us," Sontag writes.[49] The journey of Zapruder's images suggests that she is right, but also that we should continue to ask ourselves *how* they haunt us, *who* makes them appear for us, and in *what way*; how they are projected, exposed, confiscated, and quoted—in short, how they travel.

NOTES

INTRODUCTION

1. Steve Blow, "A City in the Spotlight," *Dallas Morning News*, Friday, November 21, 2003.

2. This account is drawn from Trask, *National Nightmare on Six Feet of Film*; Motyl, *Image of an Assassination*; and Wrone, *The Zapruder Film*, a well-researched and meticulously detailed version.

3. Black, *The Reality Effect*, 30.

4. Wrone, *The Zapruder Film*, 35. Wrone gives a detailed account of how Zapruder struggled to get his film processed. He tried to get it done at the offices of the *Dallas Morning News* as well as at the newspaper's television station, WFAA-TV, an ABC affiliate; finally, the film was processed at the Eastman Kodak Processing Laboratory. To get the film duplicated, Zapruder had to visit a laboratory in a different part of town. Of the three copies, two were given to the federal government—to the Secret Service offices in Dallas and in Washington, D.C. The third copy and the original went into the possession of Time Inc.

5. In his immensely influential essay "Das Kunstwerk im Zeitalter seiner technischen Reproduzierbarkeit," Walter Benjamin argues that reproduced artworks suffered a loss of "aura" after the advent of photography. "In photography," Benjamin wrote, "exhibition value begins to drive back cult value on all fronts" ("The Work of Art in the Age of Reproducibility (Third Version)," 257).

6. According to Bolter and Grusin: "Each act of mediation depends on other acts of mediation. Media are continually commenting on, reproducing, and replacing each other, and this process is integral to media"(*Remediation*, 55).

7. Richard Stolley, "Zapruder Rewound," *Life*, September 1998, 43.

8. Both the *Dallas Times Herald* and the *Dallas Morning News* soon approached Zapruder to obtain publication rights; he was offered a major figure by the president of the *Times Herald* over the phone, but insisted that he would hand over the film only to the Secret Service or the FBI, both of which ended up receiving copies the next morning (see Wrone, *The Zapruder Film*, 16–17).

9. *Iconology*, 10. Mitchell describes graphic, optical, perceptual, mental, and verbal images as branches of a family tree.

10. Belting, "Image, Medium, Body," 302, 304. What Mitchell calls "graphic images," Belting refers to as "physical images" (304). The essay is a condensed English-language version of the central arguments of his book *Bild-Anthropologie*, in which the distinction is between *Bild* ("picture"), *Medium*, and *Körper* ("body").

11. Mitchell, *Iconology*, 33.

12. Sontag, *Regarding the Pain of Others*, 86.

13. Sturken, *Tangled Memories*, 3. According to Wulf Kansteiner, the sociologically informed attempts to define collective memory that are heavily informed by the theories of Halbwachs worry historians because of his "determined anti-individualism" ("Finding Meaning in Memory," 181). Cultural memory, on the other hand, "consists of objectified culture, that is, the texts, rites, images, buildings, and monuments which are designed to recall fateful events in the history of the collective" (182). See also Zelizer, "Reading the Past Against the Grain."

14. Antze and Lambek, *Tense Past*.

15. Huyssen, *Twilight Memories*, 2–3.

16. Sturken, *Tangled Memories*, 3; Bal, Crewe, and Spitzer, *Acts of Memory*, vii.

17. Mayhew, *World's Tribute to John F. Kennedy in Medallic Art*, xv.

18. Mitchell, *What Do Pictures Want?* 318.

19. Sturken, *Tangled Memories*, 29.

20. Hirsch, *Family Frames*, 22.

21. Sturken observes how several Vietnam veterans say they forget where their memories come from and confuse whether the source of their memory is their own experiences or photographs or movies (*Tangled Memories*, 20).

22. Sturken, *Tangled Memories*, 33. Indeed, my own first encounter with the images occurred in a movie theater in Norway, where I saw *JFK* the year that I was twenty, in 1992.

23. Lubin, *Shooting Kennedy*, 4. The imagery in the extensive photographic record of Kennedy is so resonant because it echoes canonized images from the history of art, Lubin argues in his book. Thus, pictures of Kennedy are not famous "because they show famous events," but because they "look like or call to mind or somehow otherwise invoke and engage a wide range of previous pictures (and

literatures and historical actors and events) that have already staked a claim on the cultural imagination" (xi).

24. Black, *Reality Effect*, 1. Tom Mullin pronounces Zapruder "the most influential filmmaker" of the last half of the twentieth century, since his film "established a new code of reality for the representation of death" ("Livin' and Dyin' in Zapruderville," 12).

25. Bruzzi, *New Documentary*, 26.

26. Chanan, *The Politics of Documentary*, 49.

27. Fletcher, *Allegory*, 2.

28. Austin, *How To Do Things with Words*.

29. Simon, *Dangerous Knowledge*, 31, 46. Simon's book-length study of the assassination in art and film is informed by its focus on how this lack of stability has produced "both a faith and a crisis in representation" (31).

30. The film, David Lubin points out, "divulges so many 'objective' truths, so many 'indisputable' proofs, so many 'authoritative' interpretations of who fired the bullets and from where that anyone who is not a die-hard believer of one particular theory or another faces an array of conclusions so bewildering that choosing among them seems all but impossible" (*Shooting Kennedy*, 172–173). "The existence of the film opened the door to scientific inquiry, but the sequence clearly has defied such analysis," Sturken writes. "The image withholds its truth, clouds its evidence, and tells us, finally, nothing. Science cannot fix the meaning of the Zapruder film precisely because the narrative of national and emotional loss outweighs empirical investigation. We cannot have, perhaps ultimately do not want to have, a definitive answer to why and how it happened—the answer is potentially overwhelming. Hence, fantasies about what happened are as important in national meaning as any residue of the 'truth'" (*Tangled Memories*, 29).

31. Michelangelo Antonioni's *Blow-Up* (1966) is widely believed to have been inspired by the epistemological frustration this ongoing scrutiny entailed (see Lubin, *Shooting Kennedy*, 26–28).

32. Lubin, *Shooting Kennedy*, 182.

33. Beck, "Zapruder, Warhol, and the Accident of Images," 189.

34. Barthes, *Camera Lucida*, 79.

35. Gingeras, "The Mnemonic Function of the Painted Image."

36. Beck, "Zapruder, Warhol, and Images," 188. "The transformation of art practice—and art theory—since Pop, along with the way this transformation has been absorbed into the broad visual culture of the United States, has made it possible to conceive of something like the Zapruder film as a kind of *objet trouvé* that can be read, to all intents and purposes, as art," Beck points out (184).

37. Lyotard, *The Postmodern Condition*, xxiv.

38. The assassination was unique, Jameson claims in *Postmodernism*, not least because Kennedy's "posthumous public meaning" could best be grasped "as the projection of a new collective experience of reception," one that represented "the

coming of age of the whole media culture that had been set in place in the late 1940s and the 1950s" (355).

39. Carmichael, "Lee Harvey Oswald and the Postmodern Subject," 207.

40. Hayden White, *Figural Realism*, 66.

41. Ibid., 70. According to White, "Any attempt to provide an objective account of the event [the assassination], either by breaking it up into a mass of its details or by setting it within its context, must conjure with two circumstances: one is that the number of details identifiable in any singular event is potentially infinite; and the other is that the context of any singular event is infinitely extensive, or at least is not objectively determinable" (70–71). There is only one book that can be called a historical narrative of the assassination: Kurtz, *Crime of the Century*.

42. Ballard, *A User's Guide to the Millennium*, 277; DeLillo, *Libra*, 181. A week after the assassination, President Lyndon Johnson established the President's Commission on the Assassination of President Kennedy, chaired by Chief Justice Earl Warren; a year later, it concluded that Lee Harvey Oswald had acted alone. Consisting of twenty-six volumes and more than ten million words, the report remains controversial.

43. Mitchell, *Picture Theory*, 11–34. The term intentionally echoes Richard Rorty's description in *Philosophy and the Mirror of Nature* of a final stage of the history of philosophy marked by a "linguistic turn." Gottfried Boehm has described what he observes to be an "iconic turn," in "Die Wiederkehr der Bilder." For a discussion of these terms, see the interview with Mitchell by Asbjørn Grønstad and Øyvind Vågnes.

44. Mitchell, *Picture Theory*, 16.

45. Mitchell, "Interdisciplinarity and Visual Culture," 542.

46. Lubin, *Shooting Kennedy*, 14.

47. In this, I follow Mitchell's distinction: "You can hang a picture, but you cannot hang an image," he writes. "The image seems to float without any visible means of support, a phantasmatic, virtual, or spectral appearance. It is what can be lifted off the picture, transferred to another medium" (*What Do Pictures Want?* 85).

48. Thus, I think of various and very diverse visual phenomena in the history of pictorial representation as traveling images. They can be found in precivilizational figures and statues, in religious iconography (as in the crucifix), or in art (as in paintings such as Edvard Munch's *Scream* [1893] or Grant Wood's *American Gothic* [1930], to pick a couple of relatively recent versions). Far from even being a sketch of a genealogy of such images—such a thing seems to me impossible— the point of this willfully short and hasty list is thus to suggest that images that travel are not an exclusively "modern" or "postmodern" phenomenon.

49. Bal, "Interdisciplinary Approaches to Narrative," 250.

50. Ginzburg, "Vetoes and Compatibilities," 534; Mitchell, "Interdisciplinarity and Visual Culture," 540.

51. Ginzburg, "Vetoes and Compatibilities," 534.

52. Bal, *Travelling Concepts in the Humanities*, 5.

53. Bal, *Travelling Concepts*, 3–5. Toward the end of "Philosophy and Literature," Culler concludes that "rather than try to restrict or simplify the performative's domain by choosing one strand of reflection as the correct one, we ought to accentuate and to pursue the differences between them—so as to increase our chances of grasping the different levels and modes in which events occur" (518).

54. Bal, *Travelling Concepts*, 51, 11. In describing this processual aspect of concepts, Bal is inspired not only by Austin, but also by Deleuze and Guattari's *What Is Philosophy?* Philosophy, they write, "is the discipline that involves *creating* concepts" (5), and every concept "is a multiplicity," "at least double or triple, etc." (15), a "fragmentary whole" (16).

55. Said, "Traveling Theory," 195.

56. Bal, *A Mieke Bal Reader*, xxii.

57. Ibid., xxii–xxiii.

58. Simon, *Dangerous Knowledge*, 221, 219, 32.

59. Ibid., 32–33.

60. Bal, *Double Exposures*, 3.

61. "The gesture of exposing," Bal insists, "involves the authority of the person who knows" (*Double Exposures*, 2).

62. Zelizer, *Covering the Body*, 201.

63. Lubin, *Shooting Kennedy*, xi.

64. Mitchell, *Picture Theory*, 35.

65. Hutcheon, *A Poetics of Postmodernism*, 8.

66. Simon, *Dangerous Knowledge*, 1.

67. See Burke, *Eyewitnessing*, for a broad array of examples in several forms of pictorial representation.

CHAPTER ONE

1. This account is based on a transcript of the broadcast in Trask, *National Nightmare*, 138.

2. Bal, *Double Exposures*, 2, 3.

3. According to Paul B. Sheatley and Jacob J. Feldman, the event seemed to represent "a golden opportunity . . . to collect a body of data with both immediate and long-term significance" (*The Assassination of President Kennedy*, 2). When social scientists called a meeting, the National Opinion Research Center (NORC) at the University of Chicago responded, and it was held in Washington two days after the assassination. The director of NORC left with a preliminary draft of a questionnaire. Of the 1,384 nationwide interviews, 97 percent were undertaken by November 30 (4). The results showed that practically everyone interviewed had

heard about the assassination less than four hours after it happened. The way the media shaped public response to the event was thus recognized as significant by researchers immediately after the assassination and in the next few years, and a wealth of studies have followed. For example, Ruth Leeds Love's "Television and the Death of a President," a doctoral dissertation from 1970, presents an analysis of interviews with persons from, among other institutions, ABC, NBC, the Associated Press, and United Press International. Both it and the NORC report reflect an early interest in the assassination as a form of "cultural memory" and in the construction of such a memory.

4. About half of those interviewed by NORC received the news from radio or television, the other half through phone calls or "personal messages"; only 4 percent first learned about the event from newspapers or other unspecified sources (Sheatley and Feldman, *Assassination of Kennedy*, 6). NORC estimated that the average adult spent between eight and ten hours on the day of the assassination and each of the next three days following the coverage (12).

5. The Kennedy assassination, Arthur Neal argues, is a "national trauma" (*National Trauma and Collective Memory*, 111).

6. Bal, *Double Exposures*, 2.

7. Ibid., 8.

8. Sontag, *Regarding the Pain of Others*, 69.

9. Mitchell, "The Unspeakable and the Unimaginable," 292.

10. Mitchell, "Unspeakable and Unimaginable," 293, 294; the reference is to Wittgenstein's *Tractatus Logico-Philosophicus*.

11. Leys, *Trauma*, 9.

12. Bal, *Narratology*, 147.

13. The NORC report gives a clear indication of the tremendous impact the event had on individuals as well as the public: the majority of respondents "could not recall any other time in their lives when they had the same sort of feelings" as when they heard of Kennedy's death; of those who could, the majority referred to "the death of a parent, close friend or other relative" (Sheatley and Feldman, *Assassination of Kennedy*, 8).

14. Rather, *The Camera Never Blinks*, 123.

15. According to Rather: "There is something that kicks over inside you—like the omni on an airplane where you switch on the remote control—on a certain kind of story that causes the adrenalin [sic] to pump so strong you are acting almost purely by instinct, by training" (*Camera Never Blinks*, 121).

16. Mitchell, "Unspeakable and Unimaginable," 295.

17. Schudson, *The Power of News*, 14, 54.

18. Rather, *Camera Never Blinks*, 111.

19. Schudson, *Power of News*, 109, 103.

20. In fact, Rather was not assigned to cover the presidential visit to Dallas, but as a local correspondent with CBS News, he returned from another job just in time

to be lingering in the area around Dealey Plaza when the motorcade arrived. In *The Camera Never Blinks: Adventures of a TV Journalist*, he describes how he called Parkland Hospital, where Kennedy had been taken, and tried to get people there to say more than they should. This investigative approach turned out to be very successful, since it made it possible for him to learn, before any official statement was issued, that the president had been declared dead (*Camera Never Blinks*, 116). The reporting from Dallas that ensued has remained a matter of controversy over the years. Rather recalls in his memoir how he was "plugged into three or four lines at once," talking both to a local reporter, Eddie Barker, and to the CBS station in New York City; in the confusion that arose, it was hard to know who said or heard what (118). To Rather, the story illustrates the "imperfection of the telephone as an instrument of communication" (121). He has continued to accept that the report is described as his first journalistic triumph, in spite of the fact that it has been established that it was Barker, not Rather, who first delivered the unconfirmed report to Cronkite; see Zelizer, *Covering the Body*, 41.

21. Rather, *Camera Never Blinks*, 125.
22. Zelizer, *Covering the Body*, 41.
23. Ibid., 68.
24. For an important ethnographic reading of Dealey Plaza and the twenty-fifth anniversary of the assassination there, see Trujillo, "Interpreting November 22." It should be mentioned that the Kennedy family repeatedly has called for national commemorations to be held on Kennedy's birthday rather than on the date of his death (Zelizer, *Covering the Body*, 103).
25. A year after his return to Dealey Plaza for the fortieth anniversary, on September 20, 2004, Rather issued a statement in which he admitted that he had lost confidence in the authenticity of the documents he had used to support a *60 Minutes Wednesday* story about George W. Bush's time in the Texas Air National Guard. "It was an error that was made," he wrote in the statement, "in good faith and in the spirit of trying to carry on a CBS News tradition of investigative reporting without fear or favoritism." When he quit the next spring, after twenty-four years with CBS, several narratives of his life and career appeared online on CBSnews.com, and these continued to describe his reporting from Dallas as his breakthrough.
26. Schudson, *Power of News*, 71.
27. Zelizer, *Covering the Body*, 35.
28. Schudson, *Power of News*, 108.
29. Wrone, *Zapruder Film*, 32; Rather, *Camera Never Blinks*, 124.
30. See Wagner, introduction, 14. Wagner gives a good overview of what he calls "ekphrastic studies."
31. Grant F. Scott observes that "everywhere in ekphrastic studies we encounter the language of subterfuge, of conspiracy; there is something taboo about moving

across media, even as there is something profoundly liberating" (*The Sculpted Word*, xiii).

32. Ruth Webb suggests that the predominant focus on poetry is partly accidental and that the delimitation of the ekphrastic object as an artwork is a modern phenomenon ("*Ekphrasis* Ancient and Modern," 7). In fact, as Webb demonstrates, ekphrasis was originally not conceived as a form of writing dedicated to art objects—in fact, it was not even "restricted to objects" (13).

33. Bal, *Quoting Caravaggio*, 118. In a much-quoted definition, James Heffernan refers to ekphrasis as "a verbal representation of a visual representation" (*Museum of Words*, 3). Mitchell suggests that "the effort to translate any visual experience into words, whether it involves art works or images or not, is involved in the problematic of ekphrasis" (interview by Grønstad and Vågnes).

34. Mitchell, *Picture Theory*, 158.

35. This is Trask's observation (*National Nightmare*, 144).

36. Quoted in ibid., 139.

37. That several conspiracy theorists eventually would come to suggest that the reporter was involved in a setup and that his misdescription of what happened was deliberate—an insinuation that Rather himself addresses in his memoir (*Camera Never Blinks*, 125)—is clearly an example of the level of paranoia the assassination has inspired.

38. Quoted in Trask, *National Nightmare*, 140.

39. Baym, "Packaging Reality," 284.

40. Zelizer, *Covering the Body*, 35.

41. Trask, *National Nightmare*, 142–144.

42. Feuer, "The Concept of Live Television," 13, 14. In his book on what he calls "liveness," Philip Auslander describes how, in the early years of television, its "intimacy was seen as a function of its immediacy—the close proximity of viewer to event that it enables—and the fact that events from outside are transmitted into the viewer's home" (*Liveness*, 16).

43. Doane, "Information, Crisis, Catastrophe," 229.

44. Barthes, "The Reality Effect," 148. According to Barthes, "the very absence of the signified, to the advantage of the referent alone, becomes the very signifier of realism: the *reality effect* is produced" (148).

45. Rather, *Camera Never Blinks*, 124.

46. Wrone, *The Zapruder Film*, 32.

47. Stolley, "The Zapruder Film," 411.

48. Rather describes his worry that someone would purchase the film before him: "My instructions were, one, to get a preview of the film, and two, bring it back to the station if I could. All sorts of crude ideas rushed through my mind. What if he gave it to NBC? What if he sold it to someone else? . . . For a moment I thought, if I have to, I'll just knock him down and grab the film, run back to the

station, show it one time and then let him sue us. Later someone at the network suggested half jokingly, but only half, that I should have done just that" (Rather, *Camera Never Blinks*, 124).

49. Stolley, "The Zapruder Film," 410.

50. Wrone, *The Zapruder Film*, 33.

51. Ibid., 36. Wrone's book describes the terms of the contract in detail; Zapruder donated the first $25,000 to the widow of a police officer, J. D. Tippit, who had been killed by Oswald after trying to stop him.

52. Wrone, *The Zapruder Film*, 51–66.

53. Lubin, *Shooting Kennedy*, 168.

54. In particular, the fact that some of the frames from the original film are missing and that others were treated carelessly has brought Time Inc. much criticism; see Wrone, *The Zapruder Film*, 51–67.

55. Sontag, *Regarding the Pain of Others*, 68.

56. Wrone, *The Zapruder Film*, 284.

57. Kracauer, *The Mass Ornament*, 48.

58. Doss, *Looking at "Life" Magazine*, 1.

59. The only exception was a public projection when the film was subpoenaed by Louisiana district attorney Jim Garrison; see Chapter Four.

60. Mitchell, *Picture Theory*, 89n.

61. Ibid., 91.

62. In his history of Time Inc., Robert T. Elson suggests that the staff of *Life* referred to sets of pictures as "acts" and that the editor therefore "was in some ways more a producer than an editor," an observation that reflects the performativity of these image-texts (*Time Inc.*, 304).

63. Kozol, "Gazing at Race in the Pages of *Life*," 160. Even though Wilson Hicks quit this job in 1950, after holding it for thirteen years, and even though another thirteen years would pass before Zapruder's images found their way into the pages of the magazine, his description in 1952 of what the picture editor does gives an idea of how powerful this role was: "Having determined the story he wishes to tell, the editor selects those pictures which relate themselves most readily and effectively to other pictures in developing the story's theme or advancing its action. . . . In addition to answering the question, 'Does the picture say what it is intended to say?,' the editor asks and answers another question, 'Does it say what I want it to say?'" (*Words and Pictures*, 60).

64. The lasting impact of the founder of *Life* and head of Time Inc. never fails to be mentioned in any narrative about the magazine; his vision of reportage, not entirely unlike Rather's, is that it sees, shows, and tells—there is a distinctive didactic bent to his idea of journalism. Doss describes how *Life*'s birth on November 23, 1936, on the day twenty-seven years before Stolley convinced Zapruder to sell him his film, was preceded by a prospectus in which Luce describes his

ambition "to see life, to see the world; to eyewitness great events . . . to see and to take pleasure in seeing; to see and be amazed; to see and be instructed. Thus to see, and to be shown, is now the will and new expectancy of half mankind" (quoted in Doss, *Looking at "Life" Magazine*, 15).

65. Simon, *Dangerous Knowledge*, 36.
66. Mitchell, *Iconology*, 47.
67. Doss, *Looking at "Life" Magazine*, 15.
68. Kozol, "Gazing at Race," 160.
69. This might have been according to Zapruder's own wish; I have not seen any record of how he regarded his anonymity.
70. Zelizer, *Covering the Body*, 68.
71. Sontag, *Regarding the Pain of Others*, 38.
72. Vials, "The Popular Front in the American Century," 89.
73. Ford, "Piecing Together the Evidence," 51.
74. The fact that "three different combinations of image and text went to press," Art Simon writes, brought "a confusion that required the unorthodox practice of breaking and resetting plates twice" (*Dangerous Knowledge*, 37–38). Simon describes how critics were enraged that individual frames of the film were printed out of sequence (38).
75. Simon, *Dangerous Knowledge*, 43.
76. *Life*, November 25, 1966, 53.
77. Lubin, *Shooting Kennedy*, 182.
78. Vials, "Popular Front," 81.
79. Sontag, *Regarding the Pain of Others*, 21.
80. Sturken, *Tangled Memories*, 89.
81. The broadcast has many of the characteristics of what Hanne Bruun calls "the debate," one of four dramaturgic models she identifies in talk shows ("The Aesthetics of the Television Talk Show," 248).
82. My transcription.
83. I return to this screening in Chapter Four.
84. Trask, *National Nightmare*, 207–208.
85. John O'Connor, "Two Programs Exploit Subjects," *New York Times*, March 27, 1975.
86. Lubin, *Shooting Kennedy*, 167.
87. Simon, *Dangerous Knowledge*, 40.

CHAPTER TWO

1. The film is available commercially only as part of a DVD produced by the Bay Area Video Coalition, *Playback: Preserving Analog Video*, which details the story of a recent restoration of its master tape onto a digital format for preservation.

2. Sturken, *Tangled Memories*, 30.

3. Bolter and Grusin, *Remediation*, 55.

4. Sturken, *Tangled Memories*, 32.

5. Bal, *Quoting Caravaggio*, 8. "Quoting" can thus be seen as traveling from literary theory to cultural analysis, from theories of intertextuality to theories of intermediality. Whereas an intertextual quotation is often referred to as "homo-medial," an intermedial quotation is "heteromedial"—it involves more than one medium (see Wolf, "Intermediality," 252).

6. Hall and Fifer, *Illuminating Video*, 14.

7. Ant Farm, interview by Lewallen, 41.

8. Sorkin, "Sex, Drugs, and Rock and Roll, Cars, Dolphins, and Architecture," 6.

9. Lewallen and Seid, *Ant Farm, 1968–1978*, 3.

10. Bal, *Quoting Caravaggio*, 13. Bal echoes Jacques Derrida's notion of *supplement* in *Of Grammatology*.

11. Mitchell, *Picture Theory*, 35.

12. Gross, *The Dream of the Moving Statue*, 15.

13. Belting, "Image, Medium, Body," 307. Images, Belting writes, "on behalf of the missing body, occupied the place deserted by the person who had died" (307).

14. Bazin, "The Ontology of the Photographic Image," 15. "At the origin of painting and sculpture there lies a mummy complex," Bazin suggests (9). The first Egyptian statue was a mummy, he observes—however, "substitute mummies" were produced "which might replace the bodies if these were destroyed" (9). According to Bazin, this suggests that the very function of statuary is "the preservation of life by a representation of life" (10). In a similar manner, he suggests, photography "embalms time, rescuing it simply from its proper corruption" (14). Moving images, however, are not "content to preserve the object, enshrouded as it were in an instant" (14).

15. Barthes, *Camera Lucida*, 9, 77.

16. McEvilley, "Ask Not What," 68, 71.

17. Kennedy was diagnosed with Addison's disease in 1947; see Perret, *Jack*, 147.

18. Perret, *Jack*, 352, 353. The moment brings to mind Norman Mailer's memorable depiction of Kennedy's arrival at the Democratic National Convention in Los Angeles in the summer of 1960: "The television cameras were out, and a Kennedy band was playing some circus music. One saw him immediately. He had the deep orange-brown suntan of a ski-instructor, and when he smiled at the crowd his teeth were amazingly white and clearly visible at a distance of fifty yards" (*The Presidential Papers*, 37–38).

19. The "Kennedy team" remains a loosely defined group, but at its definitive core were Theodore Sorensen, Kennedy's speechwriter, and press secretary Pierre Salinger.

20. Hellmann, *The Kennedy Obsession*, ix.

21. Mailer's "Superman Comes to the Supermarket," an expression of ambivalent exhilaration, is of particular significance here; it was published by *Esquire* three weeks before the election in 1960.

22. Mailer, "The Leading Man," 169. Victor Lasky's problem, according to Mailer in his review of his book, was that he lacked the capacity to "entertain a poetic concept of his subject" ("Leading Man," 169); he had not fully realized that Kennedy was fundamentally "divided" (165), that his persona had to be understood as metaphor rather than symbol. Whereas the latter is static and "exists eternally, immutably," Mailer insisted, the former is a "relation" and "changes as our experience changes" (169).

23. Baty, *American Monroe*, 10.

24. Hellmann, *The Kennedy Obsession*, x. In the sixties and seventies, "creating one's public self as an almost literary character" became "profoundly important for the change-directed politician," according to Jerome Klinkowitz (*The American 1960s*, 3). Over a relatively brief period of time, the Kennedy team developed a distinct iconography through consistent imaging—but also a new kind of performance—to the degree that Kennedy's life has been referred to by a biographer as "a work of performance art" (Perret, *Jack*, 354).

25. McEvilley, "Ask Not What," 68.

26. The four televised debates in which Kennedy confronted Richard Nixon live on CBS, NBC, and ABC are of particular significance here; all came to be seen as steps toward his victory as well as landmarks in television history. Indeed, that Kennedy defeated Nixon in the 1960 election because of his debate performances has been repeated so frequently that Michael Schudson refers to it as "telemythology" (*Power of News*, 116).

27. In 1960, television sets could be found in 87 percent of all American living rooms; television, as Philip Auslander observes, "was thought to make the home into a kind of theatre characterized, paradoxically, by both absolute intimacy and global reach" (*Liveness*, 16). Kennedy thus appeared on-screen during a transformative period, Mary Ann Watson argues —one in which the major events of American history and the development of American television were "inextricably intertwined" (*The Expanding Vista*, 3).

28. All dialogue from *The Eternal Frame* is my transcription.

29. Watson, *Expanding Vista*, 72.

30. Halberstam, introduction to *The Kennedy Presidential Press Conferences*, ii. "Previous Presidents had used the press conference as a means of reaching and informing and listening to the country all at the same time. Kennedy took it one step further, he used it to build himself up personally. The politician not just as leader, but as star" (ii–iii).

31. Belting, "Towards an Anthropology of the Image," 47.

32. Mellencamp, "Video Politics," 91.

33. Indeed, video defined itself, Marita Sturken suggests, "against and in spite of the overwhelming presence of television" ("Paradox in the Evolution of an Art Form," 102). "Regardless of the intentions (which were heterogeneous) of artists who turned to television technologies, especially the portable equipment introduced into North America in the late 1960's," Martha Rosler writes, "these artists' use of the media necessarily occurred in relation to the parent technology: broadcast television and the structures of celebrity that locked it into place" ("Video," 31).

34. Video art was rooted in the "practices of the counter-culture of the 1960s and 1970s," and "was understood to be a necessary step in the development of a reinvigorated participatory democracy" (Mellencamp, "Video Politics," 79; Hill, "Performing Video," 1).

35. No video history fails to stress the significance of the 1968 debut of the Sony Portapak, a portable, battery-operated video device that was, in the words of Deirdre Boyle, both "widely available, and relatively affordable" (*Subject to Change*, 4).

36. Complete with a guide to using the Portapak as a "tool," Shamberg's *Guerilla Television* functioned as a "meta-manual" with the express aim of contributing to "the decentralization of the means of production as well as those of distribution" (32). Shamberg had quit a job at *Life* magazine because he felt constrained by a "form of writing where individual authorship is less important than a 'house voice'" (Joselit, "An Allegory of Criticism," 5). Shamberg and Ant Farm worked together as TVTV on a documentary, *Four More Years* (1972), about the Democratic and Republican National Conventions in 1972. For a history of guerilla television, see Boyle, *Subject to Change* (which contains a chapter on *Four More Years*).

37. According to Shamberg, network television is a "squandering" of a "primary information resource," but "not so much because of what broadcast does, but because of how it is done" (*Guerilla Television*, 35).

38. Nichols, *Introduction to Documentary*, 118. *Primary* was shot by D. A. Pennebaker, Albert Maysles, Terence Macartney-Filgate, and Richard Leacock. An uninterrupted shot that follows Kennedy from outside a building and into it, down a long corridor, up a flight of stairs, and out onto a stage, ending with a shot of the enthusiastic audience, is well known; it was shot by Maysles. Incidentally, Drew was also employed by *Life* for years, as a news reporter and photo editor, and his approach in making *Primary* was in part informed by this experience, according to P. J. O'Connell (*Robert Drew and the Development of Cinema Verite in America*, 62–66).

39. Ant Farm was not first in addressing Zapruder's images in such a manner; John Waters's *Eat Your Makeup* (1968) includes a Baltimore reenactment in which Divine plays the role of Jackie Kennedy. The film was not released commercially and has been screened only rarely; see Leighton and Büchler, *Saving the Image*, for stills and an interview with Waters about the film.

40. Sontag, "Notes on 'Camp,'" 275, 280.
41. Belting, "Anthropology of the Image," 47.
42. Butler, *Excitable Speech*, 152, 160.
43. McEvilley, "Ask Not What," 72.
44. Miller, "On Politics and the Art of Acting."
45. Troy, "JFK: Celebrity-in-Chief or Commander-in-Chief?" 636.
46. Schechner, "Six Axioms for Environmental Theatre." Ant Farm knew Schechner's writings (Ant Farm, interview by Lewallen, 46).
47. Benjamin, "What Is the Epic Theater? (II)," 305.
48. Television "has transcended its identity as a particular medium and is suffused through the culture as 'the televisual,'" according to Auslander (*Liveness*, 2). "Televisual space," Anne Friedberg and Raiford Guins suggest, "is both the space of the televisual and the changes produced by the televisual to space itself" ("Televisual Space," 131).
49. Mellencamp, "Video Politics," 88.
50. Marin, *Portrait of the King*, 7.
51. Lasch, "The Life of Kennedy's Death."
52. Neal, *National Trauma*, 120. Indeed, the processes that brought about an "elevation" of the Kennedy image began immediately after his death. A brief essay by Theodore White, "An Epilogue," in the December 6, 1963, issue of *Life*, is particularly significant in that it was the first to give expression to Jackie Kennedy's evocation of the Camelot myth. White was summoned for an exclusive interview, and it was during their conversation that Jackie Kennedy suggested that Kennedy's vision of the New Frontier was that of an incarnation of the kingdom of Camelot (Hoffmann, *Theodore H. White and Journalism as Illusion*, 145–175). "For one brief shining moment there was Camelot": thus White concludes his essay, which is written in the present tense, and describes Jackie Kennedy's loss of her husband in a third-person-singular narrative that never mentions her name: she is merely referred to as "she." Several articles and books by Arthur Schlesinger, Jr. (including his much-cited eulogy in the *Saturday Evening Post*, December 14, 1963), William Manchester, and Theodore Sorensen also try, in the words of Hellmann, to "transcend the apparent meaninglessness" of the assassination (Hellmann, *Kennedy Obsession*, 146); see Manchester's *The Death of a President* and Sorensen's *The Kennedy Legacy*.
53. Neal, *National Trauma*, 118. "Following his death, the images and memories of Kennedy became selective and more vivid as they took on sacred qualities," Neal observes; "criticism of the man and his tenure of office was no longer socially acceptable" (117).
54. Sturken, "Reenactment, Fantasy, and the Paranoia of History," 72.
55. Hellmann, *Kennedy Obsession*, 146.
56. Baty, *American Monroe*, 3–4.

57. Latour, "What Is Iconoclash?" 14.

58. Mitchell, *What Do Pictures Want?* 18.

59. Belting, "Image, Medium, Body," 308.

60. Taussig, *Defacement*, 1.

61. Mellencamp, "Video Politics," 91.

62. Edwards, "Echoes of Camelot," 180. Edwards presents an analysis of how the photograph of John F. Kennedy Jr.'s saluting his father's coffin during the funeral on November 25, 1963, figured in the media coverage of Kennedy Jr.'s death in 1999.

63. Koerner, "The Icon as Iconoclash," 190.

64. Taussig, *Defacement*, 1.

65. Mitchell, *What Do Pictures Want?* 21.

66. McEvilley, "Ask Not What," 68, 71.

67. Bal, *Quoting Caravaggio*, 6.

68. "The true image of the past flits by," Benjamin writes in the fifth of his eighteen theses on the "philosophy of history": "The past can be seized only as an image that flashes up at the moment of its recognizability, and is never seen again" ("On the Concept of History," 390). "The image Benjamin writes about in 'Theses on the Philosophy of History' is an instant image, conjured up in a flash," Sturken writes. "It is the image of history arrested, a moment of historical rupture when everything stops and is irrevocably altered" (*Tangled Memories*, 23).

69. In writing about the idea of eternal return in Benjamin's theses, Eduardo Cadava suggests that "eternal repetition does not mean 'the return of the same' but rather the return of what is never simply itself. What returns is the movement through which something or other is inscribed within the same, which, now no longer the same, names what is always other than itself" (*Words of Light*, 31).

70. According to Benjamin, "In the field of allegorical intuition the image is a fragment, a rune" (*The Origin of German Tragic Drama*, 176). "Allegories are, in the realm of thoughts, what ruins are in the realm of things" (178).

71. "The Allegorical Impulse," a two-part essay, was originally printed in *October* (nos. 12 [1979] and 13 [1980]); my references are to its publication in *Beyond Recognition*, a collection of his writings. Allegory, Owens claimed, is characterized by "its capacity to rescue from historical oblivion that which threatens to disappear"; it operates "in the gap between a present and a past which, without allegorical reinterpretation, might have remained foreclosed" (54).

72. Benjamin, "Karl Kraus," 455; According to Owens, "Allegorical imagery is appropriated imagery; the allegorist does not invent images but confiscates them. He lays claim to the culturally significant, poses as its interpreter. And in his hands the image becomes something other (*allos* = other + *agoreuei* = to speak) . . . The allegorical meaning supplants an antecedent one; it is a supplement" ("The Allegorical Impulse," 54)

73. Mellencamp, "Video Politics," 87. Mellencamp is wrong when she writes that the Zapruder film had been "endlessly rerun on television and scrutinized for clues" after the assassination (*High Anxiety*, 96), and seems unaware of the fact that the film had just been broadcast on television for the first time when *The Eternal Frame* was made. The fact that the images were fresh to a television audience when Ant Farm visited Dealey Plaza is significant. The video comments on an endless rerun of the images that is in the process of beginning.

74. The year after the Nixon-Kennedy debates, Boorstin worried that the advent of what he called the "pseudo-event," the product of a creative transition from "news gathering" to "news making," would involve a new kind of staging in the news world. Pseudo-events promoted celebrity, according to Boorstin, and the Nixon-Kennedy debates became symbolic in this respect, since they represented a "clinical example" of the pseudo-event. Public interest centered on the event itself: "Far more interest was shown in the performance than in what was said" (*The Image*, 41).

75. Lewallen, quoted in Ant Farm's interview with her, 76.

76. Ant Farm's "stance toward mass or popular culture, like their response to technology, was in fact ambivalent"; "they used it while condemning it. . . . While Baudrillard awaits the apocalypse . . . a celebratory Ant Farm critiques catastrophe" (Mellencamp, "Video Politics," 87, 88). According to Mellencamp, "Ant Farm's policy was to record real or imaginary events, disregarding distinctions between them . . . [but they] did not need Baudrillard to tell them that TV confused the real with the imaginary and conflated reality and fiction as simulation" (86–87). Ant Farm members were not familiar with Baudrillard's writings, which had not yet been published in English when *The Eternal Frame* was made.

77. Mitchell, interview by Grønstad and Vågnes.

78. Larsen, "Junky and Important," 223.

79. Sturken, "Evolution of an Art Form," 113.

80. Boyle and Media Alliance, *Video Preservation*, 3, 13. In partnership with the Electronic Media and Film Program (part of the New York State Council on the Arts), Media Alliance, a nonprofit organization that works to develop the media arts, convened a symposium at the Museum of Modern Art in New York on June 14, 1991, where video preservation was discussed. *Video Preservation* is Boyle's report from the symposium.

81. Gamboni, "Preservation and Destruction, Oblivion and Memory," 164–165.

82. As Gamboni notes, however, and as David Carrier observes, "that an object is preserved does not show that the work of art survives" (*Museum Skepticism*, 7).

83. It was in the nineties, British video artist Catherine Elwes observes, that video art "broke through into the mainstream of the museum and gallery system, taking up a central position as the twentieth century came to a close"; contemporary video now thrives, having moved from "a marginal practice" to "the default

medium of twenty-first-century gallery art" (*Video Art*, 2, 191). Over the last few decades, video art has contributed to a major development within the art world, Shirin Neshat observes, since "artists are finally relieved of the task of making 'objects,' and can now conceive their ideas in a way that becomes 'experiential'" (foreword to Elwes, *Video Art*, ix).

84. Owens, "From Work to Frame," 126, 135.

85. A photograph of *Now* figured on the cover of the *Paris Review*'s first issue of 2005. A brief online text posted by the Carnegie suggested that Cattelan was "iconoclastic in his choice of weapons": "*Now*, according to the artist, is a commentary on the state of American politics today, a moment in which the United States lacks precisely the kind of internationally popular figurehead that President John F. Kennedy represented. But like all of Cattelan's best work, *Now* transcends its most obvious reading to touch on more universal concerns. Depicting a contemporary martyr, the work questions the existence of redemption in this and other sacrifices made over the past 50 years. Meant to inspire nostalgia, perhaps even anger, *Now* implicitly evokes a longing for a time vastly different from the present" (http://www.cmoa.org/international/the_exhibition/artist .asp?cattelan).

86. Lasch, "Life of Kennedy's Death," 32.

87. Gross, *Dream of the Moving Statue*, 71.

88. Freedberg, *The Power of Images*, 224. The wax figure embodied the dead so well because it allowed the artist to "achieve the closest possible approximation of real flesh," Freedberg points out: "When real hair was added to the wax image, the illusion of tangible fleshly reality could still further be enhanced" (224).

CHAPTER THREE

1. DeLillo, *Underworld*, 487.

2. DeLillo, "'An Outsider in This Society,'" 56; see also DeLillo, "American Blood: A Journey through the Labyrinth of Dallas and JFK."

3. N. H. Reeve, "Oswald our Contemporary," 149.

4. See LeClair, *In the Loop*, and Keesey, *Don DeLillo*.

5. DeLillo, "The American Strangeness."

6. Hamon, *Expositions*, 103.

7. Among the crime novels are Stephen Frey's *The Legacy*, which tells the story of how a bond trader, Cole Egan, inherits from his father a key to a safe-deposit box that contains a tape that turns out to resemble but not be identical with the Zapruder film. In Doug Swanson's humorous *Umbrella Man*, private investigator Jack Flippo finds a black-and-white film supposedly of the assassination, hitherto undiscovered, only to see it thrown into the fireplace by an owner who would rather see it destroyed than give it away

8. Vollmann, *Thirteen Stories and Thirteen Epitaphs*, 265.

9. Ballard, interview by Douglas Reed, 154.

10. David Pringle, "The Fourfold Symbolism of J. G. Ballard," 132.

11. Ballard, *Atrocity Exhibition*, 34. This edition contains extensive commentary by Ballard as well as illustrations by Phoebe Gloeckner.

12. Ibid., 108–109; Acker, "Weaver of Dreams from the Stuff of Nightmares," 140.

13. Ballard, *Atrocity Exhibition*, 89.

14. DeLillo, *Underworld*, 495, 496.

15. DeLillo, *Libra*, 181, 441.

16. DeLillo, *Underworld*, 495.

17. Maltby, "The Romantic Metaphysics of Don DeLillo," 258. "To postmodernize DeLillo is to risk losing sight of the (conspicuously unpostmodern) metaphysical impulse that animates his work," according to Maltby (260).

18. Begley, "The Art of Fiction CXXXV: Don DeLillo," 103–104.

19. DeLillo, *Underworld*, 488.

20. Mitchell, "Unspeakable and Unimaginable," 293; DeLillo, *Underworld*, 496.

21. DeLillo, *Underworld*, 487, 488–489.

22. For a discussion of the event as "object," see Bal, "Visual Essentialism and the Object of Visual Culture."

23. Nel, "'A Small Incisive Shock,'" 725, 727.

24. Osteen, *American Magic and Dread*. Both Nel's and Osteen's close readings of the descriptions of the projection of Eisenstein's film pay little attention to the Zapruder event.

25. Owens, "The Allegorical Impulse," 53.

26. DeLillo, *Underworld*, 495.

27. Lavender, "The Moment of Realized Actuality," 187.

28. DeLillo, *Underworld*, 495.

29. Thorburn and Jenkins, *Rethinking Media Change*, 10.

30. Owens, "The Allegorical Impulse," 57.

31. Cohen, *Spectacular Allegories*, 17, 10, 18. Cohen argues that Benjamin's theses suggest that a "new relation between past and present can be registered in the form of images. . . . Blasted out of the continuum of time, the image is that which resists narrative resolution and which interrupts its explanatory logic" (14).

32. See DeLillo, "The Power of History," originally published in the *New York Times Magazine* upon the publication of *Underworld*.

33. Owens, "The Allegorical Impulse," 52–53.

34. DeLillo, "The Power of History."

35. DeLillo, *Underworld*, 495.

36. Goodwin and Bronfen, *Death and Representation*, 4.

37. Carmichael, "Oswald and the Postmodern Subject," 207.

38. DeLillo, *Underworld*, 488–489.

39. Owens, "The Allegorical Impulse," 60.

40. DeLillo, "'An Outsider in This Society,'" 56. The *punctum* represents "the pressure of the unspeakable which wants to be spoken in the photograph" (Barthes, *Camera Lucida*, 19); it "bruises" the viewer (27).

CHAPTER FOUR

1. All dialogue from *Seinfeld* in this chapter is my own transcription.
2. Hutcheon, *A Theory of Parody*, 8.
3. O'Brien, "The Republic of *Seinfeld*," 142.
4. Berman, "Sitcoms," 5.
5. O'Brien, "Republic of *Seinfeld*," 145.
6. Marc, "*Seinfeld*," 27. William Irwin explores how *Seinfeld* "does" philosophy, connecting the "show about nothing" to the metaphysics of Nothingness; "everything and nothing are sometimes not so terribly far apart," Irwin argues, suggesting that the show highlights "the commonplace and mundane, drawing our attention to things that would otherwise go unnoticed" (*"Seinfeld" and Philosophy*, xi).
7. This is Marita Sturken's genre description (*Tangled Memories*, 85).
8. McWilliams, "Genre Expectation and Narrative Innovation in *Seinfeld*," 80.
9. Kaplan, "Angry Middle-Aged Man," 69. When "The Boyfriend" aired, the show was well into its third season, and it was at this point that it began to develop episodes with several parallel story lines. Often, as many as five "would intersect in some sort of weirdly organic way" (Larry Charles, quoted in Kaplan, "Angry Middle-Aged Man," 69). According to Irwin Hirsch, *Seinfeld* develops something like a light-hearted nihilism, a form of "humor noir," and provides an "examination of the universality of the dark characteristics that lie within all of us" ("*Seinfeld*'s Humor Noir," 116).
10. O'Brien, "Republic of *Seinfeld*," 145.
11. Indeed, the makers of *Seinfeld* staged a monumental mock closure and an ironic collective mourning ritual when creating a spectacle around their final episode (Morreale, "Sitcoms Say Good-bye").
12. Dunne, *Intertextual Encounters in American Fiction, Film, and Popular Culture*, 125. Such an encounter, Dunne points out, "should be distinguished from the customary rhetorical situation in which texts are considered by artists and audience alike to be mimetic analogs or representations of real-life people, places, and things" (3). Dunne cites Robert Morris, Umberto Eco, and Fredric Jameson and suggests that however different, these critics "recognize the presence of frequent and perhaps ironic intertextual encounters. . . . Nowhere is this assumption more valid than in the more sophisticated comedy available on American television in the 1990s" (160). An ever-widening accumulation of quotations shapes the web of what Dunne calls "the intertextual encyclopedia" (3).
13. Ibid., 3.

14. Cherones explained: "In preparing the scenes for the *JFK* sequence, we watched the film and staged it in a way and a time frame that matched what Mr. Stone had done" ("The Boyfriend").

15. Two-thirds of Oliver Stone and Zachary Sklar's *"JFK": The Book of the Film*, a six-hundred-page "documented screenplay," contain "reactions and commentaries" to the movie and give a good introduction to the controversy surrounding it. See also a special edition of *Cineaste* (vol. 19, no. 1 [1992]), a forum in the *Journal of American History* (vol. 79, no. 3 [1992]), and two special issues of *Film and History* (vol. 28, nos. 1–2 [1998]).

16. Bordwell, *The Way Hollywood Tells It*, 76.

17. Several critics have addressed what has been called the "homophobia" of *JFK* (see in particular Rogin, "Body and Soul Murder: *JFK*").

18. Mitchell, interview by Grønstad and Vågnes.

19. Bordwell, *Hollywood Tells It*, 77.

20. Tim Kaiser, a producer on the show, explains in the bonus material to the DVD release of the episode ("Inside Look") how this quality was achieved: "To get the reality of the scratchy, grainy footage, we made a positive film print and then spooled it out on the ground in the lab. And I literally dragged it up and down the hallway to get dirt on it. . . . [We were] stamping on it and whipping it around and playing catch with it, and cleaned it off and sent it back through the transferrer. We overexposed it, added a lot of chroma, and it worked out beautifully."

21. See, for example, Swanson, *Umbrella Man*, and Marrs, *Crossfire*.

22. Ludwin's comment is quoted from the DVD bonus segment "Inside Look," Alexander's from the audio commentary.

23. With the Stone parody, Seinfeld was afraid that the show had turned into a "cartoon," Louis-Dreyfus explains in the audio commentary: "It didn't resemble the show we'd made up to this point."

24. Dika, *Recycled Culture in Contemporary Art and Film*, 222, 223.

25. Sturken, "Reenactment, Fantasy, and Paranoia," 73.

26. Bordwell, *Hollywood Tells It*, 77, 76.

27. Trask, *National Nightmare*, 289; I return to this point in the next chapter.

28. Hutcheon, *Theory of Parody*, 6.

29. McWilliams, "Genre Expectation," 81.

30. Gunster, "'All About Nothing,'" 210.

31. Harries, *Film Parody*, 7.

32. Benjamin, "What Is the Epic Theater? (II)," 305. For a Benjaminian reading of physical comedy, see McCall, "'The Dynamite of a Tenth of a Second.'"

33. Hutcheon, *Theory of Parody*, 13, 6, 10.

34. Gray, *Watching with the Simpsons*, 12, 13, 55.

35. Quoted in Virginia Heffernan, "Life after *Seinfeld*," *New Yorker*, October 28, 2002, 114.

36. Docker, "*Seinfeld*" (Museum of Broadcast Communications). *Seinfeld*'s antiresolve toward the end of its plots, Docker argues, "recalls a long comic tradition of farce that descends from Elizabethan drama. In the plays and the jigs following, the audience was presented with a contestation of ideals and perspectives. Whatever moral order is realized in the play is placed in tension with its parody in the closing jig."

CHAPTER FIVE

1. Johnson is quoted in Ellen Joan Pollock, "Reel Value: Is It a Home Movie or National Treasure?" *Wall Street Journal*, May 20, 1999.
2. Mitchell, *What Do Pictures Want?* 87.
3. Trask, *National Nightmare*, 207.
4. Ibid., 288. Among the advocates for such a step were fourteen former Warren Commission staff members as well as former presidents Gerald Ford and Richard Nixon.
5. Ibid., 289.
6. Ibid., 291. Because of several delays, in part related to a change of presidential administrations, the Assassination Records Review Board did not terminate its work until September 30, 1998. Concluding that neither Zapruder's original film nor the first-generation copies had been tampered with (although treated at times with carelessness), expert Roland Zavada laid to rest years of rumors as well as theories of manipulation (ibid., 314).
7. Ibid., 315. According to Trask, officials at the Archives declined to return the film to the family on two occasions.
8. Ibid., 316, 317.
9. *Image of an Assassination* was also released on VHS. The video "is far less concerned with Kennedy's assassination than with the history of its signature form of representation . . . If *Image of an Assassination* is any indication it would appear that the historiography of the event has become as significant as the event itself" (Simon, review of *Image of an Assassination*, 84). Simon's review is of the VHS release.
10. Kompare, "Publishing Flow," 337, 346.
11. Ibid., 335.
12. Culler, *Framing the Sign*, ix. Whereas context refers to "something static," Bal suggests, the act of framing produces an "event" (*Travelling Concepts*, 135).
13. "I could not help thinking that the tape . . . belongs in that new video genre—the restored wide-screen director's cut" (Simon, review of *Image of an Assassination*, 84).
14. Mitchell, *What Do Pictures Want?* 320. "In a world where the very idea of the unique original seems a merely nominal or legal fiction, the copy has every chance

of being an improvement or enhancement of whatever counts as the original,"
Mitchell suggests. This involves a conception of the auratic different from that of
Benjamin, he hastens to add: "Of course, this would still constitute a loss of the
aura that Benjamin associated with the accretion of history and tradition around
an object; but if aura means recovering the original vitality, literally, the 'breath'
of life of the original, then the digital copy can come closer to looking and sound-
ing like the original than the original itself" (320).

15. Wrone, *The Zapruder Film*, 61.
16. Trask, *National Nightmare*, 328; Wrone, *The Zapruder Film*, 268.
17. The original release date for *Image of an Assassination* was August 25, 1998
    (Trask, *National Nightmare*, 330). By May 1999, the DVD had sold 130,000 cop-
    ies (Pollock, "Reel Value").
18. Trask, *National Nightmare*, 319.
19. Mitchell, *What Do Pictures Want?* 85.
20. See Wrone, *The Zapruder Film*, 268, 274; Trask, *National Nightmare*, 326. Wrone
    describes what he finds to be an "abysmal federal failure to acquire the essential
    copyright" (274).
21. Trask, *National Nightmare*, 327.
22. Appadurai, *The Social Life of Things*, 3.
23. Mitchell, interview by Grønstad and Vågnes.
24. Ballard, "The Film of Kennedy's Assassination Is the Sistine Chapel of Our Era,"
    25. "It's become part of the everyday iconography of the late twentieth century,"
    Ballard says of the film. "At the time [of his death], Kennedy himself was a cre-
    ation of the mass media. I think that the significance of his tragic death was
    that it was on the cusp of the old print-based newspaper/magazine world and
    the cunning new world of the electronic media, television in particular. . . . Now
    what happened with this imagery is that it was rapidly translated into the world
    of popular publishing. . . . Now it's almost a visual cliché, which itself is a sad
    comment" (25).
25. Quoted in Trask, *National Nightmare*, 325.
26. See Mary Panzer, "What Price History?" and Pollock, "Reel Value."
27. Quoted in George Lardner, Jr., "Haggling Over History; Zapruders, U.S. Far
    Apart on Price of Kennedy Film," *Washington Post*, June 13, 1998.
28. Trask, *National Nightmare*, 329.
29. See Panzer, "What Price History?" Pollock, "Reel Value," and Trask, *National
    Nightmare*.
30. "No one—the attorneys for LMH or for the Justice Department—addressed the
    film as evidence in a crime" (Wrone, *The Zapruder Film*, 274).
31. Panzer, "What Price History?" 69.
32. Kula, *Appraising Moving Images*, 23.
33. The films selected must be at least ten years old and "culturally, historically, or

aesthetically significant" (quoted from the web pages of the Library of Congress, www.loc.gov). Nominations are made by the public.

34. Kula, *Appraising Moving Images*, 95.

35. C.M.M. Associates. *Zapruder Film Appraisal*, 68, 74.

36. Mitchell, *What Do Pictures Want?* 76.

37. Lubin, *Shooting Kennedy*, 15.

38. Quoted in Pollock, "Reel Value."

39. Lubin, *Shooting Kennedy*, 168.

40. Bennett is quoted in Panzer, "What Price History?" 69.

41. Ibid.

42. Strauss, *Between the Eyes*, 51.

43. Sontag, *Regarding the Pain of Others*, 97. Bataille "is saying that he can imagine extreme suffering as something more than just suffering, as a kind of transfiguration," Sontag posits, "a view of suffering, of the pain of others, that is rooted in religious thinking" (99).

44. "If major works of cinematic art combine beauty, tragedy, happiness, and horror so as to move and instruct spectators and show them dimensions of reality they have not previously seen or understood," Lubin observes, "then the Zapruder film may qualify as such a work" (*Shooting Kennedy*, 15). "The crux of [the] dispute," Beck writes, "is not that the Zapruder film is art but that it should ever have been considered as art" ("Zapruder, Warhol, and Images," 188). One of the implications of this is a paradoxical, circular logic: the film is unique because it is described as such, and is described as such because it is unique. John Berger observed this logic in addressing how the artwork is "enveloped in an atmosphere of entirely bogus religiosity": "Works of art are discussed and presented as though they were holy relics: relics which are first and foremost evidence of their own survival" (*Ways of Seeing*, 21).

45. Kula, *Appraising Moving Images*, 102. In fact, Kula uses these hearings as a starting point for a discussion of "appraisal methodology." As Robert Vianello observes in a review of Kula's book, it demonstrates how "financial incentive and preservation are inextricably bound" (140).

46. Pollock, "Reel Value"; Panzer, "What Price History?" 69.

47. Kula, *Appraising Moving Images*, 95.

48. Quoted in Pollock, "Reel Value." In a comparative analysis of Zapruder frame 182 and Stieglitz's *The Steerage*, Wolf suggested that this single frame has "far more dramatic and emotive power" than the photograph.

49. Kula, *Appraising Moving Images*, 25.

50. Panzer, "What Price History?" 71.

51. Ibid., 67, 69. The film, Panzer observes, "must be stored in a vault at zero degrees Fahrenheit and 30 percent humidity—conditions that would freeze your ice cream hard as rock" (69). In fact, the government's lawyers passed around "a

reel of ordinary movie film that was the size and length of the one in question," Panzer points out, to illustrate that the film could not be exhibited in any normal sense (69).

52. Quoted in Pollock, "Reel Value."

CHAPTER SIX

1. See Phelan, *Unmarked*, and Auslander, *Liveness*.
2. Hellmann, *The Kennedy Obsession*, x.
3. Hoberman, "Jump Cuts."
4. See Kelly Vance, "Burning Sensation," *East Bay Express*, March 17, 2004. Vance's text is a preview for a screening in April 2004 at the Berkeley Art Museum of *The Eternal Frame*, *Death in Dallas*, and several other works quoting the Zapruder film. It was arranged by Steve Seid to coincide with the "Ant Farm, 1968–1978" exhibition and introduced by Marita Sturken.
5. Gary Shteyngart, "The Whole World Is Watching," *New York Times*, July 13, 2003.
6. Becker, "Heading for Collisions."
7. Shteyngart, "Whole World," 26.
8. Heartney, "America, Real and Imagined."
9. Chanan, *Repeated Takes*, 137.
10. "Found audio" is Bill Horrigan's description ("Zoran Naskovski: *Death in Dallas*").
11. Ibid.
12. Quoted from the museum's own presentation (my translation from the German original).
13. Osborn, "*Death in Dallas*."
14. Vincent, "Resisting the 'American Effect.'"
15. Kim Levin, "A Foreign Affair," *Village Voice*, August 5, 2003.
16. Desmond, "'As Others See Us?'" 1051.
17. Rinder, "The American Effect," 21.
18. Shteyngart, "Whole World," 26. "America is rendered in the eyes of its beholders as both the last utopia and the root cause of the world's economic, social and military disasters. . . . Because of our global reach, these artists already live in a kind of ersatz America, consuming our disposable products, debating our government's policies while their homelands are often host to our hyperactive military. In contrast, the majority of our populace has little interest in the world beyond our borders" (26).
19. Grace Glueck, "Subject Is U.S., Object Is Art," *New York Times*, July 4, 2003.
20. Frank Rich, "Ground Zero or Bust," *New York Times*, July 13, 2003.
21. Desmond, "'As Others See Us?'" 1061. "The looming presence of that site hovered in my mind," Desmond writes, "and in the mind of most museum visitors I would

expect, as we walked through the Whitney exhibit. Perhaps, we secretly hoped, the Whitney could explain it for us" (1061).

22. After Bush's visit to the aircraft carrier USS *Abraham Lincoln* on May 1, 2003, where he gave what has been widely referred to as the "mission accomplished" speech, there were several attacks on coalition troops; daily, the papers reported on chaos in Iraq, massive looting, and an upsurge in crime. Three days after I visited "The American Effect," the television networks reported that Saddam Hussein's sons, Uday and Qusay, high on the Pentagon's "most wanted" list, had been killed.

23. Shteyngart, "Whole World," 26.

24. Vincent, "Resisting the 'American Effect.'"

25. Giuliano, "God Bless America More or Less."

26. Desmond, "'As Others See Us?'" 1060. Desmond also found that Naskovski's work stood out: "It is impossible to reduce this piece to a visually depicted one-liner. Unfortunately, the overall effect of the show too often lacks this level and complexity of impact" (1060).

27. Shteyngart, "Whole World," 26.

28. Desmond, "'As Others See Us?'" 1064.

29. Pollock, "Reel Value."

30. Cotter, "Chris Burden," *New York Times*, March 18, 1994. This was a review of an exhibition at the Gagosian Gallery in New York.

31. Barthes, *Mythologies*, 53.

32. Benjamin, "Toys and Play," 120. Benjamin writes about Karl Gröber's *Kinderspielzeug aus alter Zeit: Eine Geschichte des Spielzeugs* (1928).

33. Carrier, *Museum Skepticism*, 7. "We view one painting in relation to others and recall what we have just seen or are about to view. We learn who owned art before it entered the museum and its setting in ways that contribute to our experience of individual paintings" (7).

34. Beck, "Zapruder, Warhol, and Images," 185.

35. Simon, *Dangerous Knowledge*, 110.

36. McShine, *Andy Warhol*, 18.

37. Foster, *The Return of the Real*, 131–132.

38. Phelan, "Performances of *Death in America*," 224, 225.

39. Numbered 151, the print was purchased in November 1969 for $1,075, and is part of the Spencer Collection.

40. Simon, *Dangerous Knowledge*, 116.

41. Crimp, "Getting the Warhol We Deserve," 49. The essay Crimp refers to was written by Robert Rosenblum.

42. Crimp, "The Warhol We Deserve," 49, 50. Simon Watney argues that "Warhol simply cannot be reconciled to the type of the heroic originating Fine Artist required as the price of admission to the Fine Arts tradition" ("The Warhol Effect," 118).

43. Crimp, "The Warhol We Deserve," 64. See also the interview with Crimp by Margaret Dikovitskaya, in which he argues for an "emotional or subjective relation to an object of study. . . . That is to say, it could be that one is angered by an object, it could be that one is enlightened by an object, it could be that one is excited by an object" (*Visual Culture*, 136).

44. Stephen Kinzer, "Mixing Tragedy with Art in Dallas; Book Depository Site Now Includes Gallery," *New York Times*, March 3, 2003.

45. Beck, "Zapruder, Warhol, and Images," 184.

46. Warhol Museum, press release. *Death in Dallas* was exhibited at two other U.S. galleries that fall, the fortieth anniversary of the assassination: the Wexner Center in Columbus, Ohio, and the Williams College Museum of Art in Williamstown, Massachusetts, where it was exhibited with two of Warhol's Flash prints.

47. Beck, "Zapruder, Warhol, and Images," 189.

48. David Carrier observes the rise of what he calls "the contemporary public museum" as being interrelated with the decline of "the modernist art museum": "The history of art has ended; the historical expansion of the museum has been completed; and high art must cohabit and compete with the novel culture of mass art" (*Museum Skepticism*, 16, 207). Carrier places himself somewhere between what he describes as "orthodox art history" and "museum skepticism" (7). The skeptics, among whom he identifies Arthur Danto and Douglas Crimp, think of museums as institutions that "preserve old objects, but fail to preserve the works of art constituted by these objects" (51). As Susan A. Crane points out, our experiences of visiting museums are distinctly shaped by our expectations about what kind of a place the museum is, and the "attempt to create a dialogue between museums and their publics reflects a change in attitudes since the nineteenth century" ("Memory, Distortion, and History in the Museum," 47). Eilean Hooper-Greenhill envisions a "postmuseum," an institution that is able to question and rethink its own expository poetics in an ongoing dialogue with the visitor: "In the postmuseum, multiple subjectivities and identities can exist as part of a cultural practice that provides the potential to expand the politics of democratic community and solidarity. By being able to listen critically, museum workers can become border-crossers by making different narratives available, by bridging between disciplines, by working in the liminal spaces that modernist museum practices have produced" (*Museums and the Interpretation of Visual Culture*, 7).

CHAPTER SEVEN

1. Chaney, *Fictions of Collective Life*, 112, 81.

2. Hunt, *A Visitor's Guide to Dealey Plaza, National Historic Landmark*, 9.

3. Desmond, "'As Others See Us?'" 1063. For a perceptive analysis of the role photography played at the WTC site in the period to immediately follow the terror attacks, see Marianne Hirsch, "I Took Pictures."

4. James E. Young, *The Texture of Memory*, 7.

5. Chaney, *Collective Life*, 82.

6. The story of the site is told in Abbott, *Dealey Plaza*.

7. The museum was also intended to represent an alternative to a number of private initiatives that were widely regarded as inappropriate. One of the better-known examples, "The JFK Presidential Limo Tour," was stopped in 2001 after numerous complaints. For twenty-five dollars, a tour guide offered to pick up tourists at Love Field in a Lincoln convertible and follow the route of the Kennedy motorcade; a tape of cheering crowds played on the car's stereo. As the tour arrived in Dealey Plaza, shots rang out from loudspeakers, and the driver then continued to Parkland Hospital, where the tape declared Kennedy dead.

8. Hunt is quoted in Kristin Kelly, "From Memory into History," a discussion at the Getty Conservation Institute in 2002.

9. Hunt, *JFK for a New Generation*, viii, 1.

10. "You see a middle-aged man and a young woman standing on a four-foot plinth at the western edge of the two little steps that lead into the columned arcade; he has a movie camera. If you stand in the grass you will be below him, not blocking his view. . . . Satisfied with your position, you turn to face the street" (Hunt, *JFK for a New Generation*, 6).

11. "Another shot! President Kennedy's head explodes, throwing his entire body violently backward and to the left. . . . Oh my God! Pieces of skull, blue-white chunks of matter, blood, and water fly up into the air!" (ibid., 11).

12. Ibid., 12, 14.

13. The audio guide, "The Sixth Floor: John F. Kennedy and the Memory of a Nation," written by David Helvarg and Char Woods, could be purchased in the museum store when I visited in 2003, as could a VHS tape, Allen Mondell and Cynthia Salzmann Mondell's *John F. Kennedy and the Memory of a Nation*, which includes all the exhibited films. These inform my analysis.

14. Brandimarte, "The Sixth Floor."

15. Chaney, *Collective Life*, 81.

16. See Justin Webb, "JFK 'Sniper Window' Fetches $3M."

17. Fanselow, Bain, Bedford, Croom, and Root, *Texas*, 138.

18. Michael E. Young, "Dallas Museum Provides Internet Bird's-Eye-View to JFK Assassination," *Dallas Morning News*, June 24, 1999.

19. Bob Greene, "A View to a Kill—But Is This Really Necessary?" *Jewish World Review*, July 27, 1999.

20. Quoted in ibid.

21. Deen, review of "Loss and Renewal," 191.

22. West, "'Wiser Heads Prevailed,'" 64–65, 60. Dallas, West observes, was also "consumed by a single act of violence," but in Dealey Plaza "there were no heroes, only bystanders"; the city, he argues, "was held accountable" (62).

23. Sontag, *Regarding the Pain of Others*, 88.

24. West, "Wiser Heads," 65.

25. Quoted in Kelly, "From Memory into History."

26. LaCapra, *Writing History, Writing Trauma*, 48, 49, 45, 46.

27. Sontag, *Regarding the Pain of Others*, 115.

28. Sturken, *Tangled Memories*, 32.

29. Sontag, *Regarding the Pain of Others*, 115.

30. See Michael Leccese, Notebook section, *Historic Preservation* 39, no. 6 (1987): 7; and David Dillon, "Organizations Debate Addition to Texas Schoolbook Depository," *Architecture* 76, October 1987, 21–22.

31. Deluca, "New Gallery Opens in JFK Assassination Site."

32. West is quoted in Deluca, "New Gallery Opens in JFK Assassination Site."

33. Abbott, *Dealey Plaza*, 50. "Working with a task force of dedicated individuals representing the City of Dallas Park and Recreation Department, the Dallas Park Board, the Downtown Improvement District, and the Belo Foundation, the Museum summarized and recorded historical research on the Plaza. The consultant team of MESA Design Group and Good Fulton & Farrell developed a master plan documenting the specific restoration needs and associated costs. The plan addresses the historic site in context of architectural and structural conditions, fountain restoration and repair, hardscape conditions and handicap access (ADA), lighting, landscape, irrigation, utilities, and graphic signage" (50).

34. O'Keeffe, "Landscape and Memory," 10.

35. "As the confines of the prison, the convent, the family home, the neighborhood, the executive suite, the university campus, and the Oval Office are all invaded through electronics, we must expect a fundamental shift in our perceptions of our society, our authorities, and ourselves," Meyrowitz observed in 1985, arguing that electronic media had "led to the overlapping of many social spheres that were once distinct." As a consequence, an "old 'sense of place'" has been lost (*No Sense of Place*, viii, 5, ix, 310).

36. Kinzer, "Mixing Tragedy with Art In Dallas."

37. Culler, *Framing the Sign*, 167, 164.

38. Sorkin, *Variations on a Theme Park*, xi. "TV's main event is the cut," Sorkin writes, "the elision between broadcast bits, the seamless slide from soap opera to docudrama to a word from our sponsor" (xi–xii, xiv).

39. Gottdiener, *The Theming of America*, 6.

40. Sorkin, "The Theming of the City," 15.

41. The first-person shooter game was downloadable from a website, www.jfkreloaded.com, for $9.99, and for that price, the player got an entry into a competition to win a sum between $10,000 and $100,000. The competition closed in February 2005; in August of that year, the site closed, after having offered the game to the public for free.

42. See Fullerton, "Documentary Games." For a discussion of *JFK Reloaded* as a "documentary videogame," see Poremba, "Frames and Simulated Documents."

43. Quoted from a press release from Traffic Management Limited, November 21, 2004.

44. Quoted in Jose Antonio Vargas, "JFK Internet Game Assailed," *Washington Post*, November 23, 2004.

45. Lieberman's and Glaubke's responses are quoted in Tuohey, "*JFK Reloaded* Game Causes Controversy."

46. Jennings, *Beyond Conspiracy*.

47. All quotations from *Beyond Conspiracy* are from my transcription of the broadcast.

48. Vargas, "JFK Internet Game Assailed." Certainly, this debate intensified with the controversy surrounding the withdrawal of Danny Ledonne's *Super Columbine Massacre Role Playing Game!* from the Guerilla Gamemaking Competition at the Slamdance festival in Park City, Utah, in 2007; several of the same questions were raised, and Fullerton and Bogost expressed many of the same sentiments to the *New York Times*. See Heather Chaplin, "Video Game Tests the Limits; The Limits Win," *New York Times*, January 28, 2007.

49. See, for example, the transcript of Jim Lehrer's *NewsHour* on July 14, 1998, in which the historians Doris Kearns Goodwin and Michael Beschloss, the journalist Haynes Johnson, and Waleed Ali, the president of MPI Home Video, debate the release; repeatedly, Ali complains that what is being criticized is "the format of distribution." "To imagine this in a video store," Beschloss says, "to some extent carries out our worst fears" (*NewsHour*, "Image of Assassination").

50. Raessens, "Reality Play," 221, 223.

CHAPTER EIGHT

1. Gerald Peary called it "a brilliant, one-of-a-kind *faux* documentary" (*Boston Phoenix*, May 2, 2003); Scott Foundas suggested that it set "something of a high bar for the mockumentary subgenre" (*Variety*, February 24, 2002). On Fox News, Neil Cavuto interviewed Laurie Pike, one of the central actors in *Nothing So Strange*, in a segment titled "Art or Junk?": "Are you sending a scary message, particularly to Bill Gates and his family?" Cavuto asked. "The film doesn't advocate someone shooting Bill Gates at all," Pike answered, arguing, "Bill Gates is an icon, and icons have always been used throughout history by artists in every medium to tell a story, to make observations about our culture, to prove points, and that's the way he is used in this film." Indeed, the Kennedy assassination has produced a faux documentary of its own, Neil Burger's *Interview with the Assassin*, in which an ex-marine, Walter Ohlinger (Raymond J. Barry), comes forward as a second shooter; the movie's central question is whether Ohlinger is telling

the truth. Shot in digital video on location in twenty-two days on a $700,000 budget, *Interview with the Assassin* won the New York Independent International Film and Video Festival's awards for best experimental film, best director, and best actor in 2002. Zapruder's images do not figure much in the film; a few minutes into the story, five frames are shown. In the audio commentary, Burger explains why: the frames were "very expensive to get a hold of," and "a huge part of our budget" was spent "to get the rights" for the five frames that appear.

2. Aida Ahmed, "Reactions to Erykah Badu's Nude Dealey Plaza Video Range from Groans to Yawns," *Dallas Morning News*, March 30, 2010.

3. Reddin, *Frame 312*.

4. Gibson, *Pattern Recognition*, 20, 24.

5. Sontag, *Regarding the Pain of Others*, 54.

6. Mitchell, interview by Grønstad and Vågnes.

7. Mitchell, *What Do Pictures Want?* 14.

8. Horsburgh and Meadows, "Diary of Valor," 117.

9. The Naudets had been working on the project for months, and turned down multimillion-dollar offers for the footage because they wanted control over it. The "rookie" and the other firefighters the Naudets had been filming were stationed at Engine 7, Ladder 1, in Manhattan. Although the film, for obvious reasons, hardly can be said to consistently be about the rookie throughout, its main focus remains on the firefighters and on the filmmakers themselves.

10. Its canonization was performed by critics such as Caryn James, who described the film as much in terms of what it was as what it was not, for the way in which the filmmakers had confronted difficult ethical choices during recording, production, and post-production: *9/11* was an "important, firsthand piece of history" and "also amazing to watch." The broadcast was "timely because it reveals how quickly even the most horrifying images of Sept. 11 have been absorbed, have come to seem ordinary: a necessary way to grasp a terrible reality but also a dangerously forgetful change. You only have to watch another, more typical documentary to see the difference" ("Experiencing the Cataclysm, from the Inside," *New York Times*, March 6, 2002). David Bianculli called it "an astonishing, riveting, remarkable piece of filmmaking" ("Vivid View of '9/11,'" *New York Daily News*, March 5, 2002).

11. Roth, interviewed by Jean-Louis Turlin. James Poniewozik claimed that the documentary "plays more like an independent film than a slick network news special" ("Within Crumbling Walls"). *9/11* was considered moving but not overtly sentimental in the moments when it easily could have become just that. Its omissions were widely considered a demonstration of good taste, evidence of a refusal to cynically use the spectacular: Jules Naudet turned his camera away from burning bodies, thinking spontaneously that no one should see what he saw. Images of bodies hitting the pavement were edited out. *9/11* was thus felt to stand in

marked contrast to the many television productions that seemed symptomatic of consumerism's governing ethics and aesthetics.

12. Wrone, *The Zapruder Film*, 36.

13. Rather, *The Camera Never Blinks*, 111.

14. My transcription.

15. Martin, "The Year in TV."

16. Poniewozik, "Within Crumbling Walls."

17. James Glanz, "A Rare View of 9/11, Overlooked," *New York Times*, September 7, 2003.

18. Ibid. Furthermore, the driver of the SUV, Mike Cohen, who, incidentally, also was Hlava's boss, "had strong objections to releasing the tape." Cohen commented to the *Times*, "Three thousand people died in that place. . . . I told him the day he's gonna sell that film, he's not gonna work for me anymore."

19. Zapruder was born in czarist Russia in 1905 (Wrone, *The Zapruder Film*, 9).

20. Glanz, "Rare View of 9/11."

21. Berger, *Ways of Seeing*, 9–10.

22. Sontag, *Regarding the Pain of Others*, 89.

23. Hayden White, *Figural Realism*, 70.

24. Desmond, "'As Others See Us?'" 1063.

25. Eric Lipton and James Glanz, "From the Rubble, Artifacts of Anguish," *New York Times*, January 27, 2002. This happened, the *Times* wrote, "at the behest of the city and the Port Authority of New York and New Jersey."

26. Marianne Hirsch points out that photographers have suggested that the iconic image from September 11 "would be the picture of the three firemen raising the flag on top of the rubble because it echoes the famous prize-winning photograph of American GI's raising the flag at Iwo Jima. In their search for the one lasting iconic image they were looking for the conventional, the coded, not the new" (Hirsch, "I Took Pictures").

27. Lipton and Glanz, "From the Rubble": "Dozens of museums and artists, from the Smithsonian Institution to a museum in France to a sculptor in Greensboro, N.C.," articulated interest in the fragments.

28. Sontag, *Regarding the Pain of Others*, 86–87.

29. One does not have to read many of the books of photography from September 11 before one can see that photographs are powerfully surrounded by words, and by a lot of them. Books from *Life* (*One Nation: America Remembers September 11, 2001*), Magnum (*New York: September 11*), and Reuters (*September 11: A Testimony*) are good examples when it comes to professional photography. *Above Hallowed Ground: A Photographic Record of September 11, 2001*, consisting of photographs taken by officers from the New York City Police Department, is a good example of amateur efforts. All these books are essentially narratives, and they try to convey, rather than a gallery experience, the tragedy that unfolded

in Manhattan itself. The introductions to these books are often by prominent guest writers. *Life*'s book has an introduction by Rudolph Giuliani; Magnum's is by David Halberstam.

30. This information is gathered from the websites; see hereisnewyork.org and www .sep11photo.org.

31. Paul Richard, "A Stunned City's Collected Grief," *Washington Post*, September 6, 2002.

32. The release was reported widely in the U.S. media; see the Associated Press, "Aerial Photos of Trade Center on 9/11 Released," February 10, 2010.

33. Ramirez is quoted in Associated Press, "Aerial Photos of Trade Center on 9/11 Released."

34. Beck, "Zapruder, Warhol, and Images," 184.

35. Gillmor, *We the Media*, xv.

36. Braiker, "History's New First Draft."

37. *Time*, "The Top 10 Everything of 2009." Mahr listed Agha-Soltan as one of the top 10 heroes of the year.

38. Hansen, "Why Media Aesthetics?" When Colin Powell addressed the United Nations on February 5, 2003, instructions were given, Hansen observes, to cover up a reproduction of Pablo Picasso's *Guernica*, which is displayed at the entrance of the Security Council and which thus would have served as backdrop for Powell; this kind of act urges a particular kind of analysis, she argues—a sharp attention to aesthetics and performativity.

39. Latour, "What Is Iconoclash?" 14.

40. Bill Carter, "Hard Choices over Video of Execution," *New York Times*, January 1, 2007.

41. Hassan M. Fattah, "Images of Hanging Make Hussein a Martyr to Many," *New York Times*, January 6, 2007.

42. Latour, "What Is Iconoclash?" 15.

43. The exhibition lasted from January 28 to April 30, 2006.

44. Reinhardt, Edwards, and Duganne, *Beautiful Suffering*, 11.

45. Reinhardt, "Picturing Violence," 15.

46. Bal, "The Pain of Images," 96–97.

47. Reinhardt, "Picturing Violence," 15.

48. Ibid., 20.

49. Sontag, *Regarding the Pain of Others*, 115.

BIBLIOGRAPHY

Abbott, Arlinda. *Dealey Plaza: The Front Door of Dallas*. Dallas: Sixth Floor Museum, 2003.

Acker, Kathy. "Weaver of Dreams from the Stuff of Nightmares." *RE/Search*, nos. 8–9 (1984): 140. Originally published in the *Guardian*, October 26, 1979.

Ant Farm. "Interview with Ant Farm: Constance M. Lewallen in Conversation with Chip Lord, Doug Michels, and Curtis Schreier." In Lewallen and Seid, *Ant Farm*, 38–87.

Antze, Paul, and Michael Lambek. *Tense Past: Cultural Essays in Trauma and Memory*. New York: Routledge, 1996.

Appadurai, Arjun, ed. *The Social Life of Things: Commodities in Cultural Perspective*. Cambridge: Cambridge Univ. Press, 1986.

Architecture. "Organizations Debate Addition to Texas Schoolbook Depository." October 1987.

Auslander, Philip. *Liveness: Performance in a Mediatized Culture*. London: Routledge, 1999.

Austin, J. L. *How to Do Things with Words: The William James Lectures Delivered at Harvard University in 1955*. Cambridge, Mass.: Harvard Univ. Press, 1962.

Bal, Mieke. *Double Exposures: The Subject of Cultural Analysis*. New York: Routledge, 1996.

———. "Interdisciplinary Approaches to Narrative." In *Routledge Encyclopedia of Narrative Theory*, edited by David Herman, Manfred Jahn, and Marie-Laure Ryan, 250–252. London: Routledge, 2005.

———. *A Mieke Bal Reader*. Chicago: Univ. of Chicago Press, 2006.

———. *Narratology: Introduction to the Theory of Narrative*. 2nd ed. Toronto: Univ. of Toronto Press, 1997.

———. "The Pain of Images." In Reinhardt, Edwards, and Duganne, *Beautiful Suffering*, 93–115.

———. *Quoting Caravaggio: Contemporary Art, Preposterous History*. Chicago: Univ. of Chicago Press, 1999.

———. *Travelling Concepts in the Humanities: A Rough Guide*. Toronto: Univ. of Toronto Press, 2002.

———. "Visual Essentialism and the Object of Visual Culture." *Journal of Visual Culture* 2, no. 1 (2003): 5–32.

Bal, Mieke, Jonathan Crewe, and Leo Spitzer, eds. *Acts of Memory: Cultural Recall in the Present*. Hanover, N.H.: Univ. Press of New England, 1999.

Ballard, J. G. *The Atrocity Exhibition*. San Francisco: RE/Search Publications, 1990.

———. "The Film of Kennedy's Assassination Is the Sistine Chapel of Our Era." Interview by William Feaver. *Art Newspaper* 94 (July–August 1999): 24–25.

———. Interview by Douglas Reed. *RE/Search*, nos. 8–9 (1984): 154.

———. *A User's Guide to the Millennium*. New York: Picador, 1996.

Barthes, Roland. *Camera Lucida: Reflections on Photography*. Translated by Richard Howard. New York: Hill and Wang, 1983.

———. *Mythologies*. Translated and edited by Annette Lavers. New York: Hill and Wang, 1970.

———. "The Reality Effect." In *The Rustle of Language*, 141–148. Translated by Richard Howard. New York: Hill and Wang, 1986.

Baty, S. Paige. *American Monroe: The Making of a Body Politic*. Berkeley and Los Angeles: Univ. of California Press, 1995.

Bay Area Video Coalition. *Playback: Preserving Analog Video*. DVD. San Francisco: BAVC, 2004.

Baym, Geoffrey. "Packaging Reality." *Journalism* 5, no. 3 (2004): 279–299.

Bazin, André. "The Ontology of the Photographic Image." In *What Is Cinema?* translated and edited by Hugh Gray, 9–16. Berkeley and Los Angeles: Univ. of California Press, 1967.

Beck, John. "Zapruder, Warhol, and the Accident of Images." In *American Visual Cultures*, edited by David Holloway and John Beck, 183–189. London: Continuum, 2005.

Becker, Kathrin. "Heading for Collisions: On Staging, Black Boxes, Video and Great Expectations." In *Zivilisatorische Konflikte im Medium Video* (exhibition catalogue). Berlin: Neuer Berliner Kunstverein, 2003.

Begley, Adam. "The Art of Fiction CXXXV: Don DeLillo." In DePietro, *Conversations with Don DeLillo*, 86–108.

Belting, Hans. *Bild-Anthropologie*. Munich: Wilhelm Fink Verlag, 2001.

———. "Image, Medium, Body: A New Approach to Iconology." *Critical Inquiry*, 31, no. 2 (Winter 2005): 302–319.

———. "Towards an Anthropology of the Image." In *Anthropologies of Art*, edited by Mariet Westermann. Clark Studies in the Visual Arts. Williamstown, Mass.: Clark Art Institute, 2005.

Benjamin, Walter. "Karl Kraus." Translated by Edmund Jephcott. In *Selected Writings*, 2:433–458. Cambridge, Mass.: Harvard Univ. Press, 1999.

———. "On the Concept of History." Translated by Harry Zohn. In *Selected Writings*, 4:389–400. Cambridge, Mass.: Harvard Univ. Press, 2003.

———. *The Origin of German Tragic Drama*. Translated by John Osborne. 1963. London: New Left Books, 1977.

———. "Toys and Play." In *Selected Writings*, 2:117–121. Translated by Rodney Livingstone. Cambridge, Mass.: Harvard Univ. Press, 1999.

———. "What is the Epic Theater? (II)." In *Selected Writings*, 4:302–309. Translated by Harry Zohn. Cambridge, Mass.: Harvard Univ. Press, 2003.

———. "The Work of Art in the Age of Reproducibility (Third Version)." In *Selected Writings*, 4:251–283. Translated by Harry Zohn and Edmund Jephcott. Cambridge, Mass.: Harvard Univ. Press, 2003.

Berger, John. *Ways of Seeing*. London: Penguin, 1972.

Berman, Ronald. "Sitcoms." *Journal of Aesthetic Education* 21, no. 1 (1987): 5–19.

Black, Joel. *The Reality Effect: Film Culture and the Graphic Imperative*. New York: Routledge, 2002.

Boehm, Gottfried. "Die Wiederkehr der Bilder." In *Was Ist Ein Bild*, edited by Gottfried Boehm, 11–38. Munich: Wilhelm Fink Verlag, 1995.

Bolter, David Jay, and Richard Grusin. *Remediation: Understanding New Media*. Cambridge, Mass.: MIT Press, 1999.

Boorstin, Daniel. *The Image, or What Happened to the American Dream*. London: Weidenfeld and Nicholson, 1962.

Bordwell, David. *The Way Hollywood Tells It: Story and Style in Modern Movies*. Berkeley and Los Angeles: Univ. of California Press, 2006.

Boyle, Deirdre. *Subject to Change: Guerilla Television Revisited*. New York: Oxford Univ. Press, 1997.

Boyle, Deirdre, and Media Alliance. *Video Preservation: Securing the Future of the Past*. New York: Media Alliance, 1993.

Braiker, Brian. "History's New First Draft." *Newsweek*, July 8, 2005.

Brandimarte, Cynthia B. "The Sixth Floor: John F. Kennedy and the Memory of a Nation." *Journal of American History* 78, no. 1 (June 1991): 268–274.

Bruun, Hanne. "The Aesthetics of the Television Talk Show." In *The Aesthetics of Televi-sion*, edited by Gunhild Agger and Jens F. Jensen, 229–255. Aalborg, Denmark: Aalborg Univ. Press, 2001.

Bruzzi, Stella. *New Documentary: A Critical Introduction.* 2nd ed. London: Routledge, 2006.

Burger, Neil. *Interview with the Assassin.* DVD. Showtime Home Entertainment, 2003.

Burke, Peter. *Eyewitnessing: The Uses of Images as Historical Evidence.* London: Reak-tion, 2001.

Butler, Judith. *Excitable Speech: A Politics of the Performative.* New York: Routledge, 1997.

Cadava, Eduardo. *Words of Light: Theses on the Photography of History.* Princeton, N.J.: Princeton Univ. Press, 1997.

Carmichael, Thomas. "Lee Harvey Oswald and the Postmodern Subject: History and Intertextuality in Don DeLillo's *Libra, The Names,* and *Mao II.*" *Contemporary Litera-ture* 34, no. 2 (1993): 204–218.

Carrier, David. *Museum Skepticism: A History of the Display of Art in Public Galleries.* Durham, N.C.: Duke Univ. Press, 2006.

C.C.M. Associates. *Zapruder Film Appraisal.* For Civil Division, U.S. Department of Justice. Washington, D.C.: C.C.M. Associates, 1997.

Chanan, Michael. *The Politics of Documentary.* London: BFI, 2007.

———. *Repeated Takes: A Short History of Recording and Its Effects on Music.* London: Verso, 1995.

Chaney, David. *Fictions of Collective Life: Public Drama in Late Modern Culture.* London: Routledge, 1993.

Cherones, Tom, dir. "The Boyfriend." *Seinfeld.* Written by Larry Levin and Larry David. DVD. *Seinfeld Season 3.* Sony Pictures, 2004.

Cohen, Josh. *Spectacular Allegories: Postmodern American Writing and the Politics of See-ing.* London: Pluto, 1998.

Cotter, Holland. "Chris Burden." *New York Times,* March 18, 1994.

Crane, Susan A. "Memory, Distortion, and History in the Museum." *History and Theory* 36, no. 4 (1997): 44–63.

Crimp, Douglas. "Getting the Warhol We Deserve." *Social Text* 17, no. 2 (1999): 49–66.

———. Interview by Margaret Dikovitskaya. In *Visual Culture: The Study of the Visual after the Cultural Turn,* edited by Margaret Dikovitskaya, 131–141. Cambridge, Mass.: MIT Press, 2005.

Culler, Jonathan. *Framing the Sign: Criticism and Its Institutions.* Oxford: Blackwell, 1988.

———. "Philosophy and Literature: The Fortunes of the Performative." *Poetics Today* 21, no. 3 (2000): 503–519.

Deen, Rebecca E. Review of the exhibition "Loss and Renewal: Transforming Tragic Sites." *Journal of American History* 90, no. 1 (2003): 191–193.

Deleuze, Gilles, and Félix Guattari. *What Is Philosophy?* Translated by Hugh Tomlinson and Graham Burchell. New York: Columbia Univ. Press, 1994.

DeLillo, Don. *Americana*. New York: Penguin, 1971.

———. "American Blood: A Journey through the Labyrinth of Dallas and JFK." *Rolling Stone*, December 8, 1983, 21–28, 74.

———. "The American Strangeness." Interview by Gerald Howard. In DePietro, *Conversations with Don DeLillo*, 119–130.

———. *Libra*. New York: Viking, 1988.

———. "'An Outsider in This Society.'" Interview by Anthony DeCurtis. In DePietro, *Conversations with Don DeLillo*, 52–74.

———. "The Power of History." *New York Times Magazine*, September 7, 1997.

———. *Underworld*. New York: Scribner, 1997.

Deluca, Salvatore. "New Gallery Opens in JFK Assassination Site." *Preservation*, March 2003.

DePietro, Thomas, ed. *Conversations with Don DeLillo*. Jackson: Univ. of Mississippi Press, 2005.

Derrida, Jacques. *Of Grammatology*. Translated by Gayatri Chakravorty Spivak. Baltimore: Johns Hopkins Univ. Press, 1997.

Desmond, Jane C. "'As Others See Us?' Fetishizing the Foreign at the Whitney." *American Quarterly* 56, no. 4 (2004): 1051–1066.

Deutschman, Alan. "Doing the Sundance Shuffle." Salon.com, January 23, 2002. http://www.salon.com/people/feature/2002/01/23/sundance.

Dika, Vera. *Recycled Culture in Contemporary Art and Film: The Uses of Nostalgia*. Cambridge: Cambridge Univ. Press, 2003.

Dikovitskaya, Margaret. *Visual Culture: The Study of the Visual after the Cultural Turn*. Cambridge, Mass.: MIT Press, 2005.

Doane, Mary Ann. "Information, Crisis, Catastrophe." In *Logics of Television: Essays in Cultural Criticism*, edited by Patricia Mellencamp, 222–239. Bloomington: Indiana Univ. Press, 1990.

Docker, John. "*Seinfeld*." Museum of Broadcast Communications. http://www.muse um.tv/eotvsection.php?entrycode=seinfeld.

———. "*Seinfeld*." In Lavery and Dunne, "*Seinfeld*," 42–43.

Doss, Erica, ed. *Looking at "Life" Magazine*. Washington and London: Smithsonian Institution Press, 2001.

Dunne, Michael. *Intertextual Encounters in American Fiction, Film, and Popular Culture*. Bowling Green, Ohio: Bowling Green State Univ. Popular Press, 2001.

Edwards, Janis. "Echoes of Camelot: How Images Construct Cultural Memory through Rhetorical Framing." In *Defining Visual Rhetorics*, edited by Charles A. Hill and Marguerite Helmers, 179–194. Philadelphia: Erlbaum, 2004.

Elson, Robert T. *Time, Inc.: The Intimate History of a Publishing Enterprise, 1923–1941.* New York: Atheneum, 1968.

Elwes, Catherine. *Video Art: A Guided Tour.* London: Tauris, 2005.

Fanselow, Julia, Carolyn Bain, Neal Bedford, Tracey Croom, and Don Root, eds. *Texas.* 2nd ed. Victoria, Australia: Lonely Planet, 2002.

Feuer, Jane. "The Concept of Live Television: Ontology as Ideology." In *Regarding Television: Critical Approaches*, edited by E. Ann Kaplan, 12–22. Frederick, Md.: University Publications of America, 1983.

Flemming, Brian. *Nothing So Strange.* DVD. Unsharp Mask, 2004.

Fletcher, Angus. *Allegory: The Theory of a Symbolic Mode.* Ithaca, N.Y.: Cornell Univ. Press, 1964.

Ford, Gerald R. "Piecing Together the Evidence." *Life*, October 2, 1964, 42–51.

Foster, Hal. *The Return of the Real: The Avant-Garde at the End of the Century.* Cambridge, Mass.: MIT Press, 1996.

Foundas, Scott. Review of *Nothing So Strange. Variety*, February 24, 2002.

Freedberg, David. *The Power of Images: Studies in the History and Theory of Response.* Chicago: Univ. of Chicago Press, 1989.

Frey, Stephen. *The Legacy.* New York: Onyx, 1998.

Friedberg, Anne, and Raiford Guins. "Televisual Space." *Journal of Visual Culture* 3, no. 2 (2004): 131–132.

Fullerton, Tracy. "Documentary Games: Putting the Player in the Path of History." In *Playing the Past: Nostalgia in Videogames and Electronic Literature*, edited by Zach Whalen and Laurie N. Taylor, 215–238. Nashville, Tenn.: Vanderbilt Univ. Press, 2008.

Gamboni, Dario. "Preservation and Destruction, Oblivion and Memory." In *Negating the Image: Case Studies in Iconoclasm*, edited by Anne McClanan and Jeffrey Johnson, 163–177. Burlington, Vt.: Ashgate, 2005.

Gibson, William. *Pattern Recognition.* New York: Berkeley, 2003.

Gillmor, Dan. *We the Media: Grassroots Journalism by the People, for the People.* 2nd ed. Sebastopol, Calif.: O'Reilly, 2006.

Gingeras, Alison M. "The Mnemonic Function of the Painted Image." In *The Triumph of Painting: Albert Oehlen, Thomas Scheibitz, Wilhelm Sasnal, Kai Althoff, Dirk Skreber, Franz Ackermann*, edited by Alison M. Gingeras. London: Koenig, 2005.

Ginzburg, Carlo. "Vetoes and Compatibilities." *Art Bulletin* 77, no. 4 (1995): 534–536.

Giuliano, Charles. "God Bless America More or Less." *Maverick Arts Magazine*, July 15, 2003.

Goodwin, Sarah Webster, and Elisabeth Bronfen. *Death and Representation.* Baltimore: Johns Hopkins Univ. Press, 1993.

Gottdiener, Mark. *The Theming of America: Dreams, Visions, and Commercial Spaces.* Boulder, Colo.: Westview, 1997.

Gray, Jonathan. *Watching with the Simpsons: Television, Parody, and Intertextuality*. New York: Routledge, 2006.

Grant, Steven, and Vince Giarrano. *Badlands*. Milwaukee: Dark Horse, 1993.

Greene, Bob. "A View To a Kill—But Is This Really Necessary?" *Jewish World Review*, July 27, 1999.

Gross, Kenneth. *The Dream of the Moving Statue*. Ithaca, N.Y.: Cornell Univ. Press, 1992.

Gunster, Shane. "'All About Nothing': Difference, Affect, and *Seinfeld*." *Television and New Media* 6, no. 2 (2005): 200–223.

Halberstam, David. Introduction to *The Kennedy Presidential Press Conferences*. New York: Coleman, 1978.

Halbwachs, Maurice. *The Collective Memory*. Translated by Francis J. Ditter Jr. and Vida Yazdi Ditter. New York: Harper and Row, 1980.

Hall, Doug, and Sally Jo Fifer, eds. *Illuminating Video: An Essential Guide to Video Art*. Danville, Calif.: Aperture, in association with the Bay Area Video Coalition, 1990.

Hamon, Philippe. *Expositions: Literature and Architecture in Nineteenth-Century France*. Berkeley and Los Angeles: Univ. of California Press, 1992.

Hansen, Miriam. "Why Media Aesthetics?" *Critical Inquiry* 30, no. 2 (2004): 391–395.

Harries, Dan. *Film Parody*. London: BFI, 2000.

Heartney, Eleanor. "America, Real and Imagined." *Art in America*, September 2003, 102–103.

Heffernan, James. *Museum of Words: The Poetics of Ekphrasis from Homer to Ashbery*. Chicago: Univ. of Chicago Press, 1993.

Heffernan, Virginia. "Life after Seinfeld." *New Yorker*, October 28, 2002, 114–116.

Hellmann, John. *The Kennedy Obsession: The American Myth of JFK*. New York: Columbia Univ. Press, 1997.

Helvarg, David, and Char Woods. "The Sixth Floor: John F. Kennedy and the Memory of a Nation." Audiotape. Dallas: Antenna Theater and Dallas County Historical Foundation, 1989.

Hicks, Wilson. *Words and Pictures: An Introduction to Photojournalism*. New York: Harper and Brothers, 1952.

Hill, Chris. "Attention! Production! Audience! Performing Video in Its First Decade, 1968–1980." Video Data Bank, 2008. http://www.vdb.org/resources/attention.pdf.

Hirsch, Irwin. "*Seinfeld*'s Humor Noir: A Look at Our Dark Side." *Journal of Popular Film and Television* 28, no. 3 (2000): 116.

Hirsch, Marianne. "I Took Pictures: September 11 and Beyond." *Scholar and Feminist Online* 2, no. 1 (2003). http://www.barnard.edu/sfonline/ps/hirsch.htm.

———. *Family Frames: Photography, Narrative, and Postmemory*. Cambridge, Mass.: Harvard Univ. Press, 1997.

Historic Preservation. Notebook. Vol. 39, no. 6 (1987): 7.

Hoberman, J. "Jump Cuts." *Village Voice*, September 10–16, 2003.

Hoffmann, Joyce. *Theodore H. White and Journalism as Illusion*. Columbia: Univ. of Missouri Press, 1995.

Hooper-Greenhill, Eilean. *Museums and the Interpretation of Visual Culture*. London: Routledge, 2001.

Horrigan, Bill. "Zoran Naskovski: *Death in Dallas*." Essay accompanying an exhibit at the Wexner Center for the Arts, Ohio State University, Columbus, November–December 2003. http://www.wexarts.org/ex/2003/zoran_naskovski/zoran_nask ovski.swf.

Horsburgh, Susan, and Bob Meadows. "Diary of Valor." *People*, March 18, 2002, 117.

Hunt, Conover. *JFK for a New Generation*. Dallas: Sixth Floor Museum and Southern Methodist Univ. Press, 1996.

———. *A Visitor's Guide to Dealey Plaza, National Historic Landmark*. Dallas: Sixth Floor Museum, 1995.

Hutcheon, Linda. *A Poetics of Postmodernism: History, Theory, Fiction*. New York: Routledge, 1988.

———. *A Theory of Parody: The Teachings of Twentieth-Century Art Forms*. New York: Methuen, 1985.

Huyssen, Andreas. *Twilight Memories: Marking Time in a Culture of Amnesia*. New York: Routledge, 1995.

Irwin, William, ed. *"Seinfeld" and Philosophy: A Book about Everything and Nothing*. Chicago: Open Court, 2000.

Jameson, Fredric. *Postmodernism, or the Cultural Logic of Late Capitalism*. London: Verso, 1991.

Jennings, Peter, senior ed. *Peter Jennings Reporting: The Kennedy Assassination—Beyond Conspiracy*. DVD. Port Washington, N.Y.: Springs Media/ABC, 2003.

Joselit, David. "An Allegory of Criticism." *October* no. 103 (2003): 3–13.

Kansteiner, Wulf. "Finding Meaning in Memory: A Methodological Critique of Collective Memory Studies." *History and Theory* 41, no. 2 (May 2002): 179–197.

Kantorowicz, Ernst H. *The King's Two Bodies: A Study in Medieval Political Theology*. Princeton, N.J.: Princeton Univ. Press, 1957.

Kaplan, James. "Angry Middle-Aged Man." *New Yorker*, January 19, 2004, 66–73.

Keesey, Ken. *Don DeLillo*. New York: Twayne, 1993.

Kellner, Douglas. *Media Culture: Cultural Studies, Identity, and Politics between the Modern and the Postmodern*. London: Routledge, 1995.

Kelly, Kristin. "From Memory into History: A Discussion About the Conservation of Places with Difficult Pasts." *Getty Conservation Institute Newsletter* 17, no. 2 (2002). http://www.getty.edu/conservation/publications/newsletters/17_2/dialogue.html.

Klinkowitz, Jerome. *The American 1960s: Imaginative Acts in a Decade of Change*. Ames: Iowa State Univ. Press, 1980.

Koerner, Joseph. "The Icon as Iconoclash." In *Iconoclash: Beyond the Image Wars in Science, Religion, and Art*, edited by Bruno Latour and Peter Weibel, 164–213. Cambridge, Mass.: MIT Press, 2002.

Kompare, Derek. "Publishing Flow: DVD Box Sets and the Reconception of Television." *Television and New Media* 7, no. 4 (2006): 335–360.

Kozol, Wendy. "Gazing at Race in the Pages of *Life*." In *Looking at Life Magazine*, edited by Erica Doss, 159–175. Washington: Smithsonian Institution Press, 2001.

Kracauer, Siegfried. *The Mass Ornament: Weimar Essays*. Translated and edited by Thomas Y. Levin. Cambridge, Mass.: Harvard Univ. Press, 1995.

Kula, Sam. *Appraising Moving Images: Assessing the Archival and Monetary Value of Film and Video Records*. Lanham, Md.: Scarecrow, 2003.

Kurtz, Michael L. *Crime of the Century: The Kennedy Assassination from a Historian's Perspective*. Brighton, UK: Harvester, 1982.

LaCapra, Dominick. *Writing History, Writing Trauma*. Baltimore: Johns Hopkins Univ. Press, 2001.

Larsen, Ernest. "Junky and Important: The Collective Model in the Rearview Mirror." *American Quarterly* 57, no. 1 (2005): 223–236.

Lasch, Christopher. "The Life of Kennedy's Death." *Harper's*, October 1983, 32–40.

Latour, Bruno. "What Is Iconoclash? Or Is There a World beyond the Image Wars?" In *Iconoclash: Beyond the Image Wars in Science, Religion, and Art*, edited by Bruno Latour and Peter Weibel, 14–37. Cambridge, Mass.: MIT Press, 2002.

Lavender, Andy. "The Moment of Realized Actuality." In *Theatre in Crisis? Performance Manifestos for a New Century*, edited by Maria M. Delgado and Caridad Svich, 183–190. Manchester, UK: Manchester Univ. Press, 2002.

Lavery, David, and Sara Lewis Dunne, eds. *"Seinfeld": Master of Its Domain; Revisiting Television's Greatest Sitcom*. New York: Continuum, 2006.

LeClair, Tom. *In The Loop: Don DeLillo and the Systems Novel*. Urbana: Univ. of Illinois Press, 1987.

Leighton, Tanya, and Pavel Büchler, eds. *Saving the Image: Art after Film*. Glasgow: Centre for Contemporary Arts and Manchester Metropolitan University, 2003.

Levin, Kim. "A Foreign Affair." *Village Voice*, August 5, 2003, 48.

Lewallen, Constance M., and Steve Seid, eds. *Ant Farm, 1968–1978*. Berkeley and Los Angeles: Univ. of California Press, 2004.

Leys, Ruth. *Trauma: A Genealogy*. Chicago: Univ. of Chicago Press, 2000.

Love, Ruth Leeds. "Television and the Death of a President: Network Decisions in Covering Collective Events." PhD diss., Columbia University, 1970.

Lubin, David. *Shooting Kennedy: JFK and the Culture of Images*. Berkeley and Los Angeles: Univ. of California Press, 2003.

Lyotard, Jean-François. *The Postmodern Condition: A Report on Knowledge*. Translated by Geoff Bennington and Brian Massumi. Minneapolis: Univ. of Minnesota Press, 1984.

Mailer, Norman. "The Leading Man: A Review of *J.F.K.: The Man and the Myth*." In *Cannibals and Christians*, 165–171. New York: Dial, 1966.

———. *The Presidential Papers*. New York: Berkley, 1970.

———. "Superman Comes to the Supermarket." *Esquire*, November 1960, 119–127.

Maltby, Paul. "The Romantic Metaphysics of Don DeLillo." *Contemporary Literature* 37, no. 2 (1996): 258–277.

Manchester, William. *The Death of a President*. London: Harper and Row, 1967.

Marc, David. "*Seinfeld*: A Show (Almost) about Nothing." In Lavery and Dunne, "*Seinfeld*," 23–27.

Marin, Louis. *Portrait of the King*. Translated by Martha M. Houle. Minneapolis: Univ. of Minnesota Press, 1988.

Marrs, Jim. *Crossfire: The Plot That Killed Kennedy*. New York: Carroll and Graf, 1989.

Martin, James, "The Year in TV." *America*, June 17, 2002.

Mayhew, Aubrey. *The World's Tribute to John F. Kennedy in Medallic Art*. New York: Morrow, 1966.

McCall, Tom. "'The Dynamite of a Tenth of a Second': Benjamin's Revolutionary Messianism in Silent Film Comedy." In *Benjamin's Ghosts: Interventions in Contemporary Literary and Cultural Theory*, edited by Gerhard Richter, 74–94. Stanford, Calif.: Stanford Univ. Press, 2002.

McEvilley, Thomas. "Ask Not What." *Artforum*, February 1986, 68–75.

McShine, Kynaston, ed. *Andy Warhol: A Retrospective*. New York: Museum of Modern Art, 1989.

McWilliams, Amy. "Genre Expectation and Narrative Innovation in *Seinfeld*." In Lavery and Dunne, "*Seinfeld*," 77–86.

Mellencamp, Patricia. *High Anxiety: Catastrophe, Scandal, Age and Comedy*. Bloomington: Indiana Univ. Press, 1992.

———. "Video Politics: *Guerilla TV*, Ant Farm, *Eternal Frame*." *Discourse*, Spring–Summer 1988, 78–100.

Meyrowitz, Joshua. *No Sense of Place: The Impact of Electronic Media on Social Behavior*. Oxford: Oxford Univ. Press, 1985.

Miller, Arthur. "On Politics and the Art of Acting." The 30th Jefferson Lecture in the Humanities, National Endowment for the Humanities, March 26, 2001. http://www.neh.gov/whoweare/miller/lecture.html

Mitchell, W. J. T. *Iconology: Image, Text, Ideology*. Chicago: Univ. of Chicago Press, 1986.

———. "Interdisciplinarity and Visual Culture." *Art Bulletin* 77, no. 4 (1995): 540–544.

———. Interview by Asbjørn Grønstad and Øyvind Vågnes. *Image and Narrative* 7, no. 2 (2006). http://www.imageandnarrative.be/inarchive/iconoclasm/gronstad_vagnes.htm.

———. *Picture Theory: Essays on Visual and Verbal Representation*. Chicago: Univ. of Chicago Press, 1994.

———. "The Unspeakable and the Unimaginable: Word and Image in a Time of Terror." *ELH: English Literary History* 72, no. 2 (2005): 291–308.

————. *What Do Pictures Want? The Lives and Loves of Images*. Chicago: Univ. of Chicago Press, 2005.

Mondell, Allen, and Cynthia Salzmann Mondell. *John F. Kennedy and the Memory of a Nation*. VHS tape. Dallas: Sixth Floor Museum, 1989.

Morreale, Joanne. "Sitcoms Say Good-bye: The Cultural Spectacle of *Seinfeld*'s Last Episode." In *Critiquing the Sitcom: A Reader*, edited by Joanne Morreale, 274–285. Syracuse, N.Y.: Syracuse Univ. Press, 2003.

Motyl, Howard D. *Image of an Assassination: A New Look at the Zapruder Film*. DVD. Orland Park, Ill.: MPI Video, 1998.

Mullin, Tom. "Livin' and Dyin' in Zapruderville." *Cineaction*, no. 38, 1995, 12–15.

Naskovski, Zoran. *Death in Dallas*. Installation at the Wexner Center for the Arts, Ohio State University, Columbus, November–December 2003.

Neal, Arthur G. *National Trauma and Collective Memory: Major Events in the American Century*. Armonk, N.Y.: Sharpe, 1998.

Nel, Philip. "'A Small Incisive Shock': Modern Forms, Postmodern Politics, and the Role of the Avant-Garde in *Underworld*." *Modern Fiction Studies* 45, no. 3 (1999): 724–752.

Neshat, Shirin. Foreword to *Video Art: A Guided Tour*, by Catherine Elwes. London: Tauris, 2006.

NewsHour. "Image of Assassination." July 14, 1998. http://www.pbs.org/newshour/bb/white_house/july-dec98/zapruder_7-14.html.

Nichols, Bill. *Introduction to Documentary*. Bloomington: Indiana Univ. Press, 2001.

Nora, Pierre. "Between Memory and History: *Les Lieux de Mémoire*." *Representations*, no. 26 (1989): 7–25.

O'Brien, Geoffrey. "The Republic of *Seinfeld*." In Lavery and Dunne, "*Seinfeld*," 139–147.

O'Connell, P. J. *Robert Drew and the Development of Cinema Verite in America*. Carbondale: Southern Illinois Univ. Press, 1992.

O'Keeffe, Tadhg. "Landscape and Memory: Historiography, Theory, Methodology." In *Heritage, Memory, and the Politics of Identity: New Perspectives on the Cultural Landscape*, edited by Niamh Moore and Yvonne Whelan, 3–18. Hampshire, UK: Ashgate, 2007.

Osborn, Ed. "*Death in Dallas*." *Stretcher*, January 27, 2003.

Osteen, Mark. *American Magic and Dread: Don DeLillo's Dialogue with Culture*. Philadelphia: Univ. of Pennsylvania Press, 2000.

Owens, Craig. "The Allegorical Impulse: Toward a Theory of Postmodernism." In *Beyond Recognition: Representation, Power, and Culture*, 52–87.

————. *Beyond Recognition: Representation, Power, and Culture*. Berkeley and Los Angeles: Univ. of California Press, 1994.

————. "From Work to Frame, or, Is There Life after 'The Death of the Author'?" In *Beyond Recognition: Representation, Power, and Culture*, 122–139.

Panzer, Mary. "What Price History?" *Art in America*, October 1999, 67–71.

Perret, Geoffrey. *Jack: A Life like No Other*. New York: Random House, 2001.

Petersen, Wolfgang. *In the Line of Fire*. DVD. Special Edition, 2001.

Phelan, Peggy. "Performances of *Death in America*." In *Performing the Body/Performing the Text*, edited by Amelia Jones and Andrew Stephenson, 223–236. London: Routledge, 1999.

———. *Unmarked: The Politics of Performance*. London: Routledge, 1993.

Poniewozik, James. "Within Crumbling Walls," *Time*, March 3, 2002. http://www
.time.com/time/magazine/article/0,9171,214111,00.html.

Poremba, Cindy. "Frames and Simulated Documents: Indexicality in Documentary Videogames." *Loading . . .* 3, no. 4 (2009). http://journals.sfu.ca/loading/index
.php/loading/article/viewFile/61/60.

Pringle, David. "The Fourfold Symbolism of J. G. Ballard." *RE/Search*, nos. 8–9 (1984): 126–137.

Raessens, Joost. "Reality Play: Documentary Computer Games Beyond Fact and Fiction." *Popular Communication* 4, no. 3 (2006): 213–224.

Rather, Dan. *The Camera Never Blinks: Adventures of a TV Journalist*. With Mickey Herskowitz. New York: Morrow, 1977.

Reddin, Keith. *Frame 312*. London: Methuen, 2002.

Reeve, N. H. "Oswald Our Contemporary: Don DeLillo's *Libra*." In *An Introduction to Contemporary Fiction: International Writing in English since 1970*, edited by Rod Mengham, 135–149. Cambridge: Polity Press, 1999.

Reinhardt, Mark. "Picturing Violence: Aesthetics and the Anxiety of Critique." In Reinhardt, Edwards, and Duganne, *Beautiful Suffering*, 13–36.

Reinhardt, Mark, Holly Edwards, and Erina Duganne, eds. *Beautiful Suffering: Photography and the Traffic in Pain*. Chicago: Williams College Museum of Art, in association with the Univ. of Chicago Press, 2007.

Rinder, Lawrence. "The American Effect." In *The American Effect: Global Perspectives on the United States, 1990–2003*, 15–45. Exhibition catalogue. New York: Whitney Museum of American Art, 2003.

Rogin, Michael. "Body and Soul Murder: *JFK*." In *Media Spectacles*, edited by Marjorie Garber, Jann Matlock, and Rebecca L. Waskowitz, 3–21. New York: Routledge, 1993.

Rorty, Richard. *Philosophy and the Mirror of Nature*. Princeton, N.J.: Princeton Univ. Press, 1979.

Rosler, Martha. "Video: Shedding the Utopian Moment." In Hall and Fifer, *Illuminating Video*, 30–50.

Roth, Philip. "I Feel like Saying: Stop, That's Enough . . ." Interview by Jean-Louis Turlin. *Independent*, October 16, 2002.

Russell, Catherine. *Narrative Mortality: Death, Closure, and New Wave Cinemas*. Minneapolis: Univ. of Minnesota Press, 1995.

Said, Edward. "Traveling Theory." In *The Edward Said Reader*, edited by Moustafa Bay-oumi and Andre Rubin, 195–217. New York: Vintage, 2000.

Schechner, Richard. "Six Axioms for Environmental Theatre." *Drama Review* 12, no. 2 (1968): 41–64.

Schlesinger, Arthur Jr. "A Eulogy: John Fitzgerald Kennedy." *Saturday Evening Post*, December 14, 1963.

———. *A Thousand Days: John F. Kennedy in the White House*. London: Deutsch, 1965.

Schudson, Michael. *The Power of News*. Cambridge, Mass.: Harvard Univ. Press, 1995.

Scott, Grant. *The Sculpted Word: Keats, Ekphrasis, and the Visual Arts*. Hanover, N.H.: Univ. Press of New England, 1994.

Seid, Steve. "Tunneling through the Wasteland: Ant Farm Video." In Lewallen and Seid, *Ant Farm*, 22–37.

Shamberg, Michael. *Guerilla Television*. New York: Holt, Rinehart and Winston, 1971.

Sheatley, Paul B., and Jacob J. Feldman. *The Assassination of President Kennedy: A Preliminary Report on Public Reactions and Behavior*. Chicago: National Opinion Research Center, 1964.

Simon, Art. *Dangerous Knowledge: The JFK Assassination in Art and Film*. Philadelphia: Temple Univ. Press, 1996.

———. Review of *Image of an Assassination*. *Cineaste* 24, no. 1 (1998): 83–84.

Sontag, Susan. "Notes on 'Camp.'" In *Against Interpretation*, 275–292. London: Vintage, 1994.

———. *Regarding the Pain of Others*. New York: Farrar, Straus and Giroux, 2003.

Sorensen, Theodore. *The Kennedy Legacy*. New York: Macmillan, 1969.

Sorkin, Michael. "Sex, Drugs, and Rock and Roll, Cars, Dolphins, and Architecture." In Lewallen and Seid, *Ant Farm*, 4–21.

———. "The Theming of the City." In *Lotus: International Quarterly Architectural Review*, no. 109 (2001): 6–13.

———, ed. *Variations on a Theme Park: The New American City and the End of Public Space*. New York: Hill and Wang, 1992.

Stolley, Richard. "The Zapruder Film: Shots Seen Round the World." In *"JFK": The Book of the Film*, edited by Oliver Stone and Zachary Sklar, 410–413. New York: Applause, 1992.

———. "Zapruder Rewound." *Life*, September 1998, 43.

Stone, Oliver. *JFK*. DVD. Special Edition Director's Cut. Warner Home Video, 2001.

Stone, Oliver, and Zachary Sklar, eds. *"JFK": The Book of the Film*. New York: Applause, 1992.

Strauss, David Levi. *Between the Eyes: Essays on Photography and Politics*. New York: Aperture, 2003.

Sturken, Marita. "Paradox in the Evolution of an Art Form: Great Expectations and the Making of a History." In Hall and Fifer, *Illuminating Video*, 101–121.

————. "Reenactment, Fantasy, and the Paranoia of History: Oliver Stone's Docudramas." *History and Theory* 36, no. 4 (1997): 64–79.

————. *Tangled Memories: The Vietnam War, the AIDS Epidemic, and the Politics of Remembering*. Berkeley and Los Angeles: Univ. of California Press, 1997.

Swanson, Doug. *Umbrella Man: A Jack Flippo Mystery*. New York: Putnam, 1999.

Taussig, Michael. *Defacement: Public Secrecy and the Labor of the Negative*. Stanford, Calif.: Stanford Univ. Press, 1999.

Thorburn, David, and Henry Jenkins, eds. *Rethinking Media Change: The Aesthetics of Transition*. Cambridge, Mass.: MIT Press, 2003.

Time. "The Top 10 Everything of 2009." December 8, 2009. http://www.time.com /time/specials/packages/0,28757,1945379,00.html.

Traffic Management Limited. *JFK Reloaded*. Computer game. Glasgow, Scotland: Traffic, 2004.

Trask, Richard B. *National Nightmare on Six Feet of Film: Mr. Zapruder's Home Movie and the Murder of President Kennedy*. Danvers, Mass.: Yeoman, 2005.

Troy, Gil. "JFK: Celebrity-in-Chief or Commander-in-Chief?" *Reviews in American History* 26, no. 3 (1998): 630–636.

Trujillo, Nick. "Interpreting November 22: A Critical Ethnography of an Assassination Site." *Quarterly Journal of Speech* 79, no. 4 (1993): 447–466.

Tuohey, Jason. "*JFK Reloaded* Game Causes Controversy." *PC World*, November 24, 2004.

Vials, Chris. "The Popular Front in the American Century: *Life* Magazine, Margaret Bourke-White, and Consumer Realism, 1936–1941." *American Periodicals* 16, no. 1 (2006): 74–102.

Vianello, Robert. Review of *Appraising Moving Images: Assessing the Archival and Monetary Value of Film and Video Records*, by Sam Kula. *Moving Image* 4, no. 2 (2004): 138–141.

Vincent, Steven. "Resisting the 'American Effect.'" *National Review*, September 9, 2003.

Vollmann, William T. *Thirteen Stories and Thirteen Epitaphs*. New York: Grove, 1991.

Wagner, Peter. Introduction to *Icons-Texts-Iconotexts: Essays on Ekphrasis and Intermediality*, edited by Peter Wagner, 1–42. Berlin: De Gruyter, 1996.

Watney, Simon. "The Warhol Effect." In *The Work of Andy Warhol*, edited by Gary Garrels, 115–123. Seattle: Bay Press, 1989.

Watson, Mary Ann. *The Expanding Vista: American Television in the Kennedy Years*. New York: Oxford Univ. Press, 1990.

Webb, Justin. "JFK 'Sniper Window' Fetches $3M." BBC News, February 17, 2007. http://news.bbc.co.uk/2/hi/americas/6370549.stm.

Webb, Ruth. "*Ekphrasis* Ancient and Modern: The Invention of a Genre." *Word and Image* 15, no. 1 (1999): 7–18.

West, Jeff. "'Wiser Heads Prevailed.'" *American History*, December 2003, 60–65.

White, Hayden. *Figural Realism: Studies in the Mimesis Effect*. Baltimore: Johns Hopkins Univ. Press, 1999.

White, Theodore. "An Epilogue." *Life*, December 6, 1963, 158–159.

Wolf, Werner. "Intermediality." In *Routledge Encyclopedia of Narrative Theory*, edited by David Herman, Manfred Jahn, and Marie-Laure Ryan, 252–256. London: Routledge, 2005.

Wrone, David R. *The Zapruder Film: Reframing JFK's Assassination*. Lawrence: Univ. Press of Kansas, 2003.

Young, James E. *The Texture of Memory: Holocaust Memorials and Meaning*. New Haven, Conn.: Yale Univ. Press, 1993.

Zelizer, Barbie. *Covering the Body: The Kennedy Assassination, the Media, and the Shaping of Collective Memory*. Chicago: Univ. of Chicago Press, 1992.

———. "Reading the Past against the Grain: The Shape of Memory Studies." *Critical Studies in Mass Communication* 12, no. 2 (1995): 214–239.

INDEX

Page numbers in *italics* indicate illustrations.

Ballard, J. G., 16, 71-73, 97, 174n24
Balzac, Honoré de, 70
Barker, Eddie, 158–159n20
Barney, Matthew, 67
Barry, Raymond J., 181–182n1
Barthes, Roland, 14, 32, 49, 113, 160n44
Bataille, Georges, 100
Baty, S. Paige, 51, 60
Baudrillard, Jean, 64, 168n76
Bay of Pigs, 123
Baym, Geoffrey, 31
Bazin, André, 49, 163n14
BBC, 149
Beautiful Suffering: Photography and the Traffic in Pain, 151
Beck, John, 14, 100, 113, 116, 149, 175n44
Becker, Kathrin, 104
Beers, Jack, 9
Begley, Adam, 74
Belting, Hans, 8, 49, 53, 57, 61
Benjamin, Walter, 6, 9, 58, 63, 89, 113, 153n5, 167nn68–70, 170n31, 173–174n14
Bennett, Robert S., 98, 99, 101
Berger, John, 144, 175n44
Berman, Ronald, 80
Beschloss, Michael, 181n49
Bethesda Naval Hospital, 106
Beyond Conspiracy, 132, 133
Bianculli, David, 182n10
Black, Joel, 4
Blockbuster, 141
Blow-Up (Antonioni), 155n31
Boehm, Gottfried, 156n43
Bogost, Ian, 133, 181n48
Bolter, Jay David, 6, 47, 154n6
Boorstin, Daniel, 64, 168n74
Booth, John Wilkes, 10
Bordwell, David, 82, 85
Bourdin, Michel, 68
"The Boyfriend." See *Seinfeld*
Boyle, Deirdre, 65

Brady, Mathew, 139
Brandimarte, Cynthia, 123
Brecht, Bertolt, 88
Bronfen, Elisabeth, 77
Brown, Christopher, 14
Bruun, Hanne, 162n81
Bruzzi, Stella, 12, 22
Bugaev, Sergei, 110, 111
Burden, Chris, 103, 112
Burke, Edmund, 100
Burroughs, William S., 72
Burrows, Larry, 39
Bush, George W., 66, 110, 159n25, 177n22
Butler, Judith, 57

Cadava, Eduardo, 167n69
Cadillac Ranch (Ant Farm), 48
The Camera Never Blinks (Rather), 26, 158n15, 158–159n20, 160–161n48
Carrier, David, 113, 168n82, 178n48
Castro, Fidel, 71
Cattelan, Maurizio, 66, 67, 168n85
Cavuto, Neil, 181–182n1
CBS, 31, 164n26; News, 28, 29, 158–159n20; Radio, 24
Chanan, Michael, 12, 22, 107
Chaney, David, 119, 120, 123–124
Charles, Larry, 80
Cherones, Tom, 81, 172n14
Children NOW, 130
Christianity, 62
Christie's, 100
civil rights movement, 123
Civil War, photography of, 139
Clooney, George, 66
C.M.M. Associates, 99
CNN, 3–4
Codex Leicester (da Vinci), 100
Cohen, Josh, 77, 170n31
Cohen, Mike, 183n18
Congress. See U.S. Congress
Connally, John, 9, 40, 42, 74, 85, 132
Connally, Nellie, 9

Flemming, Brian, 136
Fletcher, Angus, 13
Ford, Gerald R., 40, 173n4
Ford's Theater, 126
Foster, Hal, 114
Foundas, Scott, 181–182n1
Frame 312 (Reddin), 138
Freedberg, David, 68, 168n88
Freedom of Information Act, 148
Freudianism, 114
Friedberg, Anne, 166n48
Fullerton, Tracy, 130, 133, 181n48

Gamboni, Dario, 65, 66, 168n82
Garrison, Jim, 82, 84–86, 88, 161n59
Gates, Bill, 100, 136–137, 181–182n1
Gibson, William, 138
Gillmor, Dan, 149
Gingeras, Alison M., 14
Ginzburg, Carlo, 18
Giuliani, Rudolph, 183–184n29
Giuliano, Charles, 111
Glaubke, Christy, 130, 132
Glueck, Grace, 110
Good Night America, 43–45
Goodwin, Doris Kearns, 181n48
Goodwin, Sarah Webster, 77
Gottdiener, Mark, 129
"grassy knoll," 58, 81, 82, 130, 137
Gray, Jonathan, 89
Greer, Philip, 114
Gregory, Dick, 43
Groden, Robert J., 43, 44, 47, 92, 132
Gross, Kenneth, 49, 67
Ground Zero. *See* September 11 terrorist
   attacks
Grusin, Richard, 6, 47, 154n6
Guardian, 149
Guerilla Television (Shamberg), 55
Guernica (Picasso), 184n38
Guins, Raiford, 166n48
Gunster, Shane, 88

Halberstam, David, 52, 164n30,
   183–184n29
Halbwachs, Maurice, 8, 154n13
Hall, Diane Andrews, 47
Hall, Doug, 47, 48, 50, 53, 56–59, 61, 63,
   119
Hamon, Philippe, 70
Hanlon, James, 141
Hansen, Miriam, 150
Harries, Dan, 89
Hartley, Eleanor, 106
A Harvest of Death, Gettysburg (O'Sullivan),
   23
Heffernan, James, 160n33
Hellmann, John F., 51
Here Is New York, 146–148
Hernandez, Keith, 79, 89
Hersh, Seymour, 106
Hicks, Wilson, 161n63
Hill, Clinton J., 10
Hiroshima bombing, 112
Hirsch, Irwin, 171n9
Hirsch, Marianne, 10, 183n26
Hirst, Damien, 66
Hlava, Josef, 143
Hlava, Pavel, 143, 144, 183n18
Hoberman, J., 103
Holocaust Memorial Museum, 127
Hooper-Greenhill, Eilean, 178n48
Horrigan, Bill, 108, 176n10
Hotelett, Richard C., 24, 29
House of Representatives. *See* U.S.
   Congress
Houston Street (Dallas, Texas), 1, 2, 4
How to Do Things with Words (Austin), 13
Hunt, Conover, 121, 122, 124, 126, 127,
   132
Hurr, Douglas, 47
Hussein, Saddam, 150, 177n22
Hutcheon, Linda, 21, 80, 88
Huyssen, Andreas, 8